Critical Visions

Legacies of Social Thought
Series Editor: Charles Lemert

Critical Visions

New Directions in Social Theory

Anthony Elliott

ROWMAN & LITTLEFIELD PUBLISHERS, INC.
Lanham • Boulder • New York • Toronto • Oxford

ALSO BY ANTHONY ELLIOTT

Psychoanalysis in Contexts: Paths between Theory and Modern Culture (1995)
 Coeditor with Stephen Frosh
Subject to Ourselves: Social Theory, Psychoanalysis, and Postmodernity (1996)
Freud 2000 (1998)
 Editor
Social Theory and Psychoanalysis in Transition: Self and Society from Freud to Kristeva (1999)
The Mourning of John Lennon (1999)
The Blackwell Reader in Contemporary Social Theory (Blackwell, 1999)
 Editor
Psychoanalysis at Its Limits: Navigating the Postmodern Turn (2000)
 Coeditor with Charles Spezzano
Profiles in Contemporary Social Theory (2001)
 Coeditor with Bryan S. Turner
Concepts of the Self (2001)
Psychoanalytic Theory: An Introduction (2002)
Key Contemporary Social Theorists (2003)
 Coeditor with Larry Ray
Imaginings: Social Theory since Freud (2003)

ROWMAN & LITTLEFIELD PUBLISHERS, INC.

Published in the United States of America
by Rowman & Littlefield Publishers, Inc.
A wholly owned subsidiary of The Rowman & Littlefield Publishing Group, Inc.
4501 Forbes Boulevard, Suite 200, Lanham, Maryland 20706
www.rowmanlittlefield.com

P.O. Box 317, Oxford OX2 9RU, United Kingdom

Library of Congress Cataloging-in-Publication Data

Elliott, Anthony.
 Critical visions : new directions in social theory / Anthony Elliott.
  p. cm.— (Legacies of social thought)
 Includes bibliographical references (p.) and index.
 ISBN 0-7425-2689-5 (cloth : alk. paper)—ISBN 0-7425-2690-9 (paper :
alk. paper)
  1. Social sciences—Philosophy. I. Title. II. Series.
H61.E4285 2003
300′.1—dc21   2002156610

Printed in the United States of America

♾ ™ The paper used in this publication meets the minimum requirements of American National Standard for Information Sciences—Permanence of Paper for Printed Library Materials, ANSI/NISO Z39.48-1992.

For
Anthony Moran
and
Nick Stevenson

Contents

The Direction of Social Theory Is Always New: Series Editor's Foreword

Charles Lemert

In *Critical Visions,* Anthony Elliott writes emphatically of the *New Directions in Social Theory.* There is no want of those who question the idea that social theory might have any direction at all, much less new ones. It was not all that long ago, well within current memory, that social theory was at best a marginal, vaguely leftist, uncertainly *nouveau* activity. It was done, if at all, in but a few European or bicoastal North American outposts. I am old enough to have been young when one put his career at some risk by claiming social theory as a sphere of competence.

Today, early in the twenty-first century, all that is changed. Whether it has changed enough for the title of Anthony Elliott's brilliant new book to bear easy scrutiny is, thus, a worthy question. Social theory has at least become a considered object of derision in academic quarters, while standing as a totem for a host of seriously interesting intellectual labors by the younger inhabitants of those quarters. One imperfect measure of the change is the notable sullenness of a certain colleague of mine. For years, whenever I put forth a book or a public lecture containing the phrase "social theory," this quite good man would seek me out to ask, "What is social theory? Would you please tell me?" Sometime in the last years of the previous century he declined into his current state of gloom. He no longer asks the questions. We hardly talk at all, except for a distant greeting across the crowded hallway. I never once convinced this man, an economist, as to the what or whereof of social theory. His gloom today descends, I suppose, not so much from the brilliance of my account of the subject as from all the younger people crowding our hallways for whom "social theory" is a badge of honor.

A more durable index of the new-found verisimilitude of the subject of Elliott's *Critical Visions: New Directions in Social Theory* is that social theory is on the verge of coming into its own as an established academic thing in its own right. One may go, for example, to a website (www.socialtheory.org) to find listings of programs in and on the subject in universities the world over. Many of these are, it seems, gathered into an International Consortium of Social Theory Programs, which begins its self-announcement with the following: "Social Theory has always had an uneasy relationship to the disciplines." Thereafter, the names Marx, Mill, Spencer, Comte, and Nietzsche are invoked as among the classic figures to whom this uneasy relationship is owed. Thereafter, the website serving these programs of uneasy relationship to the tight sphincter of academic normalcy calls forth social theory's institutional lineage: the Frankfurt Institute for Social Research in Germany, the University of Chicago's Committee on Social Thought, and the now-defunct British program in Cultural Studies at Birmingham. These are, one might observe, three twentieth-century variants of institutional social theory that could not possibly be more severely at theoretical odds one with the other.

Hence, the dilemma invoked by the current book. Social theory has, indeed, come to be a household phrase in the academy. Yet it remains (thank goodness) in the toddler stage of development. Even its most esteemed institutional sites are themselves in scant accord as to what their common subject might be—and this quite apart from the fact that one of them is extinct, another hopelessly lost in a conservative backwater, and the third holding onto life by the largess of the German state and the longevity of Jürgen Habermas, its one remaining theoretical giant.

Against such a background one must be daring, as Anthony Elliott most certainly is, to speak so soon of *new directions in social theory.* And ever more so when the claim is made that sociology, an academic discipline not recently known for daring, is somehow at the heart of the direction social theory is newly taking so early in its moral career and against the inertia of traditional disciplinary habits.

Anthony Elliott makes his case with the blinding clarity that readers of his ten or so previous books have come to expect. It is hard to think of others his age (he has not yet enjoyed his fortieth birthday) who have achieved so much, in so many fields, as has Elliott. But it is not clarity or even ambition and hard work that account for the importance of *Critical Visions: New Directions in Social Theory.*

Unlike other books seeking to present a critical introduction to new ideas and those who think them, this book adds the third dimension too often left out. Ordinary writers (who very often are quite extraordinary minds) have no trouble setting forth the ideas as they are associated with those who brought them into being. Exceptional writers (who necessarily are exceptional thinkers as well) are those who tackle the riddle that has yet to be solved as to the origin of new ideas, namely: *Why does this or that idea come into play in a given time by the hand of a given thinker?*

The riddle turns on two principles, both of which are central to good social theory: (1) Ideas are things of their own, intractable kind. This is to say that new ideas are unlike technological innovations; fashion or culinary or other departures in the design of commodities; new, more plastic methods of construction in architecture; and such like. Naturally, new directions in any field depart from a new idea, but the idea itself is almost always something apart from what it has wrought. Once, years ago, *nouvelle cuisine* was actually new. The food itself was striking for the reduction of the butter and other fats that were formerly considered the *sine qua non* of culinary art. But what is the idea that stood behind the innovation? Or was there any one idea?

Hence the second distinguishing quality of an idea: (2) Once an idea is thought through and widely accepted, it seems (to those with a stake in its success) perfectly obvious. Those with a sufficient stake in my personal health—that is, my wife and my physician—are quite convinced that, whatever cuisine I may indulge, it ought to be from among those that share one essential principle with *nouvelle cuisine*, namely, reduced fat. The idea is, of course, that saturated fats like butter will kill you in the long run of life. Personally, I hate this idea, but even I cannot dispute it. But, reverting to the first point, there was a time when wives and physicians could not figure out what it was about certain foods that killed certain husbands and patients. The idea, now clear (if appalling), was once quite unthinkable, in the strict sense of the word—that is, quite beyond comprehension. Note also that, though the idea is both clear and distinct, it remains quite a separate thing from its applications to the invention of cuisines, exercise equipment, health clubs, and all the other commodities that are failing to keep people at risk to fats from dying. You may note, finally, that this is not to say that the idea (or, if you prefer, the theory) is aloof and abstract. Ideas of such applicability are neither. The point is that they are things of their own kind.

The business of social theory might, therefore, be said to be thinking ideas about social things that have not hitherto been thought. Social theory, thereby, would be the work of thinking the Unthinkable. If there were, for example, a social theory of culinary fats (and there may well be), it would be a theory of why and how complex social things (such as cultures or societies or global environments) produce and reproduce the risks associated with commodities likely to destroy health and life itself. It could even be said that social theory, put even more simply, is the work of thinking through the hard-to-believe fact of social life that people merrily join forces with the powers that put them at risk.

If we were to think of social theory in this way, then one can see just how apt the book at hand is. *Social theory* is, by its nature, *always* looking for new angles, which is to say, precisely, *new directions*. In this sense, Anthony Elliott and those whose ideas he discusses are at the heart of social theory as it *must* be practiced at this time. He does not tell us why such men and women as Ulrich Beck, Anthony Giddens, Jacques Lacan, Cornelius Castoriadis, Julia Kristeva, among others, are the precise thinkers whose ideas help us to think the Unthinkable. As I say, his purpose is the even more demanding one of accounting for the fact that ideas of the kind associated with the thinkers he discusses are *necessarily* the new directions social theory must be (and is) taking.

Hence, the special value of Part Two of *Critical Visions,* where the new ideas (previously introduced in Part One, in connection with the thinkers) are compiled into what is, in effect, a short list of urgent concerns of those willing honestly to face the new realities of a global environment. Once you read through this book, you will immediately see what Anthony Elliott means by the new directions of social theory. Who, today, in the early years of the twenty-first century, would deny that the most spectacular social questions are as follows: (1) Who am I and to whom or what do I belong? (2) If I belong at all to a given society, in what might subsist my citizenship rights? (3) If I am said to have such rights and responsibilities, then how can this be, given the surprising ways that power and politics seem always to come back to haunt me, as if I were constantly conjuring up that which cuts me down? (4) Given the risks I experience as one who is both the source and victim of the general political ineptitude of the times, how am I to think of my actions as correct, if not exactly good, especially now that the global environment as a whole is somehow, implausibly but evidently, the sphere of my moral action?

In short, the list of imponderables today is the nature of *human identity* itself—a question provoked not by philosophy so much as the struggle to come to terms with the nature of sexualities, citizenship, and politics—provoked now not so much by the pure ideals of patriotic desire as by the risks of political engagement in a world of strangely configured inequalities and impotencies; and *ethics*—no longer a question of the right and the good, so much as of the very possibility of moral recognition in a world where individualism is at once more and less than it was a century ago.

Critical Visions gives account of those ideas that, for the time being, must pre-occupy social theory (even when, like the theory of fat and heart disease, most of us refuse to think through their terrifying applications). The book is written by Anthony Elliott, who is certainly among the rising stars in the early morning sky of social theory. The book and the man will reward you precisely because the man has written the book out of his determined refusal to ignore the social realities by which we flawed citizens of the global spaces put ourselves at risk in the inscrutable play of power and values that no longer fit the centuries-old wineskins from which we first drank of them. *Critical Visions* demonstrates, by the freshness of its arguments, that the direction of social theory is, necessarily, always toward the new.

Preface and Acknowledgments

This book was written between 1997 and 2002, and consequently it owes its existence to a considerable number of institutions of various kinds. Initial work on the volume was conducted during the tenure of an Australian Research Council Fellowship in the Faculty of Arts at the University of Melbourne. Further research was carried out at the welcoming environment of the Centre for Comparative Literature and Cultural Studies at Monash University. Finally, work on the volume was completed at the Centre for Critical Theory at the University of the West of England. This research also benefited, in the final stages, through an award from the British Academy—and I am grateful to the academy for its generous support.

At all these institutions, and at seminars and lectures of various and varying kinds where I have presented this research, as well as in other, more informal settings, many people have provided me with comments, criticisms, and support. I should like to thank the following individuals in particular: Alison Assiter, Zygmunt Bauman, Paul du Gay, Stephen Frosh, Alison Garrod, Anthony Giddens, Kevin Hart, Paul Hoggett, Fiore Inglese, Deborah Maxwell, Kriss McKie, Carmel Meiklejohn, Andrew Milner, Andrew Newton, Jeffrey Prager, Larry Ray, Lynne Segal, Simone Skacej, Jem Thomas, John B. Thompson, Simon Thompson, Gail Ward, Sean Watson, and Elizabeth Wood.

I am also deeply grateful to Bryan Turner, whose friendship and wise counsel over recent years have been invaluable. I wish also to thank Charles Lemert, my series editor, for his many various suggestions that have improved the arguments set out in this book; he has done so much to help me in recent times, though I doubt he fully realizes the extent of his influence.

The dedication acknowledges very deep debts of friendship and intellectual support: Anthony Moran and Nick Stevenson heard out many of these chapters half-raw, and they have been kind enough to read much of this book in manuscript. They are wonderful friends and have always advised me well.

Nicola Geraghty deserves special mention: She gave me many terrific suggestions, helped sort out a range of publishing issues, and generally enriched the daily experience of writing. I can scarcely begin to thank her enough. Jean and Keith Elliott were, as usual, generous with their time and their supportive comments. Caoimhe Elliott provided all the necessary distractions and helped me see that sometimes the best way to get somewhere is to take the long way round. And the final stages of writing just wouldn't have been the same without the input of Oscar Elliott, who pretty much grinned all the way throughout.

Some chapters, or some parts of chapters, are previously published and reprinted here by permission of the publishers or by prior agreement. Details of original publication are as follows:

Aspects of "Interdisciplinary Studies and the Fortunes of Sociology" were delivered as a keynote address at the Australasian Sociological Association Conference, University of South Australia, in December 2000.

Chapter 1 originally appeared as "Beck's Sociology of Risk: A Critical Assessment," *Sociology* 36, no. 2 (May 2002): 293–315. The chapter printed here is an expanded version of the original article.

Chapter 2 is a modified and much expanded version of my essay in *Profiles in Contemporary Social Theory*, ed. Anthony Elliott and Bryan S. Turner (London: Sage, 2001), 293–303.

Chapter 3 is a modified and expanded version of my essay in *Profiles in Contemporary Social Theory*, ed. Anthony Elliott and Bryan S. Turner (London: Sage, 2001), 140–50. The afterword on Lacan and Derrida appeared in a reduced form in *Australian Higher Education* as "Deconstructive Derrida Has His Limitations," 3 February 1999, 41.

The first part of chapter 4 was published in a reduced and altered form as "The Social Imaginary: A Critical Assessment of Castoriadis's Psychoanalytic Social Theory," *American Imago: Studies in Psychoanalysis and Culture* 59, no. 2 (2002): 141–70. The second part of chapter 4 was published in a modified and altered form in as "Subjectivity, Culture, Autonomy: Castoriadis and Social Theory," *Current Perspectives in Social Theory* 22 (2002): 369–94.

A short section on the work of Julia Kristeva in chapter 5 will be published in *History of the Human Sciences* (forthcoming) with the title "Kristeva and the Haunting of the Soul." The excursus appeared in an early and reduced form as "Excommunications," *Radical Philosophy* (Autumn 1992): 42–44.

Chapter 6 is a modified and slightly expanded version of my essay in *The Handbook of Social Theory,* ed. Barry Smart and George Ritzer (London: Sage, 2001), 428–38.

Chapter 7 originally appeared in *Culture and Citizenship*, ed. Nick Stevenson (London: Sage, 2000), 47–61.

Some sections of chapter 8 were published in a reduced and altered form with the title "Political Science, Modernity and Postmodernism," *Political Theory Newsletter* 9, no. 1 (1997): 11–19.

Chapter 9 derives from a lecture at the University of the West of England in May 2000. A section of the argument developed was previously published in a reduced and altered form as "The Ethical Antinomies of Postmodernity," *Sociology* 34, no. 2 (2000): 335–40.

Introduction: Interdisciplinary Studies and the Fortunes of Sociology

In universities around the world, interdisciplinary study is all the rage. This is true not only for comparative literature, cultural studies, political science, and history, but also increasingly for sociology. Indeed, interdisciplinary debates reach right to the heart of sociology as a discipline worldwide. Gone are the days when the theoretical underpinnings of sociological research could be neatly confined to the conceptual terrain of, say, structural-functionalism, symbolic interactionism, or ethnomethodology. Today, theoretical innovation in sociology results from a cross-referencing of disciplinary perspectives, a cross-referencing that scoops up and reconfigures many of the new social theories—poststructuralism, postmodernism, postfeminism, postcolonialism, psychoanalysis, and deconstruction. From this angle, one might reasonably expect to find that an increasing number of sociological practitioners are equally at home with the theoretical departures of Lacan, Lyotard, and Derrida as they are familiar with the standpoints of Parsons, Goffman, or Gouldner.

To advocates of the interdisciplinary turn in sociology, these new social theories are primarily valuable because they disrupt traditional disciplinary boundaries. The new theories, it is said, provoke a novel engagement with current social processes and promote an intellectual process of expansion and transformation. In the currently fashionable language, interdisciplinary perspectives offer "productive hybridities"—essentially, new concepts for thinking about our fast-changing world. Much of this relates to fairly abstract issues. For example, the suggestive blending of linguistics, poststructuralism, and psychoanalysis that has unfolded in modern European thought over the last twenty or so years has accorded a fundamental role to language in the constitution of both personal life and social relations; the study of language has, in turn, included investigation of

1

identity in terms of discursive rules and linguistic codes as well as the uses of talk in the concrete activities of day-to-day social life. Yet sociologists would be wrong to conclude that the new rules of interdisciplinary method only impact upon conceptual issues. For it is via the whole category of "interdisciplinary research" that many sociologists over recent years—Anthony Giddens, Stuart Hall, Richard Sennett, John B. Thompson, Paul Gilroy, Bryan S. Turner, Charles Lemert, and Patricia Clough, to name just a few—have made a considerable contribution to the restructuring, or perhaps even reinvention, of the discipline.

For others less impressed with this turn to theory and "productive hybridities," it is sometimes hard not to feel that all the talk about multidisciplinary studies isn't just a pseudointellectual cover for avoiding more pressing political issues. Looming ecological devastation, the depoliticization of public life, the privatization of public resources, the global restructuring of the market: many of the new discourses, according to their critics, have little or perhaps nothing to say about such pressing political concerns. Such a critique of interdisciplinary studies, it should be stressed, is primarily political in orientation; the critique is not necessarily against theory as such. In fact, many of the sharpest critics of the interdisciplinary turn in sociology have been the first to acknowledge that we now live in new times—for example, in a postsocietal era, a postindustrial economy, or a postmodern world. It is just that such critics of the interdisciplinary turn think that more interesting things can be said about global transformations than we find in many of the new social theories, with all their talk of "microstrategies," "local deconstructions," and "undecidable differences."

My own view is that a good deal of this debate over the status of interdisciplinary studies in sociology has been shaped by the declining fortunes of the discipline as a whole. By that, I mean to draw attention to the wholesale collapse of sociology's traditional audience. While sociologists once routinely conducted research and presented their findings to public policymakers, social administrators, political power shapers, and politicians, it now seems that the pronouncements of sociologists fall on deaf ears, or, at best, that the findings of sociologists are read only by other sociologists, as if what is going on in the discipline is a matter for internal consumption alone. And it is against this backdrop, I think, that we need to situate various calls from within the discipline for a radical new agenda—the demand for new interdisciplinary rules of sociological method. The erosion of the power of the nation-state; the transformation of visibility; the liquidation of the concept of "society"; the intensification of processes of globalization: the world in which we live today is a transformed social landscape, one in which the precepts of twentieth-century social science are simply unable to comprehend the networks, flows, fluidities, and representations of contemporary social processes. The problem, as I see it, then, is not that sociologists have been wrong in looking to the rise of "interdisciplinary studies" as a means of developing a new theoretical agenda (for, as I have said, this turn to theory has taken place across the disciplines). Yet it must be recognized that sociologists have encountered considerable difficulties—for reasons I'll try to briefly elaborate—in linking interdisciplinary theoretical developments to the broader forces of social change that preoccupy them.

To develop this argument a little further, I want to look briefly at John Urry's much celebrated *Sociology beyond Societies* (2000). Interestingly (or worryingly, depending on your standpoint), the book is subtitled "Mobilities for the Twenty-First Century," and it is perhaps this focus on the flows and fluidities of global capitalism that explains why the book has been widely applauded as a manifesto for the advancement of new interdisciplinary sociologies. Urry, a professor of sociology at Lancaster University in the United Kingdom, has been at the forefront of theoretical innovation in sociological discourse for some time now; he has, above all, sought to move sociology beyond a formal concern with society as an "entity," with the social as a "thing," to the analysis of what he has elsewhere termed "economies of signs and space" (Lash and Urry 1994). What really impresses one about *Sociology beyond Societies,* I think, is the deft manner in which Urry links together a whole range of complex theoretical discourses, ranging from poststructuralism and postmodernism to deconstructionist and rhizomatic analysis. The core hypothesis of the book is that sociology needs to move beyond the study of society as a set of bounded institutions. Sociology, Urry says, must switch focus instead to "imaginative and virtual movements and mobilities"—of images, flows, scapes, messages, waste products, and global temporalities.

All stirring stuff, and perhaps precisely the kind of diagnosis for the future of sociology that one might expect from mixing such a conceptual cocktail of poststructuralist, postmodern interdisciplinary discourses. Reading through the book, though, one is tempted to ask, Where, exactly, are we to find these emerging flows and fluidities inaugurated by our new world of global dynamism? For a book with such an immodest objective of defining where sociology as a discipline is heading for the twenty-first century, it is likely that one might be left with a sense of incomprehension at Urry's answer to the question, because his answer to the question turns on what he terms, in quaintly old-fashioned style, "the automobile." Amazingly, Urry sees mobilities for the twenty-first century as resting upon the car as a mode of travel. Let me quote directly from Urry:

> Automobility is a source of freedom, "the freedom of the road." . . . The flexibility of the car enables the car driver to roam at speed, at any time in any direction along the complex road systems of western societies that link together most houses, work places and leisure sites. Cars therefore extend where people can go to and hence what as humans they are able to do. Much of what many people now think of as "social life" could not be undertaken without the flexibility of the car and its availability 24 hours a day. One can travel to and from work, friends and family when one wants to. It is possible to leave late, to miss connections, to travel in a relatively time-less fashion. People travel when they want to, along routes that they choose,

finding new places unexpectedly, stopping for relatively open-ended periods of time, and moving on when they desire. (2000: 190)

Thank heavens Urry is relying so firmly on the theoretical credentials of Deleuze, Derrida, and Virilio to make such supposedly radical conjectures about the new mobilities we all inhabit. Yet I for one cannot help feeling that, in having his head so firmly buried within the textual intricacies of these discourses, Urry might not have noticed that most car drivers experience increasing worries and anxieties over, say, the escalating costs of fuel, pollution, and traffic gridlock. (In Britain in recent years, "automobilities" have been brought to a crashing halt, first by a massive fuel crisis—a crisis that, at one point, threatened to topple Blair's New Labour government—and second as a consequence of Britain's foot-and-mouth epidemic.)

I need now to enter some judicious qualifications to how I've characterized Urry's sociological analysis—partly because his remarks on automobiles form only a small component of his theory of mobilities, and partly because Urry's ideas have some interesting and instructive features. The best advertisement for Urry's critique of mobilities is surely the dramatic rise in travel (especially international travel), as well as the explosion in mass migration the world over; by testing sociological ideas on these social trends, as it were, Urry demonstrates that the discipline has important things to contribute to public political debate. Yet informing my rather snide remarks on Urry's analysis of automobilities there is a more substantive point. Urry's views, while in some respects idiosyncratic (few, surely, would identify cars as representing the *future* of travel!), exemplify for the most part some alarming aspects of "interdisciplinary sociology" in a general way. For Urry's reflections on mobilities, I want to suggest, indicate all too readily that interdisciplinary perspectives can be deployed for pseudointellectual theorizing, or for what Cambridge social theorist Bryan Turner and cultural studies analyst Chris Rojek term "decorative sociology" (Rojek and Turner 2001). Decorative theory is sociology shorn of serious engagement with the social world, its changing practices and structures. For many critics of the interdisciplinary turn in sociology, it is precisely the transcendentalism of Theory that led to the collapse of politically informed social critique, to which we might add that for those whose intellectual preoccupations incline toward social and cultural theory the simple response has been to underscore the blatant incoherence of those professional sociologies that imagine that social science can be conducted without reference to conceptual concerns.

Against the backdrop of the political despair pervading the postmodern 1990s, then, the discipline witnessed the unfolding of certain intellectual deadlocks and difficulties, with empirical sociologists bemoaning the fetishized character of Theory, and with social theorists countering by pointing to the dead-ends of indefensible empiricism. Thankfully, though, this is only part of the story. For while the dangers of turning interdisciplinary studies into a fetishistic, homogenizing sociologism are considerable, a number of genuinely exciting and novel areas of sociological research (both theoretical and substantive) have in recent years greatly benefited from, and been deepened by, an engagement with interdisciplinary perspectives. Many pressing sociological issues need to be mentioned here, including globalization, postmodernization, and new communication technologies—and I shall return to these shortly. However, it is now necessary to situate the new directions in social theory to which I have alluded within a broader conceptual history.

NEW DIRECTIONS IN SOCIAL THEORY

The perspective on social theory advanced in the pages that follow seeks to distance itself from those implacably linear, progressivist, and systematizing elements traditionally associated with classical social thought. Notwithstanding their brilliance and insights, the great sociological diagnosticians of the "golden age of modernity"—Karl Marx, Emile Durkheim, Max Weber, Georg Simmel, Sigmund Freud, and others—articulated a vision of history partly beholden to the West's ideology of progress and, in particular, societal movement with a singular direction, grasped differentially as the organizing principles of class domination, social mystification, bureaucratic regulation, repressed desire, and the like. Very often, these sociological models of modern society exaggerated the determination of social formations and cultural processes in terms of the systemic character granted to, say, reification, rationalization, or repression. Yet the unanticipated conceptual consequences of totalization—as recent studies of classical social thought have vividly demonstrated—have been much more profound and relate, above all, to the *instrumentalization of society.*

In a superb sociological confrontation with models of society created by classical sociology, Zygmunt Bauman (1991, 2000) has attempted to demonstrate that the very philosophical ambitions and theoretical assumptions of modernist social thought locked the discipline of sociology into an approach to society that was instrumentalizing, universalizing, homogenizing. Modernity could be defined as that culture in which people continually sought out better lives (and were continually promised better lives), according to Bauman, because the modernist sociological mentality was thoroughly obsessed with homogeneity, universality, monotony, clarity, and control. Hence, the "business of life" came to be attributed with a specific normative dynamic ranging from the reproduction of orderly, structured managerial practices and administrative designs through to the systematization of all social action as geared to ever-increasing levels of rationality, happiness, or organic systemness of the whole. It may further be readily admitted, says Bauman, that uncoordinated activities outside this projected orderly, structured nature of totality were, wittingly or unwittingly, rendered superfluous—as waste; disease; indeed, a flawed variant of organized modernity itself.

Perhaps nowhere has the instrumentalization of modernity been more evident within social theory than in debates concerning the status of the individual subject as regards the social totality. *Divided, fractured, split:* such terms are central to defining the state of the subject today within the evolution of the late capitalist economy itself, yet these terms are also surely evocative of competing versions of subjectivity within the social sciences and the humanities. On the one hand, the modernist, metaphysical fantasy constructs an image of individuals as self-mastering and self-contained, a conception in which selfhood is rendered whole, centered, and rational. This form of subjecthood, so vital to the political and juridical categories of the bourgeois era, is premised on the assumption that consciousness of self provides a sure foundation for knowledge, and as such critical self-reflection becomes intricately interwoven with the pursuit of individual and collective autonomy. On the other hand, it is precisely this image of the self-mastering, self-legislating liberal subject that is powerfully dispersed and derailed by the newer deconstructive theoretical operations emanating within late modern or postmodern European thought. For social theorists working from this vantage point, the individual subject is conceptualized largely as an effect of discourse, a product or construct of the ambiguous and unstable nature of language itself. Intriguingly and infuriatingly, however, both forms of subjecthood appear to remain hermetically sealed off from each other. For example, critics of modernist conceptions of selfhood, while demonstrating that the fantasied strength of the narcissistic ego is in fact a defensive sham, tend to be left celebrating the manic, fragmentary, and dispersed splitting of the subject—which, it must surely be recognized, is hardly a promising starting point for political projects concerned with the renewal of personal and cultural life.

On the most general level, contemporary theory has now almost everywhere broken with the Enlightenment idea of the self-identity of the subject by deconstructing its psychological unity, social rootedness, cultural construction and economic determination (see Cascardi 1992; Elliott 1996). The ontological modality of subjectivity in recent social thought is instead rendered a particular problematic of either discursive positions, political inconclusiveness, cultural rootlessness, and free-floating psychological operations of self-assembly. All of which is to say that the phenomenological ideal unity of subjective thinking or experience is now thought to have been undone or dismantled by the theoretical operations of newer ideological positions against which the consciousness of the individual subject can be mapped. In other words, the theme of personal identity or the coherence of the self has been replaced by the idea of never-ending self-constitution—the assembly, disassembly, and reassembly of narratives of the self.

Yet as far as sociological work is concerned at any rate, it is apparently easier to denounce the ideological terrors of the centered, self-identical subject at the level of theory than to resist the idea that personal experience is somehow primary or authentic on the level of social critique. There are two important and instructive illustrations of this tendency in the recent sociological literature. The first may be found in much contemporary hat tipping to the notion of dispersed identities or fragmented selves, on the one hand, while relying heavily on an appeal to experience as a foundational point of sociological explanation, on the other hand (see, e.g., Sennett 1998; Turkle 1999). The second example of this contradiction comes primarily, though not exclusively, from poststructural or deconstructive sociology, where the unmasking or deconstruction of modernist categories and their ideological ramifications is performed with reference to newer, postmodern benchmarks—variously termed *dissemination, libidinal economy, schizoanalysis,* or *ecriture.*

If today we are skeptical of the assumption that our societies are progressing in a unilinear direction and are reproduced and stabilized through mechanisms of order promotion and boundary maintenance (socialization, culture, ideology, etc.), we need also to resist the view that self-constitution and sociality are simply the upshot of pure social differences, randomness, unpredictability, indeterminancy, and flux. For while poststructuralist and postmodern authors usefully question the systemness of society, as well as deconstruct the deterministic logics of the social sciences and humanities, the dynamics of cultural phenomena, symbolic practices, and systems of thought do not float through time and space without anchorage in social contexts and historical habitats. Rather, to explore the interrelations between self-constitution and sociality is—as I shall argue throughout this book—to focus on the *social imaginary* dimensions of practical action, a creative medium through which social power is produced and history reproduced.

The political stimulus given to social theory and the task of its reconstruction over recent decades by poststructural, deconstructive, and postmodern methods of cultural analysis, however suggestive, should not be allowed to overshadow the contribution of contemporary social thinkers whose work has also sought to move beyond foundational, functional, or instrumental approaches to knowledge, but in a fashion that calls into question the primarily negative emphasis on identity formation and social norms (i.e., the thesis of *subjectification as subjection*) in much continental social theory through instead stressing the creative, intersubjective, recursive, and imaginary forms of living together in today's changed cultural conditions. The chapters that comprise Part One of this book critically examine a series of attempts to develop such a multidimensional social theory. Ulrich Beck's doctrine of the risk society and pervasive individualization; Anthony Giddens's notions of structuration and routinization for the rootedness of self-constitution and sociality in our posttraditional age; Cornelius Castoriadis's seminal exploration of the links between the radical imagination of the individual self and the social imaginary of culture and history; Jacques Lacan's conception of the symbolic structuring of identity, or cultural interpellation; Jürgen Habermas's ideal of communicative action or of discursive democracy; and Julia Kristeva's reflections on the dual symbolic nature of loss, mourning, and melancholia within the political domain: all of these contributions suggest a variety of possibilities for articulating a properly multidimensional social critique beyond the purely instrumentalizing logics of classical social theory. Thus, I have sought to facilitate this articulation by providing critical introductions to the work of these social theorists in the chapters that follow, paying special attention to those aspects of their social thought that I believe are of particular importance for the reconstruction of critical social theory.

The problem of the relations between the individual and society, or subject and structure, has been a core preoccupation of social and political thought. Broadly speaking, those schools of sociological thought that have paid particular attention to theorizing individual subjectivities and human actors have contributed to a unique understanding of how action and interaction are structured by broader social, political, and cultural sources. This is most obviously true of those forms of contemporary social analysis that have drawn from psychoanalytical theory, from both the various attempts to delineate the unconscious motivation of action as well as symbolic forms of interpersonal and cultural relations. Notwithstanding the importance of these affective dimensions of human experience for the social sciences and social theory, however, such frameworks encounter difficulties in providing conceptions of institutional transformation or social structure. Institutions certainly appear in the writings of major theorists of human subjectivity, such as Lacan, Kristeva, and Derrida, and in ways that problematize the connections between self and society. But as understood from the standpoint of more orthodox sociological traditions, institutions are analyzed by these authors mostly in terms of their symbolic or semiological meanings, and not in terms of social transformations or power relations.

Other branches of social theory, such as structuralism and systems theory, have sought to remedy this neglect by taking institutional structure as the core ingredient of social explanation. From this perspective, there is an explicit attempt to elucidate, in objective scientific terms, the structures and representations on which social interaction depends but that it cannot explicitly grasp or formulate. In such objectivistic approaches to social-scientific inquiry, there is a methodological break with the immediate experience of individual agents and a focus instead on the changing structural conditions of modern industrial societies.

There is, of course, an important line of continuity here with classical social thought. One central theoretical issue in classical sociology is concerned with the intrusion of structural or systemic aspects of modern society into forms of social conduct, specifically the way in which structures influence the social opportunities for, and constraints on, people. The view that economic structures are at once determinant and dominant in social life is certainly evident in the writings of Marx. "Human beings make their own history," wrote Marx (1963: 15), "but not in circumstances of their own choosing." Marx saw in the capitalist mode of production a dynamic in which people are subjected to the dull compulsion of oppressive economic relationships; writing about commodity fetishism in *Capital,* he argued that the individual subject is caught up in a social logic of mystified activity and ideology. A somewhat similar understanding of the power of structures in the lives of individuals can be found in the writings of Weber. While Weber argued that reason unleashed social critique and the demise of traditional worldviews, he, too, thought that the development of industrial societies ultimately led to the self-destruction of individuality and human agency. In Weber's sociology, the iron cage of modernity was a result of rationalization raised to the second power, in which agents functioned as mere cogs in the machine of the bureaucratic state.

Broadly speaking, many versions of modern social theory have sought to further explicate the role of structures in the maintenance of social stability. *The Social System* (1951), written by Harvard sociologist Talcott Parsons, became for many years the classic work for understanding how the actions of individuals linked to the general social system, its variety of reproductive processes and socialization patterns. Parsons's functionalism laid primary stress on a global system of common values and shared dispositions. In the wake of increasing social conflict and political violence throughout the 1960s and 1970s, however, sociologists found it increasingly difficult to defend the Parsonian theoretical tradition, with its neglect of issues of power and domination. That said, Parsonian theory has made something of a resurgence in recent times (see Schluchter 1979; Munch 1987; Robertson and Turner 1991), especially in Europe—where both Niklas Luhmann and Jürgen Habermas have refashioned Parsonian system theory for the analysis of contemporary society. Indeed, Parsonian functionalism and systems-theoretic logic is increasingly deployed in contemporary social theory as an explanation for both social stability and social change.

But if such attempts to understand institutional structures as deriving from more than repetitious patterns of human action have merit, they also have substantive limitations. The central limitation of objectivist social theory is that, by according priority to structure over action, a deterministic flavor is accorded to the social world and the practical activities of the individuals who make up that world. Many argue that this is especially obvious in the classical social thought of Emile Durkheim, in which society often appears as a force external to the agent, exercising constraint over individual action (see, e.g., Giddens 1971). Yet the tendency to grant priority to the object (structure) over the subject (agent) is sustained in various guises in contemporary social thought, principally in the work of structuralist and systems-theory analysts. It might thus be said that, while sociologists concerned with structural-functionalism or systems approaches have managed to analyze the intrusion of systemic social factors into domains of human activities, such theorists have managed less well with grasping how structural forces affect the production of everyday life in situated social contexts. That this is the case is perhaps not too surprising, for as I have said most social theorists tend to resolve the problem of the relation between human action and social structure by prioritizing one term at the expense of the other. "Few questions in social theory," laments John B. Thompson (1984: 148), "remain as refractory to cogent analysis as the question of how, and in precisely what ways, the action of individual agents is related to the structural features of the society of which they are part."

When social theorists today reflect on the changing relations between the individual and society, they generally do so in ways that are profoundly shaped by methodological concerns that underscore actor- and/or system-based models of analysis. Yet for many social theorists, these issues cannot be worked out only on a methodological level. For some theorists the transformations of modernity, such as globalization and the mediated character of the public sphere, have a direct impact on the nature of the self as well as the textures of day-to-day social life—reshaping the very definition of what is meant by the constitution of personal and social life. According to the German sociologist Ulrich Beck, for example, the antinomies between individualist and systems-based social-theoretic perspectives are themselves brought low by a new riskiness to risk, the consequences of which people confront everywhere around the globe. What Beck calls "risk society"—an emerging global technological world which generates a diversity of possible dangers, hazards, and futures—is said to bring people into a more active engagement with aspects of their lives, aspects that were previously the terrain of tradition or taken-for-granted norms. The riskiness of risk society, according to Beck, is the living of individual lives increasingly decision-dependent and in need of justification, reworking, reelaboration, and, above all, reinvention. As a consequence, problems of self/society cohesion—the integration of individualized individuals into the network of broader social relations—necessarily arise in novel forms at both the micro and macro levels. In chapter 1, I critically assess Beck's sociology of risk, and I seek to develop the view that the analysis of action and social structure can be satisfactorily pursued only in the broader context of a critical social theory.

Perhaps the most important attempt to rethink the relation between human action and social structure in our own time has been undertaken by the British sociologist Anthony Giddens. Giddens argues it is necessary for social theory to provide an account of the conditions and consequences of action as directly embroiled with structure. To do so, he suggests that action and structure should be seen as complementary terms of a duality, the "duality of structure"; social structures, he contends, are *both medium and outcome* of the practices that constitute those structures. That is, social systems are viewed by Giddens as simultaneously enabling and constraining. The structuring properties of social systems, he suggests, at once render human action possible and, through the performance of action, serve to reproduce the structural properties of society. To talk of the "structuring properties" of social systems, as Giddens does, is to adopt a radical, and indeed novel, view of the ways in which structures work in relation to human subjects. Giddens does not view structures so much as things that exist in themselves as, to use his terminology, a "virtual order" of transformative relations that exhibit themselves only in instantiated social practices and memory traces. When Giddens writes of this virtual order of structures, his analysis sometimes sounds reminiscent of a poststructuralist critique of language—as a structuring of presences against a backdrop of absences. What distinguishes Giddens's theory of structuration from poststructuralist thought, however, is a strong conception of human agency. For Giddens, subjects necessarily know a great deal about the social world in which they recursively organize their practices; such practices, he says, are socially embedded as virtual order properties of structures. This mutual dependence of structure and agency is what Giddens calls the "recursive character," or "reflexivity," of personal and social life, in which self-monitoring and self-critique are defining features. In chapter 2 I assess the strengths and weaknesses of Giddens's imaginative social theory, paying particular attention to the arts of structuration as played out in personal and cultural life.

If pressed to designate a term that encapsulates the reshaped social world of the twenty-first century, one could do worse than nominate *globalization*. The media continually refer to it; big business is full of clichéd references to its transforming power; academics busy themselves analyzing and debating it. *Globalization* is the buzzword of our era, an idea that apparently encompasses everything from the Internet to intimacy, multinational corporations to migration flows, the World Trade Organization to the demise of the welfare state. Notwithstanding the generality infusing popular rhetoric, social theorists broadly agree that *globalization* refers to the spatial and temporal "regrooving" or compression of social relations across the globe. Despite an expanding literature on whether this reshaping of social space by economic and technological forces will lead to a single global culture or alternatively plural globalizations (see Held et al. 1999), there appears little doubt that increased connections between different cultures and regions of the world are occurring.

Perhaps the more politically puzzling issues, then, are these. How fast, and how evenly, are contemporary social and economic changes developing? Has the sheer scale of global transformations outstripped the capacity of citizens, groups, or national governments to contest, control, or resist such forces? Are some regions or groups of people better able to negotiate the contradictions of globalization than others? For the German philosopher and critical theorist Jürgen Habermas, the nature, form, and impact of globalization are best conceptualized as involving the communicative reconstitution of the social-historical world, the complex ways in which individuals partake in symbolic negotiations and intersubjective settlement of democratic challenges and opportunities in the new millennium. Habermas's communicative theory of the global emergence of democratic public spheres, or what he elsewhere terms the postnational constellation, is one of the most outstanding contemporary contributions to the study of the relations between globalization, democracy, and politics. Yet some commentators have been quick to note that Habermas has given less attention to the ways in which nondiscursive, presymbolic, affective forces influence, shape, constrain or limit public political dialogue. How might an analysis of social transformations affecting the political sphere of democratic dialogue and intersubjective dispute be pursued if we are also to do justice to the emotional, unconscious desires of subjects or citizens in a world of pervasive globalization?

An interesting set of answers to this dilemma can be found in the writings of the French feminist Julia Kristeva. In numerous studies of cultural mourning, of public political dialogue, and of psychoanalysis, Kristeva has sought to integrate the analysis of psychic turmoil and personal trauma into a political understanding of public dialogue and democratic institutions. In chapter 5 I critically assess and compare the social theories of Habermas and Kristeva. I do so by situating their work in relation to contemporary debates raging over global culture and European identity.

Few areas of social inquiry are more conceptually exciting and politically important than the area staked out by imagination and the transgressive impulses of the unconscious. For it is, in part, through the symbolic and unconscious dimension of the social world that human agents represent a sense of identity to themselves, create visions of their ways of living with others, and engage in constant imaginative interpretation of their cultural, collective life. Conceptions of human imagination deployed in social theory contrast sharply. In demystifying procedures usually associated with French psychoanalysis and Lacanian theory, the "imaginary" dimensions of identity and sociality are discerned in the narcissistic, mirror distortions of identification, where lack and loss are intimately interwoven with subjective illusions, snares, fictions.

In chapter 3, I survey and critique the contribution of Jacques Lacan to social theory, paying special attention to his conception of the imaginary and the imagination. Lacan loathed the model of mental health evident in psychoanalytic formulations of the American ego psychologists: the cult of the expressive personality, the ideology of "normal" or "stable" identity. By contrast, Lacan was theoretically bold and radical, always looking for ambivalence, indeterminancy, and otherness. This makes his work important to social theory, as I seek to demonstrate in reviewing not only his theory of the imaginary but also his reformulation of the Freudian conscious/unconscious dualism as a linguistic relation, as well as his account of the intersubjective structuring of the subject in the symbolic order. However, while there is much that is fruitful for social theory in Lacan's approach, I argue that there are major shortcomings with both his negative paradigm of imagination and his linguistic reformulation of the relations between the individual subject, the unconscious and socio-symbolic order.

Another conception of "the imaginary" and imagination that is evident in recent social theory is that which emphasizes the fundamentally *creative* dimension of our personal and social lives. If Lacan's negative paradigm of "the imaginary" focuses on lack, gap, absence, and impossibility, this alternative reading of the power of social imagination confronts its generative capacity with regard to the reproduction or alteration of cultural forms. In chapter 4, I examine Cornelius Castoriadis's theory of radical imagination and the social imaginary, with particular reference to the themes of subjectivity, culture and political autonomy. Castoriadis's entire corpus is an argument for the creative and constitutive dimension of human imagination in our personal lives and cultural worlds. Imagination for Castoriadis is the excess of fantasy that escapes all social determination and ideological programming, that which slips through the very instrumental, functional, or rational forms it so surreptitiously delineates. The powers of imagination are also central to the theoretical departures of Julia Kristeva, whose influential reflections on the contradictory consequences of mourning, melancholia, and depression for public political life are considered in chapter 5.

Recently I attended an international colloquium on social theory at Cambridge University. In such a culturally exclusive and richly tranquil environment, delegates from around the world came together for several days to think through, and reflect on, new political sources for critical social thought. The aim of the conference, it appeared, was to dispute the adequacy of current perspective in social theory for analyzing late modern or postmodern culture and politics.

One presentation in particular caught my attention, if only because it seemed to condense and reflect the broader mood of delegates concerning the state of social theory. The American neofunctionalist sociologist Jeffrey Alexander, previously of UCLA and now based at Yale University, developed the contention that—notwithstanding postmodern relativism within the academy and also the broader public's general pessimism regarding intellectual assessments of the future shape of the social world—we live in an era of "critical post-Utopianism." What Alexander seemed to be driving at with the use of this unlovely term *critical post-Utopianism*, I gather, is the sense of the resilience of culture and the power of Utopian impulses and longings. While the metanarratives or big stories of the modern age (Truth, Justice, Revolution, Freedom, Reason) might have fallen on hard times, it is still the case that people hunger for better lives and better ways of living together. Around the globe, Alexander argued, a critical energizing vision infuses the activities of individuals and collectivities.

I liked the general sound of this argument, as I did Alexander's debunking of some of the more extreme claims emanating from postmodern social thought. Nonetheless, there seemed something a little forced about his argument, and hence I pondered these sociological musings further. Where, I asked myself as I listened to Alexander continue his presentation, might such critical energizing visions be found? I was, in effect, asking a fairly straightforward sociological question. What agents, or agencies, represent "critical post-Utopianism"? It transpired that Alexander's answer to this, much like those of Alain Touraine and Jürgen Habermas before him, centered on "new social movements" (feminism, peace activism, and ecological groupings) as the carriers of radical political action.

Hearing such a conclusion you might be forgiven for thinking, as indeed I did, "Here we go again!" It is certainly arguable that the new social movements (which are hardly "new" any longer) have been working overtime in sociological discourse for too long. This is a serious point, though I certainly do not wish to dismiss out of hand the potentially reformist, and sometimes radical, contribution of peace, ecological, and other social activists to public political debate. Nor do I wish to dispute Alexander's contention that collective projects and group action remain worthy of serious sociological scrutiny. But I do want to assert that there is something altogether too neat and comfortable about Alexander's conjectures concerning collective manifestations of the Utopian impulse, and further that this argument blends too easily with the traditional mainstream of sociology. Such critical comments are proffered in this context because it seems that the discipline of sociology is in danger of becoming too eagerly complicit with the grim seriousness of the social predicaments it seeks to critique. Hence, in a kind of manic quest for scientific respectability, certain highfalutin formulations ("critical post-Utopianism") are developed in order to demonstrate that sociology has immediate answers to perplexing and pressing social problems.

Perhaps what sociology *really* has to offer is less immediate answers stemming from so-called research than the disclosure—necessarily uncertain and ambivalent—of our changing engagements with the social world, and thus our everyday ways of doing sociological competence and thus the practical accomplishment of sociology itself. Signs of collective disaffection are abundant and increasing, yet, as Ulrich Beck repeatedly notes, people today are fashioning privatized solutions to the dilemmas of globalization. This search for individualized shelter is, of course, in large part defensive, manic, narcissistic—and it is the urgent task of sociology to show that the complex ways in which we take our individualized fates for destiny is itself a pressing political issue. Such engagement demands new ways of thinking, the revelation of new sites (emotional, bodily, psychosexual) of action, and not a return to social fatalism vis-à-vis blind confidence that social movements will somehow come to our rescue.

The chapters that comprise Part Two of this book may be regarded as a series of attempts to explore new sociological imaginings. The chapters focus on contemporary thinkers or numerous new sociologies proposing alternative cultural visions as well as programmatic suggestions for engagement with the clash of private and public turmoils of postmodern society. The chapters do not form a systematic overview of all of today's social-theoretical controversies, much less a review of the range of new sociologies. Rather, they present critical discussions and constructive conceptual proposals for the reformulation of specific thematic concerns. These include sexuality and identity politics, citizenship, representations of politics beyond left and right, and the renewed concern with ethics and morality in modern social thought.

Sociology, the critique of what is common, routine, and recursive in human life, is essentially the study of social action and cultural practices. It thus comes as no surprise that standardized versions of academic sociology have, for the most part, been implacably opposed to extending the reach of the sociological imagination to the analysis of subjective dispositions, sexualities, erotic fantasies, or experiments with gender identification. Yet these thematics are precisely the terrain of numerous new sociologies. In chapter 6, I turn to review such challenges to mainstream sociology by situating recent controversies over sexualities, sexual stereotypes, transgressive gender performances, and other identity politics in relation to rival social theories. I discuss psychoanalytic, Foucaultian, feminist, queer, and reflexive sociological approaches to the study of human sexuality and reflect on the conceptual advantages and limitations of each approach.

Globalization, as I mentioned earlier, is said to be one of the most contentious social-theoretical and political issues of the twenty-first century. To elevate the global over the national, with citizens squeezed between transnational forces on the one hand and local or regional movements on the other, is an increasingly common conceptual move in recent social thought. As Held (2001: 397) puts this:

> the present period is marked by a significant series of new types of "boundary problems," which challenge the distinctions between domestic and foreign affairs, internal political issues and external questions, and the sovereign concerns of the nation-state and international considerations. . . . In fact, in all major areas of government policy, the enmeshment of national political communities in regional and global processes involves them in intensive issues of transboundary coordination and control. Political space for the development and pursuit of effective government and the accountability of political power is no longer coterminous with a delimited national territory.

But how, exactly, do such "transboundary problems" affect our inherited conceptions of citizenship? Does social theory need to rethink citizenship? With the current debate split between global skeptics and hyperglobalists, the issue of how to develop a sense of connectedness to, and belonging within, the postnational community is certainly politically urgent, and chapter 7 examines recent attempts to rethink the political fostering of civic duty without states. The chapter seeks to provide an overview of recent debates on citizenship in the context of a mixed theoretical model of modern and postmodern political forms. Four new paths or frames of civic culture are identified: (1) the individualization of citizenship; (2) the intersubjective constitution of local, regional, national, and transnational civic communications in the public sphere; (3) the resetting of civic duty in the frame of what Beck terms "sub-politics"; and (4) the reinvention of citizenship as a consequence of the interlacing of the forces of regionalization and globalization.

"The state of an intellectual discipline," writes the political analyst Alan Davies (1972: 85), "like that of a distant nation, may sometimes be read off from its alliances." This may be especially true of the profession of political science, where its practitioners have sought through various engagements with other fields in the social sciences and humanities to carve out their specialism in the analysis of power. In chapter 8, I critically examine the received wisdom that political scientists can properly be regarded as specialists in the study of power and domination, partly through mapping the ways in which the discipline has sought to develop "laws" of a universal, or at least a highly generalized, nature. The interpretation of the nature of power as represented in political science can be understood in two somewhat different ways, conceiving politics to be concerned either with the discovery of immutable laws, principles, rules, and regulations or with specific techniques of poststructural deconstruction or of textual interpretation somehow peculiar to today's discontinuous, multifaceted, drifting, and unstable political environment. These contrasting interpretations I discuss in terms of modernist and postmodernist conceptualizations of political power.

This leads, finally, to changing conceptions of ethics in social and political theory today. The perfected objective apparatus of modernist academic sociology repressed ethics and morality just as successfully as mainstream representations of the discipline did the fracturing effects of decentered subjectivity. A sociological aversion to ethics went along with an objectivistically driven fear of emotion and the passions, and both were underpinned by a disciplinary devotion to social structure and cultural order rather than individual moral responsibility. If in our own time social theory has suffered an unprecedented crisis of confidence regarding such high modernist ideals, this is perhaps nowhere more evident than in recent and urgent discussions of moral duty and ethical challenges across the social sciences and humanities. A radical stress on human frailty, on widespread human misery and spectacles of suffering, has become entwined with issues concerning our ability to act globally for the common good in recent sociological debates. In chapter 9, I discuss contemporary culturalist, communitarian, and cosmopolitan standards of morality as well as revised commitments to the ethical sphere in a globalizing world. The writings of Taylor, Kymlicka, Rawls, Levinas, Melucci, and others are critically appraised, in order to advance the argument that social theories of moral responsibility can be usefully classified within a dual model as *modes of ethical construction:* "ethics as sociality" and "ethics as individualization." By examining the representation, translation, regulation, and repression of the moral impulse in terms of these social-theoretical discourses, I attempt to sketch the personal complexities and global challenges of ethics and morality in contemporary political life.

The following chapters thus trace interventions in contemporary social thought by prominent sociologists, philosophers, psychoanalysts, and the like, as well as detailing key social-theoretical issues as analyzed from poststructuralist interpretative strategies and in feminist and postmodernist discourse. In the process, I seek to develop the elements of a synthetic account of social critique, one capable of grasping the radical power of social imagination and the multidimensional nature of social life in the late modern or postmodern age. If social theorists are to meet the challenges raised by the world of the twenty-first century, such challenges on the level of theory require, above all, new ways of understanding ourselves, others, and the wider world.

I

INTERVENTIONS IN CONTEMPORARY SOCIAL THEORY

1

Risk and Reflexivity: Ulrich Beck

As competent reflective agents, we are aware of the many ways in which a generalized "climate of risk" presses in on our daily activities. In our day-to-day lives, we are sensitive to the cluster of risks that affect our relations with the self, with others, and with the broader culture. We are specialists in carving out ways of coping with and managing risk, whether this be through active engagement, resigned acceptance, or confused denial. From dietary concerns to prospective stock market gains and losses to polluted air, the contemporary risk climate is one of proliferation, multiplication, specialism, counterfactual guesswork, and, above all, anxiety. Adequate consideration and calculation of risk taking, risk management, and risk detection can never be fully complete, however, since there are always unforeseen and unintended aspects of risk environments. This is especially true at the level of global hazards, where the array of industrial, technological, chemical, and nuclear dangers that confront us grows, and at an alarming rate. Indeed, the German sociologist Ulrich Beck (1996b) defines the current situation as that of "world risk society." The rise of risk society, Beck argues, is bound up with the new electronic global economy—a world in which we live on the edge of high technological innovation and scientific development, but where no one fully understands the possible global risks and dangers we face.

My aim in this chapter is to explore some of the issues concerning the relation between risk and society by focusing on Beck's work. A profoundly innovative and imaginative social theorist, Beck (1986, 1991, 1992, 1994, 1997, 1998, 1999a, 1999b) has developed powerful analyses of the ways in which the rise of the risk society is transforming social reproduction, nature and ecology, intimate relationships, politics, and democracy. It is necessary to state, at the outset, that I am not seeking in this chapter to provide a general introduction to Beck's work as a whole. Rather, I shall offer a short exposition of his risk society thesis, in

19

conjunction with his analysis of reflexivity and its role in social practices and modern institutions.

The second, more extensive half of the chapter is then critical and reconstructive in character. I try to identify several questionable social-theoretic assumptions contained in Beck's risk society thesis, as well as limitations concerning his analysis of reflexivity, social reproduction, and the dynamics of modernity. In making this critique, I shall try to point, in a limited and provisional manner, to some of the ways in which I believe that the themes of risk and social reflexivity can be reformulated and, in turn, further developed in contemporary sociological analysis.

OUTLINE OF BECK'S SOCIAL THEORY

Let me begin by outlining the central planks of Beck's social theory. These can be divided in three major themes: (1) the risk society thesis, (2) reflexive modernization, and (3) individualization.

The Risk Society Thesis

In *Risk Society: Towards a New Modernity, Ecological Politics in an Age of Risk, The Normal Chaos of Love, The Reinvention of Politics, Democracy without Enemies, What Is Globalization?*, and *World Risk Society,* Beck argues that the notion of risk is becoming increasingly central to our global society. As Beck (1991: 22–23) writes:

> [T]he historically unprecedented possibility, brought about by our own decisions, of the destruction of all life on this planet . . . distinguishes our epoch not only from the early phase of the Industrial Revolution but also from all other cultures and social forms, no matter how diverse and contradictory. If a fire breaks out, the fire brigade comes; if a traffic accident occurs, the insurance pays. This interplay between before and after, between security in the here-and-now and security in the future because one took precautions even for the worst imaginable case, has been revoked in the age of nuclear, chemical and genetic technology. In their brilliant perfection, nuclear power plants have suspended the principle of insurance not only in the economic but also in the medical, psychological, cultural, and religious sense. The "residual risk society" is an uninsured society, in which protection, paradoxically, decreases as the threat increases.

For Beck, modernity is a world that introduces global risk parameters that previous generations have not had to face. Precisely because of the failure of modern social institutions to control the risks they have created, such as the ecological crisis, risk rebounds as a largely defensive attempt to avoid new problems and dangers.

Beck contends that it is necessary to separate the notion of risk from hazard or danger. The hazards of preindustrial society—famines, plagues, natural disasters—may or may not come close to the destructive potential of technoscience in the contemporary era. Yet for Beck this really is not a key consideration in any event, since he does not wish to suggest that daily life in today's risk society is intrinsically more hazardous than in the premodern world. What he does suggest, however, is that no notion of risk is to be found in traditional culture: preindustrial hazards or dangers, no matter how potentially catastrophic, were experienced as pregiven. They came from some "other"—gods, nature, or demons. With the beginning of societal attempts to control, and particularly with the idea of steering toward a future of predictable security, the consequences of risk become a political issue. This last point is crucial. It is societal intervention—in the form of decision making—that transforms incalculable hazards into calculable risks. "Risks," writes Beck (1997: 30), "always depend on decisions—that is, they presuppose decisions." The idea of "risk society" is thus bound up with the development of instrumental rational control, which the process of modernization promotes in all spheres of life—from individual risk of accidents and illnesses to export risks and risks of war.

In support of the contention that protection from danger decreases as the threat increases in the contemporary era, Beck (1994) discusses, among many other examples, the case of a lead crystal factory in the Federal Republic of Germany. The factory in question—Altenstadt in the Upper Palatinate—was prosecuted in the 1980s for polluting the atmosphere. Many residents in the area had, for some considerable time, suffered from skin rashes, nausea, and headaches, and blame was squarely attributed to the white dust emitted from the factory's smokestacks. Due to the visibility of the pollution, the case for damages against the factory was imagined, by many people, to be watertight. However, because there were three other glass factories in the area, the presiding judge offered to drop the charges in return for a nominal fine on the grounds that individual liability for emitting dangerous pollutants and toxins could not be established. "Welcome to the real-life travesty of the hazard technocracy!" writes Beck, underlining the denial of risks within our cultural and political structures. Such denial for Beck is deeply layered within institutions, and he calls this "organized irresponsibility"—a concept to which we will return.

The age of nuclear, chemical, and genetic technology, according to Beck, unleashes a destruction of the calculus of risks by which modern societies have developed a consensus on progress. Insurance has been the key to sustaining this consensus, functioning as a kind of security pact against industrially produced dangers and hazards. (Beck draws substantially from the work of François Ewald in developing the idea that society as a whole comes to be understood as a risk environment in insurers' terms. See Ewald 1986, 1993.) In particular, two kinds of insurance are associated with modernization: the private insurance company and public insurance, linked above all with the welfare state. Yet the changing nature of risk in an age of globalization, argues Beck, fractures the calculating of risks for purposes of insurance. Individually and collectively, we do not fully know or understand many of the risks that we currently face, let alone can we attempt to calculate them accurately in terms of probability, compensation, and accountability. In this connection, Beck emphasizes the following:

- Risks today threaten irreparable global damage that cannot be limited, and thus the notion of monetary compensation is rendered obsolete.
- In the case of the worst possible nuclear or chemical accident, any security monitoring of damages fails.
- Accidents, now reconstituted as "events" without beginning or end, break apart delimitations in space and time.
- Notions of accountability collapse.

Reflexive Modernization

Beck develops his critique of modernity through an examination of the presuppositions of the sociology of modernization. Many mainstream sociological theories remain marked, in his view, by a confusion of modernity with industrial society—seen in either positive or negative terms. This is true for functionalists and Marxists alike, especially in terms of their preoccupation with industrial achievement, adaptation, differentiation, and rationalization. Indeed, Beck finds an ideology of progress concealed within dominant social theories that equate modernization with linear rationalization. From Marx through Parsons to Luhmann, modern society is constantly changing, expanding, and transforming itself; it is clear that industrialism results in the using up of resources that are essential to the reproduction of society. But the most striking limitation of social theories that equate modernity with industrial society, according to Beck, lies in their lack of comprehension of the manner in which dangers to societal preservation and renewal infiltrate the institutions, organizations, and subsystems of modern society itself.

In contrast to this grand consensus on modernization, Beck argues that we are between industrial society and advanced modernity, between simple modernization and reflexive modernization. As Beck (1996b: 28) develops these distinctions:

In view of these two stages and their sequence, the concept of "reflexive modernization" may be introduced. This precisely does not mean reflection (as the adjective "reflexive" seems to suggest), but above all self-confrontation. The transition from the industrial to the risk epoch of modernity occurs unintentionally, unseen, compulsively, in the course of a dynamic of modernization which has made itself autonomous, on the pattern of latent side-effects. One can almost say that the constellations of risk society are created because the self-evident truths of industrial society (the consensus on progress, the abstraction from ecological consequences and hazards) dominate the thinking and behavior of human beings and institutions. Risk society is not an option which could be chosen or rejected in the course of political debate. It arises through the automatic operation of autonomous modernization processes which are blind and deaf to consequences and dangers. In total, and latently, these produce hazards which call into question—indeed abolish—the basis of industrial society.

It is the autonomous, compulsive dynamic of advanced or reflexive moderniza-tion that, according to Beck, propels modern men and women into "self-confron-tation" with the consequences of risk that cannot adequately be addressed, measured, controlled, or overcome, at least according to the standards of indus-trial society. Modernity's blindness to the risks and dangers produced by modern-ization—all of which happens automatically and unreflectingly, according to Beck—leads to societal self-confrontation—that is, the questioning of divisions between centers of political activity and the decision-making capacity of society itself. "Within the horizon of the opposition between old routine and new aware-ness of consequences and dangers," writes Beck, "society becomes self-critical" (1999b: 81).

The prospects for arresting the dark sides of industrial progress and advanced modernization through reflexivity are routinely short-circuited, according to Beck, by the insidious influence of "organized irresponsibility." Irresponsibility, as Beck uses the term, refers to a political contradiction of the self-jeopardization and self-endangerment of risk society. This is a contradiction between an emerg-ing public awareness of risks produced by and within the social-institutional sys-tem, on the one hand, and the lack of attribution of systemic risks to this system, on the other. There is, in Beck's reckoning, a constant denial of the suicidal ten-dency of risk society—"the system of organized irresponsibility"—which mani-fests itself in, say, technically orientated legal procedures designed to satisfy rigorous causal proof of individual liability and guilt. This self-created dead-end, in which culpability is passed off onto individuals and thus collectively denied, is maintained through political ideologies of industrial fatalism: faith in progress, dependence on rationality, and the rule of expert opinion.

Individualization

The arrival of advanced modernization is not wholly about risk; it is also about an expansion of choice. For if risks are an attempt to make the incalculable calcu-lable, then risk monitoring presupposes agency, choice, calculation, and respon-sibility. In the process of reflexive modernization, Beck argues, more and more areas of life are released or disembedded from the hold of tradition. That is, peo-ple living in the modernized societies of today develop an increasing engagement with both the intimate and more public aspects of their lives, aspects that were previously governed by tradition or taken-for-granted norms. This set of developments is what Beck calls "individualization," and its operation is governed by a dialectic of disintegration and reinvention. For example, the disappearance of tradition and the disintegration of previously existing social forms—fixed gender roles, inflexible class locations, masculinist work models—forces people into making decisions about their own lives and future courses of action. As traditional ways of doing things become problematic, people must choose paths for a more rewarding life—all of which requires planning and rationalization, deliberation and engagement. An active engagement with the self, with the body, with relationships and marriage, with gender norms, and with work: this is the subjective backdrop of the risk society.

The idea of individualization is the basis on which Beck constructs his vision of a "new modernity," of novel personal experimentation and cultural innovation against a social backdrop of risks, dangers, hazards, reflexivity, globalization. Yet the unleashing of experimentation and choice that individualization brings is certainly not without its problems. According to Beck, there are progressive and regressive elements to individualization, although, in analytical terms, these are extremely hard to disentangle. In personal terms, the gains of today's individualization might be tomorrow's limitation, as advantage and progress turn into their opposite. A signal example of this is offered in *The Normal Chaos of Love*, where Beck and Beck-Gernsheim (1995) reflect on the role of technological innovation in medicine and on how this impacts on contemporary family life. Technological advancements in diagnostic and genetic testing on the unborn, they argue, create new parental possibilities, primarily in the realm of health monitoring. However, the very capacity for medical intervention is one that quickly turns into an obligation on parents to use such technologies in order to secure a sound genetic starting point for their offspring. Individualization is seen here as a paradoxical compulsion, at once leading people into a much more engaged relationship with science and technology than used to be the case, and enforcing a set of obligations and responsibilities that few in society have thought through in terms of broad moral and ethical implications. It is perhaps little wonder therefore that Beck (1997: 96), echoing Sartre, contends that "people are condemned to individualization."

CRITIQUE OF BECK

Beck has elaborated a highly original formulation of the theory of risk, a formulation that links with, but in many ways is more sophisticated in its detail and application than, other sociological approaches to the analysis of risk environments in contemporary society (among other contributions, see Douglas and Wildavsky 1982; Castell 1991; Giddens 1990, 1991; Luhmann 1993; and Adam 1998). Beck's sociology of risk has clearly been of increasing interest to sociologists concerned with understanding the complex temporal and spatial figurations of invisible hazards and dangers, including global warming, chemical and petro-chemical pollution, the effects of genetically modified organisms, and culturally induced diseases such as bovine spongiform encephalopathy (BSE) (see Lash, Szerszynski, and Wynne 1996; Adam 1998). In what follows, I shall develop a critique of Beck's work around four core areas: (1) risk, reflexivity, and reflection; (2) power and domination; (3) tradition, modernity, and postmodernization; and (4) individualization, self-alteration, and critique.

Risk, Reflexivity, and Reflection

Let me begin with Beck's discussion of the "risk society" that, according to him, currently dominates sociopolitical frames thanks to the twin forces of reflexivity and globalization. There are, I believe, many respects in which Beck's vision of *Risikogesellschaft,* especially its rebounding in personal experience as risk-laden discourses and practices, is to be welcomed. In the wake of the Chernobyl disaster and widespread environmental pollution, and with ever more destructive weapons as well as human-made biological, chemical, and technological hazards, surely thinking in terms of risk has become central to the way in which human agents and modern institutions organize the social world. Indeed, in a world that could literally destroy itself, risk managing and risk monitoring increasingly influence both the constitution and calculation of social action.

As mentioned previously, it is this focus on the concrete, objective physical-biological-technical risk settings of modernity that recommends Beck's analysis as a useful corrective to the often obsessive abstraction and textual deconstruction that characterizes much recent social theory. However, one still might wonder whether Beck's theory does not overemphasize, in a certain sense, the phenomena and relevance of risk. From a social-historical perspective it is plausible to ask, for instance, whether life in society has become more risky. In "From Regulation to Risk," Turner (1994: 180–81) captures the problem well:

[A] serious criticism of Beck's arguments would be to suggest that risk has not changed so profoundly and significantly over the last three centuries. For example, were the epidemics of syphilis and bubonic plague in earlier periods any different from the modern environment illnesses to which Beck draws our attention? That is, do Beck's criteria of risk, such as their impersonal and unobservable nature, really stand up to historical scrutiny? The devastating plagues of earlier centuries were certainly global, democratic and general. Peasants and aristocrats died equally horrible deaths. In addition, with the spread of capitalist colonialism, it is clearly the case that in previous centuries many aboriginal peoples such as those of North America and Australia were engulfed by environmental, medical and political catastrophes which wiped out entire populations. If we take a broader view of the notion of risk as entailing at least a strong cultural element whereby risk is seen to be a necessary part of the human condition, then we could argue that the profound uncertainties about life, which occasionally overwhelmed earlier civilizations, were not unlike the anxieties of our own fin-de-siècle civilizations.

Extending Turner's critique, we might also ask whether risk assessment is the ultimate worry in the plight of individuals in contemporary culture. Is it right to see the means-ended rationality of risk, and thus the economistic language of preference, assessment, and choice, as spreading into personal and intimate spheres of life (such as marriage, friendship and child rearing) in such a determinate and unified way? And does the concept of risk actually capture what is new and different in the contemporary social condition?

I shall not pursue these general questions, important though they are, here. Instead, the issue I want to raise concerns the multiple ways in which risk is perceived, approached, engaged with, or disengaged from in contemporary culture. Beck's approach, however suggestive it may be, is at best a signpost that points to specific kinds of probabilities, avoidances, and unanticipated consequences, but that is limited in its grasp of the social structuring of the perception of risk. The American social theorist Jeffrey C. Alexander (1996: 135) has argued that Beck's "unproblematic understanding of the perception of risk is utilitarian and objectivist." Alexander takes Beck to task for adopting a rationalistic and instrumental-calculative model of risk in microsocial and macrosocial worlds; it can be added that such a model has deep affinities with neoclassical economics and rational-choice theory, and thus necessarily shares the conceptual and political limitations of these standpoints also. Beck has also been criticized by others for his cognitive realism, moral proceduralism, and lack of attention to aesthetic and hermeneutical subjectivity (Lash and Urry 1994); failure to acknowledge the embodied nature of the self (Turner 1994; Petersen 1996); and neglect of the psychodynamic and affective dimensions of subjectivity and intersubjective relations (Elliott 1996; Hollway and Jefferson 1997).

In a social-theoretical frame of reference, what these criticisms imply is that Beck's theory cannot grasp the hermeneutical, aesthetic, psychological, and culturally bounded forms of subjectivity and intersubjectivity in and through which risk is constructed and perceived. To study risk management and risk avoidance strategies, in the light of these criticisms, requires attention to forms of meaning making within sociosymbolically inscribed institutional fields, a problem to which I return in a subsequent section when looking at Beck's analysis of tradition, modernity, and postmodernity. In raising the issue of the construction and reconstruction of risk—in particular, its active interpretation and reconstruction—one might reference numerous studies of sociopolitical attitudes relating to the conceptualization and confrontation of risk, danger and hazard. The anthropologist Mary Douglas (1986, 1992), for example, argues that advanced industrial risks are primarily constructed through the rhetoric of purity and pollution. For Douglas, what is most pressing in the social-theoretic analysis of risk is an understanding of how human agents ignore many of the potential threats of daily life and instead concentrate only on selected aspects.

Interestingly, Beck fails to discuss in any detail Douglas's anthropology of risk. Where Beck comments on Douglas, the concentration is typically on the schism in sociology between the analysis of traditional-agrarian and modern-industrial societies (see Beck 1997: 57–58, 87). This would seem peculiar not only since Douglas's pathbreaking analyses of risk appear to have laid much of the thematic groundwork for Beck's sociological theory but also because her work is highly relevant to the critique of contemporary ideologies of risk—that is, the social forms in which risk and uncertainty are differentiated across and within social formations, as well as peculiarly individuated.

My purpose in underscoring these various limitations of Beck's theory is not to engage in some exercise of conceptual clarification. My concern, rather, is to stress the sociologically questionable assumptions concerning risk in Beck's work and to tease out the more complex, nuanced forms of risk perception that might fall within the scope of such an approach. To call into question Beck's notion of risk is, of course, also to raise important issues about the location of reflexivity between self and societal reproduction. Now it is the failure of simple, industrial society to control the risks it has created that, for Beck, generates a more intensive and extensive sense of risk in reflexive, advanced modernity. In this sense, the rise of objective, physical, global risks propels social reflexivity. But again one might wish to question the generalizations Beck makes about human agents, modern institutions, and culture becoming more reflexive or self-confronting. Much of Beck's work has been concerned to emphasize the degree of reflexive institutional dynamism involved in the restructuring of personal, social, and political life, from the reforging of intimate relationships to the reinvention of politics. But there are disturbing dimensions here as well, which the spread of cultural, ethnic, racial, and gendered conflict has shown only too well, and often in ways in which one would be hard pressed to find forms of personal or social reflexive activity.

No doubt Beck would deny—as he has done in his more recent writings—that the renewal of traditions and the rise of cultural conflicts are counterexamples to the thesis of reflexive modernization. For we need to be particularly careful, Beck contends, not to confuse reflexivity (self-dissolution) with reflection (knowledge). As Beck (1994a: 176–77) develops this distinction:

[T]he "reflexivity" of modernity and modernization in my sense does not mean reflection on modernity, self-relatedness, the self-referentiality of modernity, nor does it mean the self-justification or self-criticism of modernity in the sense of classical sociology; rather (first of all), modernization undercuts modernization, unintended and unseen, and therefore also reflection-free, with the force of autonomized modernization. . . . [R]eflexivity of modernity can lead to reflection on the self-dissolution and self-endangerment of industrial society, but it need not do so.

Thus, reflexivity does not imply a kind of hyper-Enlightenment culture, in which agents and institutions reflect on modernity, but rather an unintended self-modification of forms of life driven by the impact of autonomized processes of modernization. Reflexivity, on this account, is defined as much by "reflex" as it is by "reflection." "It is possible to detect," write Szerszynski et al. (1996) of Beck's recent sociology, "a move towards seeing reflexive modernization as in most part propelled by blind social processes—a shift, crudely, from where risk society produces reflection which in turn produces reflexivity and critique, to one where risk society automatically produces reflexivity, and then—perhaps—reflection."

Without wishing to deny the interest of this radical conception of reflexivity as self-dissolution, it still seems to me that Beck's contention that contemporary societies are propelled toward self-confrontation, split between reflex and reflection, remains dubious. In what sense, for instance, can one claim that reflection-free forms of societal self-dissolution exist independently of the reflective capacities of human agents? For what, exactly, is being dissolved, if not the forms of life and social practices through which institutions are structured? How might the analytical terms of reflexivity—that is, social reflexes (nonknowledge) and reflection (knowledge)—be reconciled? It may be thought that these difficulties can be overcome by insisting, along with Beck, on reflexivity in the strong sense—as the unseen, the unwilled, the unintended; in short, institutional dynamism. But such an account of blind social processes is surely incompatible with, and in fact renders incoherent, concepts of reflection, referentiality, and reflexivity. Alternatively, a weaker version of the argument might be developed, one that sees only partial and contextual interactions of self-dissolution and reflection. Yet such an account, again, would seem to cut the analytical ground from under itself, since there is no adequate basis for showing how practices of reflexivity vary in their complex articulations of reflex and reflection, or repetition and creativity.

Power and Domination

I now want to consider Beck's theory in relation to sociological understandings of power and domination. According to Beck, reflexive modernization combats many of the distinctive characteristics of power, turning set social divisions into active negotiated relationships. Traditional political conflicts, centered around class, race and gender, are increasingly superseded by new, globalized risk conflicts. "Risks," writes Beck (1992: 35), "display an equalizing effect." Everyone now is threatened by risk of global proportions and repercussions; not even the rich and powerful can escape the new dangers and hazards of, say, global warming or nuclear war. And it is from this universalized perspective that Beck argues political power and domination is shedding the skin of its classical forms and reinventing itself in a new global idiom.

The problematic nature of Beck's writings on this reinvention of political power and its role in social life, however, becomes increasingly evident when considering his analysis of social inequalities and cultural divisions. Take, for example, his reflections on class. Reflexive modernization does not result in the self-destruction of class antagonisms but rather in self-modification. He writes:

Reflexive modernization disembeds and re-embeds the cultural prerequisites of social classes with forms of individualization of social inequality. That means . . . that the disappearance of social classes and the abolition of social inequality no longer coincide. Instead, the blurring of social classes (in perception) runs in tandem with an exacerbation of social inequality, which now does not follow large identifiable groups in the lifeworld, but is instead fragmented across (life) phases, space and time. (1997: 26)

The present-day individualizing forces of social inequality, according to Beck, erode class consciousness (personal difficulties and grievances no longer culminate into group or collective causes) and also, to some considerable degree, class-in-itself (contemporary social problems are increasingly suffered alone). In short, class as a community of fate or destiny declines steeply. With class solidarities replaced by brittle and uncertain forms of individual self-management, Beck finds evidence for a "rule-altering rationalization" of class relationships in new business and management practices, as well as industrial relations reforms. He contends that new blendings of economics and democracy are discernible in the rise of political civil rights within the workplace, a blend that opens the possibility of a post-capitalistic world—a "classless capitalism of capital," in which "the antagonism between labour and capital will collapse."

There is considerable plausibility in the suggestion that class patterns and divisions have been altered by rapid social and political changes in recent years. These include changes in employment and the occupational structure, the expansion of the service industries, rising unemployment, lower retirement ages, as well as a growing individualization in the West together with an accompanying stress on lifestyle, consumption, and choice. However, while it might be the case that developments associated with reflexive modernization and the risk society are affecting social inequalities, it is surely implausible to suggest, as Beck does, that this involves the transfiguration of class as such. Why, as Scott Lash (in Beck, Giddens, and Lash 1994) asks, do we find reflexivity in some sectors of socioeconomic life and not others? Against the backdrop of new communication technologies and advances in knowledge transfer, vast gaps in the sociocultural conditions of the wealthy and the poor drastically affect the ways in which individuals are drawn into the project of reflexive modernization. These tensions are especially evident today in new social divisions between the "information rich" and "information poor" and in the forces and demands of such symbolic participation within the public sphere. What Beck fails to adequately consider is that individualization (while undoubtedly facilitating unprecedented forms of personal and social experimentation) may directly contribute to, and advance the proliferation of, class inequalities and economic exclusions. That is, Beck fails to give sufficient sociological weight to the possibility that individualization may actually embody systematically asymmetrical relations of class power.

Taken from a broader view of the ideals of equal opportunity and social progress, Beck's arguments about the relationship between advanced levels of reflexivity and the emergence of a new subpolitics do not adequately stand up to scrutiny. The general, tendential assertions he advances about business and organizational restructuring assume what needs to be demonstrated—namely, that these new organizational forms spell the demise of social class, as well as the viability of class analysis. Moreover, it seems implausible to point to "subpolitics," defined by Beck only in very general terms, as symptomatic of a new sociopolitical agenda. When, for example, have the shifting boundaries between the political and economic spheres not played a primary role in the unfolding of relations between labor and capital? Are decision making and consciousness really focused on a postcapitalistic rationalization of rights, duties, interests, and decisions?

A good deal of recent research shows, on the contrary, that income inequality between and within nations continues to escalate (Braun 1991; Lemert 1997); that class (together with structures of power and domination) continues to profoundly shape possible life chances and material interests (Westergaard 1995); and that the many different definitions of class as a concept, encompassing the marginal, the excluded, as well as the new underclass or new poor, are important in social analysis for comprehending the persistence of patterns of social inequality (Crompton 1996).

These difficulties would suggest that Beck's theory of risk requires reformulation in various ways. Without wishing to deny that the risk-generating propensity of the social system has rapidly increased in recent years due to the impact of globalization and technoscience, it seems to me misleading to contend that social divisions in multinational capitalist societies are fully transfigured into a new logic of risk, as if the latter disconnects the former from its institutionalized biases and processes. The more urgent theoretical task, I suggest, is to develop methods of analysis for explicating how patterns of power and domination feed into, and are reconstituted by, the sociosymbolic structuring of risk. Here I shall restrict myself to noting three interrelated forces that indicate, in a general way, the contours of how a politics of risk is undergoing transformation.

The first development is that of the privatization of risk. Underpinned by new transnational spatializations of economic relations as well as the deregulation of the government of political life (Giddens 1990; Hirst and Thompson 1996; Bauman 1998), the individual is increasingly viewed today as an active agent in the risk monitoring of collectively produced dangers; risk information, risk detection, and risk management are more and more constructed and designed as a matter of private responsibility and personal security. By and large, human agents confront socially produced risks individually. Risk is desocialized; risk exposure and risk avoidance are matters of individual responsibility and navigation. This is, of course, partly what Beck means by the individualization of risk.

However, the relations between individualized or privatized risk, material inequalities, and the development of global poverty are more systematic and complex than Beck's theory seems to recognize. In the postwar period, the shift from Keynesian to monetarist economic policies has been a key factor in the erosion of the management of risk through welfare security. The impact of globalization, transnational corporations, and governmental deregulation is vital to the social production of the privatization of risk, all of which undoubtedly have a polarizing effect on distributions of wealth and income. It has also become evident—and this is crucial—that one must be able to deploy certain educational resources, symbolic goods, cultural and media capabilities, as well as cognitive and affective aptitudes, in order to count as a "player" in the privatization of risk detection and risk management. People who cannot deploy such resources and capabilities, often the result of various material and class inequalities, are likely to find themselves further disadvantaged and marginalized in a new world order of reflexive modernization.

The second, related development concerns the commodification of risk. Millions of dollars are made through product development, advertising, and market research in the new industries of risk, which construct new problems and market new solutions for risk-fighting individual agents. "As risk is simultaneously proliferated and rendered potentially manageable," writes Nikolas Rose (1996: 342),

> the private market for "security" extends: not merely personal pension schemes and private health insurance, but burglar alarms, devices that monitor sleeping children, home testing kits for cholesterol levels and much more. Protection against risk through an investment in security becomes part of the responsibilities of each active individual, if they are not to feel guilt at failing to protect themselves and their loved ones against future misfortunes.

In other words, the typical means for insuring against risk today is through market-promoted processes. However, the fundamental point here—and this is something that Beck fails to develop in a systematic manner—is that such "insurance" is of a radically imaginary kind (with all the misrecognition and illusion that the Lacanian-Althusserian theorization of the duplicate mirror structure of ideology implies), given that one cannot really buy one's way out of the collective dangers that confront us as individuals and societies. How does one, for example, buy a way out from the dangers of global warming? The commodification of risk has become a kind of safe house for myths, fantasies, fictions, and lies.

The third development concerns the instrumentalization of identities in terms of lifestyle, consumption, and choice. Beck touches on this issue through the individualization strand of his argument. Yet because he sees individualization as an active process transforming risk society, he pays almost no attention to the kinds of affective "investments," often destructive and pathological, unleashed by an instrumentalization of identities and social relations. Of core importance here is the "culture of narcissism" (Lasch 1980) that pervades contemporary Western life and plays a powerful role in the instrumental affective investments in individuals that a risk society unleashes. Joel Kovel (1988) writes of "the de-sociation of the narcissistic character," a character lacking in depth of emotional attachment to others and communities. Unable to sustain a sense of personal purpose or social project, the narcissistic character, writes Kovel, rarely moves beyond instrumentality in dealing with other people. Such instrumental emotional investments may well be increasingly central to the management of many risk codes in contemporary culture.

Consider the ways in which some parents fashion a narcissistic relation with their own children as a kind of imaginary risk insurance (involving anxieties and insecurities over old age, mortality, etc.), rather than relating to their offspring as independent individuals in their own right. Also in risks relating to the home, personal comfort, as well as safety, hygiene, health, and domesticity, the veneer-like quality of pathological narcissism can be found. Some analytical caution is, of course, necessary here, primarily because the work on narcissistic culture of Lasch and Sennett, among others, has been criticized in terms of overgeneralization (Giddens 1991). Accordingly, it may be more plausible to suggest that narcissistic forms of identity are a tendency within contemporary cultural relations of risk management, and not a wholesale social trend.

Beck's writings, I am suggesting, are less than satisfying on issues of power and domination because he fails to analyze in sufficient depth the psychological, sociological, and political forces by means of which the self-risk dialectic takes its varying forms. To develop a more nuanced interpretative and critical approach, I have suggested, the sociological task is to analyze privatization, commodification, and instrumentalization as channels of risk management.

Tradition, Modernity, and Postmodernity

The limitations in the concept of reflexivity I have highlighted are, in turn, connected to further ambiguities concerning the nature of social reproduction in contemporary culture. The production and reproduction of contemporary social life are viewed by Beck as a process of "detraditionalization." The development of reflexive modernization, says Beck, is accompanied by an irreversible decline in the role of tradition; the reflexivity of modernity and modernization means that traditional forms of life are increasingly exposed to public scrutiny and debate. That the dynamics of social reflexivity undercut preexisting traditions is emphasized by Beck via a range of social-theoretical terms. He speaks of "the age of side-effects," of individualization, and of a sub-politics beyond left and right—a world in which people can and must come to terms with the opportunities and dangers of new technologies, markets, experts, systems, and environments. He thus argues that the contemporary age is one characterized by increased levels of referentiality, ambivalence, flexibility, openness, and social alternatives.

It might be noted that certain parallels can be identified between the thesis of detraditionalization and arguments advanced in classical social theory. Many classical social theorists believed that the development of the modern era spelled the end of tradition. "All that is solid melts into air," said Marx of the power of the capitalist mode of production to tear apart traditional forms of social life. That the dynamics of capitalism undercut capitalism's own foundations meant for Marx a society that was continually transforming and constantly revolutionizing itself.

Somewhat similar arguments about the decline of tradition can be found in the writings of Max Weber. The development of industrial society for Weber was inextricably intertwined with the rise of the bureaucratic state. Weber saw in this bureaucratic rationalization of action, and associated demand for technical efficiency, a new social logic destructive of the traditional texture of society.

The views of Marx and Weber, among others, thus advanced a general binary opposition of "the traditional" and "the modern." For proponents of the thesis of detraditionalization, such as Beck, the self-referentiality and social reflexivity of advanced modernity also necessarily imply that traditional beliefs and practices begin to break down. However, the thesis of detraditionalization is not premised on the broad contrast between "the traditional" and "the modern" that we can discern in much classical social theory. On the contrary, Beck finds the relation between tradition and modernity at once complex and puzzling. If tradition remains an important aspect of advanced modernity, it is because tradition becomes reflexive; traditions are invented, reinvented, and restructured in conditions of the late modern age.

So far I think that there is much that is interesting and important in this general orientation of Beck to understanding the construction of the present, past, and future. In particular, I think the stress placed on the reflexive construction of tradition, and indeed all social reproduction, is especially significant—even though I shall go on to argue that this general theoretical framework requires more specification and elaboration. I want, however, to focus on a specific issue raised by Beck's social theory and ask, Has the development of society toward advanced modernization been accompanied by a decline in the influence of tradition and traditional understandings of the past? Must we assume, as Beck seems to, that the social construction of tradition is always permeated by a pervasive reflexivity? At issue here, I suggest, is the question of how the concept of reflexivity should be related to traditional, modern, and postmodern cultural forms. I shall further suggest that the concept of reflexivity, as elaborated by Beck, fails to comprehend the different modernist and postmodernist figurations that may be implicit within social practices and symbolic forms of the contemporary age.

To develop this line of argumentation, let us consider in some more detail the multiplicity of world traditions, communities, and cultures as they impact on current social practices and life strategies. I believe that Beck is right to emphasize the degree to which modernity and advanced modernization processes have assaulted traditions, uprooted local communities, and broken apart unique regional, ethnic, and subnational cultures. At the level of economic analysis, an argument can plausibly be sustained that the erratic nature of the world capitalist economy produces high levels of unpredictability and uncertainty in social life and cultural relations, all of which Beck analyzes in terms of danger, risk, and hazard.

It is worth noting, however, that Beck's emphasis on increasing levels of risk, ambivalence, and uncertainty is at odds with much recent research in sociology and social theory that emphasizes the regularization and standardization of daily life in the advanced societies. George Ritzer's *The McDonaldization of Society* (1993) is a signal example. Drawing from Weber's theory of social rationalization and the Frankfurt School's account of the administered society into a reflective encounter, Ritzer examines the application of managerial techniques such as Fordism and Taylorism to the fast-food industry as symptomatic of the infiltration of instrumental rationality into all aspects of cultural life. *McDonaldization,* as Ritzer develops the term, is the emergence of social logics in which risk and unpredictability are written out of social space. The point about such a conception of the standardization of everyday life, whatever its conceptual and sociological shortcomings, is that it clearly contradicts Beck's stress on increasing risk and uncertainty, the concept of reflexive individualization, and the notion that detraditionalization produces more ambivalence, more anxiety, and more openness.

Of course, Beck insists that reflexive modernization does not mark a complete break from tradition; rather, reflexivity signals the revising, or reinvention, of tradition. However, the resurgence and persistence of ethnicity and nationality as a primary basis for the elaboration of traditional beliefs and practices throughout the world are surely problematic for those who, like Beck, advance the general thesis of social reflexivity. Certainly, the thesis would appear challenged by widespread and recently revitalized patterns of racism, sexism, and nationalism that have taken hold in many parts of the world; indeed, many serious controversies over race, ethnicity, and nationalism involve a reversion to what might be called traditionalist battles over traditional culture—witness the rise of various religious fundamentalisms in the United States, the Middle East, and parts of Africa and Asia.

These political and theoretical ambivalences have their roots in a number of analytical difficulties, specifically Beck's diagnosis of simple and advanced modernity. Beck furnishes only the barest social-historical sketch of simple modernity as a distinctive period in the spheres of science, industry, morality, and law. He underscores the continuing importance and impact of simple industrial society for a range of advanced, reflexive determinations (e.g., economically, technologically, and environmentally), yet the precise relations of such overlapping are not established or demonstrated in any detail. Exactly how we have moved into the age of reflexive modernization, although often stated and repeated, is not altogether clear. Beck's main line of explanation seems to focus on the side effects of modernization as undercutting the foundations of modernity. But, again, the dynamics of simple and reflexive modernization, together with their social-historical periodization, remain opaque.

In addition, it is not always clear how Beck is intending to draw certain conceptual distinctions between "positive" and "negative" instantiations of respectively simple and advanced modernist sociosymbolic figurations. Rejecting outright any crude opposition between traditional and modern societies, Beck relates a tale of the proliferation of reflexive biographies and practices, lives and institutions, in which creative possibilities develop and new forms of risk and hazard take shape. Yet social advancement is far from inevitable: Beck speaks of countermodernities. The question that needs to be asked here, however, is whether it is analytically useful for social theory to construct the contemporary age as characterized by interacting tropes of industrial society and reflexive modernization, on the one side, and a range of countermodernities, on the other.

Viewed from the frame of postmodern social theory, and in particular the sociology of postmodernity (see Bauman 1992a), Beck's argument concerning the circularity of the relationship between risk, reflexivity, and social knowledge appears in a more problematic, and perhaps ultimately inadequate, light. For postmodern social theorists and cultural analysts diagnose the malaise of present-day society not only as the result of reflexively applied knowledge to complex technoscientific social environments, but as infused by a more general and pervasive sense of cultural disorientation. The most prominent anxieties that underpin postmodern dynamics of social regulation and systemic reproduction include a general loss of belief in the engine of progress, as well as feelings of out-of-placeness and loss of direction. Such anxieties or dispositions are accorded central significance in the writings of a number of French theorists—notably, Foucault, Derrida, Lyotard, Baudrillard, and Deleuze and Guattari—and also in the work of sociologists and social scientists interested in the ramifications of poststructuralism, semiotics, and deconstructionism for the analysis of contemporary society (Bauman 1992a, 1992b, 2000; Smart 1992, 1993; Best and Kellner 1991; Harvey 1989; Lash and Urry 1987; Poster 1990; Elliott 1996). Postmodern anxieties or dispositions are, broadly speaking, cast as part of a broader cultural reaction to universal modernism's construction of the social world, which privileges rationalism, positivism, and technoscientific planning. Premised on a vigorous philosophical denunciation of humanism, abstract reason, and the Enlightenment legacy, postmodern theory rejects the metanarratives of modernity (i.e., totalistic theoretical constructions, allegedly of universal application) and instead embraces fragmentation, discontinuity, and ambiguity as symptomatic of current cultural conditions.

To express the implications of these theoretical departures more directly in terms of the current discussion, if the social world in which we live in the twenty-first century is significantly different from that of simple modernization, this is so because of *both* sociopolitical and epistemological developments. It is not only reflection on the globalization of risk that has eroded faith in humanly engineered progress. Postmodern contributions stress that the plurality of heterogeneous claims to knowledge carries radical consequences for the unity and coherence of social systems. Bluntly stated, a number of core issues are identified by postmodern analysts in this connection:

- The crisis of representation, instabilities of meaning, and fracturing of knowledge claims.
- The failure of the modernist project to ground epistemology in secure foundations.
- The wholesale transmutation in modes of representation within social life itself. Postmodernization in this context spells the problematization of the relationship between signifier and referent, representation and reality, a relationship made all the more complex by the computerization of information and knowledge (Poster 1990).

What I am describing as a broadly postmodern sociological viewpoint highlights the deficiency of placing "risk" (or any other sociological variable) as the central paradox of modernity. For at a minimum a far wider range of sources would appear to condition our current cultural malaise.

What is significant about these theoretical sightings, or glimpses, of the contours of postmodernity as a social system are that they lend themselves to global horizons and definitions more adequately than the so-called universalism of Beck's sociology of risk. Against a theoretical backdrop of the break with foundationalism, the dispersion of language games, coupled with the recognition that history has no overall teleology, it is surely implausible to stretch the notion of risk as a basis for interpretation of phenomena from, say, an increase in worldwide divorce rates through to the collapse of insurance as a principle for the regulation of collective life. Certainly, there may exist some family resemblance in trends surrounding new personal, social, and political agendas. Yet the seeds of personal transformation and social dislocation are likely to be a good deal more complex, multiple, discontinuous.

This is why the change of mood—intellectual, social, cultural, psychological, political, and economic—analyzed by postmodern theorists has more far-reaching consequences for sociological analysis and research into modernity and postmodernization than does the work of Beck. In Beck's sociology, the advent of advanced modernization is related to the changing social and technological dimensions of just one institutional sector: that of risk and its calculation. The key problem of reflexive modernization is one of living with a high degree of risk in a world where traditional safety nets (the welfare state, traditional nuclear family, etc.) are being eroded or dismantled. But what is left unexplored here is the possibility that today's far-reaching social transitions have occurred as a result of a broader crisis, one that involves not only the spiraling of risk but also the shattering of modernist culture, the breakdown of enlightenment faith in progress, the collapse of European imperialism, and the globalization of capital. This is not to say, of course, that anxieties arising from postindustrial and techno-logical risks are not of central importance; but it is to acknowledge that such risks form a part—albeit a very important part—of very broad social transitions currently occurring.

Many aspects of the sociology of postmodernity—emphasis on the intensifica-tion of globalization, the cult of technology, dislocating subversions of epistemo-logical closure, and the leveling of social and cultural hierarchies—also underline the significant limitations inherent in Beck's faith in the self-limitation and self-control of reflexive risk environments for the emergence of "another modernity." The criticism here is that Beck's overemphasis on a potential reflexive social future in which alternative technoscientific practices come to the fore—where institutionalized politics is displaced in favor of social sub-politics and the politi-cization of culture—follows directly from his assumption that risk can be collec-tively navigated via a modern, rationalist faith in self-control and self-monitoring. But this assumption may be misleading, for it may rest on a mistaken view of the relation between enlightened rationalities and social transformation.

"After having convincingly argued that modern solutions have become the source of our problems," as Barry Smart writes (2000: 466), "it is ironic that Beck continues to turn to aversion of the modern project in pursuit of a resolu-tion." Smart persuasively argues, pace Beck, that many aspects of our lives remain far from controllable not only due to the insidious influence of overratio-nalization and intensive global risks but primarily because contingency, ambiva-lence, and ambiguity structure the human condition in a more far-reaching fashion.

Following the sociological insights of Bauman (1991, 2000), one can plausibly argue that postmodern adherents of the paradoxes of modernity indicate that con-tingency and ambivalence are here to stay, with the implication that the sociologi-cal picture may be considerably more messy and ambiguous than Beck cares to acknowledge. The postmodern emphasis on the multiple, fragmented, discontinu-ous, and local implies that all attempts to fashion a master discourse of society are illegitimate. Is Beck's sociology of risk such a "master discourse"? Probably not, as Beck has been at pains in his writings to stress that he is seeking to elabo-rate a multidimensional account of the nature of modernity. What these theoreti-cal considerations do highlight, however, is that Beck's work leaves out various cultural, epistemological, and political forces that are contributing to current social transitions of the most fundamental kind, and in doing so perhaps overpriv-ileges the degree to which the management of risk is a key institutional value.

Viewed from this perspective, it also becomes apparent that Beck's argument against postmodernists—that is, that they make the sociologically naive mistake of equating modernity with industrial modernization—is vulnerable, and precisely for reasons which have to do with grasping the "multiple worlds" with which late modern culture increasingly engages. By rejecting all the current talk of postmodernism and postmodernity as conceptually off the mark, Beck closes off the possibility of seeing that the processes of self-reflexivity and institutional dynamism with which he is most concerned might well be propelling us beyond modernity to some new, institutionalized social order. Proper analysis of postmodern cultural conditions demands breaking with our traditional (modernist) theoretical frameworks in which social realities of the world are assimilated to certain key decisive forces (such as risk, class, or nationalism) and the development instead of more heterogeneous interpretative methods for analyzing the plurality of traditions, practices, and perspectives that constitute social life.

Individualization, Self-Alteration, and Critique

By this point, the ambivalence pervading Beck's account of the process of individualization within the broader confines of his sociology of risk will once more have become apparent. It will be recalled that Beck is, in part, concerned with the expansion of choice, calculation, and responsibility in the patterning and restructuring of reflexive modernization. He thus comprehends the increasing individualization of contemporary times in the context of the disembedding of ways of life associated with simple industrial modernity and the reembedding of new ones within reflexive modernity. In a posttraditional society, the individualized calculation of the riskiness of life has been taken from the sphere of the natural and the inevitable and is now subject to human decisions and choices. Yet because the mechanics of individualization occurs under the overall conditions and models of *two conflicting modernities* (simple and reflexive modernization), Beck is at pains to point out that the social dynamics whereby modern freedoms of various kinds are demanded and negotiated also raise normative presuppositions involving commitments, obligations, and duties. Paradoxical as it may be, the process of individualization is one that loops an explicit and unlimited self-interrogation with self-subjection, once we appreciate the manner in which networks of regulatory rules and conditions affect the self-designing and self-staging of one's own biography. From the family and marriage to tax rates, from insurance cover to the housing market—these are the institutional centers called on to negotiate the simultaneous enlargement and constriction of the scope of agency and the complexity of the self.

Beck's account of the individualized individuals of advanced modernity, split between reflex and reflexivity, makes clear the errors of much poststructuralist social theory that uncritically fuses subjectivity and agency with repression and constraint. For poststructuralists, the relations between rationality, discourse, and power, formulated along roughly neo-Nietzschean lines, involve the wholesale manipulation and coercion of thought and action, such that the whole concept of subjectivity is thought to be ideologically contaminated and politically redundant. Against poststructuralist theorists, however, Beck advances the provocative sociological argument that human subjects are reasserting agency over the rationalized and reified domains of the lifeworld at precisely the historical moment when subjectivity has been declared finished.

However, even though Beck's account of individualization uncovers many of the key theoretical and methodological limitations of poststructuralist equations of subjectivity and repression, it might still be considered sociologically vulnerable, primarily for reasons that touch on the problematics of subjectivity itself. I have already noted that several critics have argued that Beck, notwithstanding his claim of an epochal transformation from simple to reflexive modernity, is essentially analyzing the traditional subject of the Enlightenment, a subject primarily rational and cognitive rather than expressive or psychodynamic. Now because Beck refuses to theorize adequately how individualization relates to, and is structured by, noncognitive and aesthetic dimensions of human experience, he cannot ultimately provide the moment of self-reflection in the relationship between self and society. This is problematic enough, because it gives rise to the catastrophic misunderstanding that the circularity of reflexive individualization is primarily cognitive. But it also erases—and this is fundamental—the reflexive dimensions of affect and of drive in the constitution and perpetuation of "representations" in and for individualized individuals.

In this connection, the work of Cornelius Castoriadis is of special interest in the present context because it also seeks to uncover the social-historical dynamics in and through which individuals become truly individualized, or, alternatively, suffer the burdens of self-alienation and heteronomy, in the contemporary epoch. Yet, unlike Beck, Castoriadis devotes considerable analytical attention to the formation of a reflective and deliberative instance in the life of the individual and the life of society, an instance that he ties to the functioning of specific psychical mechanisms.

The core of Castoriadis's argument, which will be discussed in more detail in chapter 4, consists in the contention that the modern era is the creation of two intrinsically antinomic but related elements of the "social imaginary" (*l'imaginaire social*), at once individually and socially created representations and meanings that account for the orientation of social institutions, for the framing of motives and desires, and for the existence of symbolism, reflection, and individuality. The first element is that of autonomy, which traverses the democratic and emancipatory movements of the West and from which all self-questioning and self-interrogation flow. The second element is that of pseudorational mastery, which dominates the institutions of capitalism and technoscience and is at the center of modernist enframings of order, control, and certitude. These interlocking, and mutually dislocating, social imaginations form a world of significations—the symbols and representations in and through which the contemporary world represents its present, past, and future. Furthermore, this world of significations is the basis from which individuals develop relations of identity and difference, both intrapsychically and intersubjectively.

The relations between the notion of the social imaginary and the individualized individual are complex and contradictory, and they are explored in an important essay by Castoriadis (1991b). Like Beck, Castoriadis views tradition as repetition and argues that the normative components of tradition are antithetical to ordinary rational enquiry. "Tradition," writes Castoriadis (1991b: 163), "means that the question of the legitimacy of tradition shall not be raised." The transition from preindustrial culture to industrial society spells the weakening of tradition as repetition, and this is a phenomenon that intensifies with the maturation of bourgeois ideology in nineteenth-century Europe. At the level of the individual, and specifically the individual in society, Castoriadis paints much the same picture as Beck: Traditions become reconstructed by the individual in the present, and often deconstructed; as traditions become weakened, the creative dimension of ways of life and societal forms are raised as matters of individual and collective reflectiveness; the individual subject moves to the center of things as an individual in the planning and regulation of biographical self-framings; and the emergent question of the subject (*"What is it that we ought to think?"*) presumes increased levels of emotional autonomy. This last point, concerning emotional autonomy, crucially differentiates Castoriadis from Beck. Castoriadis himself, as we will see, is far from suggesting that emotional autonomy is fully achieved in societal processes of individualization. On the contrary, human subjects are routinely subjected to the power of reification, to which many become held in thrall. But the critical point is that Castoriadis makes autonomous thought and action, as well as genuine historical creation, central to his social and political theory.

It will be apparent that the key to Castoriadis's revision of the individualization thesis consists in his conception of radical imagination, and specifically the manner in which the psychic imaginary intervenes between self and society in the reflexive mediation of new meanings and representations. It is significant, therefore, that Castoriadis argues—*pace* Beck—that genuine self-reflexivity comprises an altered relation to the self that necessarily calls into question the structuring features of individualization in the social network. "The autonomy of the individual," Castoriadis (1991: 165) argues, "consists in the instauration of an *other* relationship between the reflective instance and the other psychical instances as well as between the present and the history which made the individual such as it is." Castoriadis's viewpoint here highlights once again that Beck's theorem that "people are condemned to individualization" depends on a set of extremely questionable psychological and sociological assumptions. For Castoriadis is not simply pointing out that the psychological dimension of reflexive individualization is more subtle and nuanced than Beck's work would suggest, but also that the process of reflexivity is not absorbed by its symbolic mediations. That is, individualized individuals do not undertake decisions, forced by others and the political sphere, that simply reinstate the logics of individualization and hyperdecisionism.

On the contrary, the critical point concerning the productive imagination is that it can be called on to question, to interrogate, and to reflect on the social institution and social regulation—and this, fundamentally, must include the institution of individualization itself. None of this can be understood within an ontology of determinacy. As Castoriadis (1991b: 165) writes:

> In other words, once formed, the reflective instance plays an active and not predetermined role in the deployment and the formation of meaning, whatever its source (be it radical creative imagination of the singular being or the reception of a socially created meaning). In turn, this presupposes again a specific psychical mechanism: to be autonomous implies that one has *psychically invested freedom and the aiming at truth.*

Thus far, we have examined Castoriadis's attempt to define the instituting reflective dimension of individualization and its transformative capacity at the level of personal and social autonomy. The other essential dimension of the contemporary social imaginary, pseudorationality, however, also requires consideration, specifically in terms of the normative integration of individualized individuals into the technological, ecological, nuclear, chemical, and genetic networks of meaning that frame the individuality and social horizon of human agents. For Castoriadis, individualization not only implies autonomy but also repression and repetition. As he (1991b: 163) develops this, "The denial of the instituting dimension of society, the covering up of the instituting imaginary by the instituted imaginary, goes hand in hand with the creation of true-to-form individuals, whose thought and life are dominated by repetition (whatever else they may do, they do very little), whose radical imagination is bridled to the utmost degree possible, and who are hardly truly individualized." This repressive emptying-out of the imaginative self-engagement of the subject might be described in Foucaultian terms as a variant of technologies of the self, the political logic of which is the increasing obligation to situate oneself in relation to wants and needs that are deemed desirable in normative discourses. Certainly, Castoriadis suggests that an individual or society dominated by repetition is incapable of reflective self-construction in anything but the most formulaic and defensive manner—what he elsewhere terms the "second-order imaginary." But, again, it is this stress on imagination and its related fantasies that differentiates Castoriadis's interpretation of the repressive self-fashioning of new types of individuals (e.g., narcissistic pathology) from Foucault's bloodless account of discourse and Beck's sociologism of institutional constraints.

CONCLUSION

In this chapter, I have presented Beck's argument about risk within the context of a broader discussion of his sociological approach to reflexivity, advanced modernization, and individualization. While criticizing various aspects of Beck's sociological theory, I have suggested throughout that the concepts of risk, hazard, and uncertainty, when couched within the framework of reflexive individualization and advanced modernization, are significant and provocative ideas that go a considerable distance in resolving some of the central problems and dichotomies within contemporary social theory. As a contribution to the further elaboration of such an approach, I have criticized Beck's account of the "risk society" for its dependence on rationalistic and instrumental models of constructions of uncertainty and unpredictability in social relations, and for its failure to adequately define the relations and interplay between institutional dynamism and social reflexes, on the one hand, and self-referentiality and critical reflection, on the other.

It can be argued plausibly that Beck's account of risk is at once reductionist and excessivist. At the subjective and cultural levels, Beck makes a number of unjustified reductions when conceptualizing the social construction of risk, specifically the cognitive, informational, and technoscientific inflections his work accords to the issue. It is clear that his work does not appreciate the full significance of interpersonal, emotional, and cultural factors as these influence and shape risk monitoring in contemporary societies. In sociological terms, Beck's theory often appears excessivist: Risk is elevated to such prominence in social reproduction and political transformation that other social forces are, by implication, downgraded in conceptual importance.

I have suggested that Beck's exclusion of wider institutional and epistemological factors affecting the shape of present-day society is nowhere more evident than in his wholesale dismissal of the idea of postmodernity. In contrast, I have tried to suggest ways in which social theory could develop the notions of risk and uncertainty in connection with an analysis of reflexivity and critical self-reflection, ideologies of power and domination, and a dialectical notion of modernity and postmodernization. "We are living," writes Beck (1997: 174), "in a self-critical risk society that is continuing, albeit with restrained pangs of consciousness, in the old routines." The social theory of Beck represents an important but restricted critique of societal attempts to break from the old routines—that is, contemporary engagements with reflexive individual and collective autonomy, the clarification and formulation of which is essential to current theoretical activity in the social sciences.

2

Social Theory and Politics in the
Writings of Anthony Giddens

Who could fail to be intellectually stimulated by the imaginative sweep and sheer breadth of the writings of the British social theorist Anthony Giddens? Over thirty years and in almost as many books, Giddens has established himself as the outstanding social theorist of his generation. Few have equaled him in originality, ambition, or comprehensiveness. His writings on the classical sociological tradition, as well as his interpretations of contemporary social theory, have had a profound impact on conceptual debates in the social sciences over recent decades. Especially in social and political theory, Giddens has expanded the terrain of debate by interpreting, deconstructing, and reconstructing such traditions as structural-functionalism, interpretative sociology, critical theory, ethnomethodology, systems theory, psychoanalysis, structuralism, and poststructuralism.

However, the contribution of Giddens to social theory rests on more than his capabilities as a first-rate hermeneuticist. For, above all, he is a "grand theorist," a sociologist whose contributions rank in importance alongside the writings of theorists including Parsons, Habermas, and Foucault. Giddens's structuration theory is a richly textured analysis of the late modern world, with particular emphasis on processes of social reproduction and political transformation.

The extensive breadth of Giddens's social theory has been employed to illuminate social, cultural and political research, although the precise relationship between structuration theory and empirical sociological research is contested (see Clark, Modgil, and Modgil 1990). Certainly Giddens's own research concerns, like his theoretical interests, are very wide ranging—stretching from his work on modernization and modernity to his analysis of sexuality and intimacy to his more recent work on the development of a "Third Way" or "radical center" as a means of managing global capitalism with greater equity and freedom.

Giddens was born on 18 January 1938 in Edmonton, north London. His father was a clerical worker at London Transport, and his mother a housewife who raised her son in a typically working-class community in the postwar era. Giddens attended a local grammar school; the first in his family to pursue higher education, he subsequently gained admission to the University of Hull, where he studied psychology and sociology. After completing his B.A. at Hull, he commenced an M.A. at the London School of Economics. The title of his master's thesis was "Sport and Society in Contemporary England." He was supervised by David Lockwood and Asher Tropp, and an emerging interest in the sociology of sport reflected much about his own background, primarily his long-standing commitment to the Spurs football (i.e., soccer) team. In the thesis Giddens attempted to demonstrate, following the work of Max Weber, that sport had become rationalized and codified, as well as permeated by class divisions. The topic of sport was a very marginal concern in mainstream sociology when Giddens started to write about it, and he subsequently commented that he felt that his supervisors did not take his work at the LSE all that seriously.

After completing his studies at the LSE, Giddens was appointed lecturer in sociology at the University of Leicester, where he worked alongside Norbert Elias and Ilya Neustadt. It was at Leicester that Giddens's interest in social theory developed, and the theme of ordinary or practical knowledge—the idea that the world holds subjective meaning for its members and that such meaning stands in a reflexive relation to the subject matter of sociology, namely human social practices—emerged as one of his central sociological concerns. In 1968 and 1969, he taught at Simon Fraser University in Vancouver and the University of California, Los Angeles. At this time, his principal research concerned the history of sociological thought, primarily the work of Marx, Weber, and Durkheim. Concentrating on the connections and divergences between the founding fathers of the discipline, Giddens started drawing up plans for his first book.

Returning to England, Giddens resigned his position at Leicester to take up a post at Cambridge University, where he remained until the mid-1990s. His first book, *Capitalism and Modern Social Theory*, appeared in 1971 and remains to this day one of the most referenced sociological textbooks on Marx, Weber, and Durkheim. In examining the origins of classical sociology, Giddens signaled his emerging ambition to reinterpret the theoretical foundations of the social sciences—a project developed from his Durkheimian-titled *New Rules of Sociological Method* (1976) to *Politics, Sociology and Social Theory* (1995). *Capitalism and Modern Social Theory* established an international reputation for Giddens as one of the foremost interpreters of classical social thought, and it was at Cambridge University that he continued this appropriation of European social theory in order to criticize orthodox American sociology.

Giddens's most ambitious work, *The Constitution of Society* (1984), proposed a vast, dramatic restructuring of the methodological and substantive concerns of social theory in the light of current problems of the social sciences. Regarded as one of the most important books since the grand sociological theorizing of Talcott Parsons, *The Constitution of Society* presented a whole new vocabulary for grasping the age of modernization: "structuration," "reflexivity," "time–space distantiation," "double hermeneutic," and "ontological security"—just to name a few terms Giddens introduced.

Subsequent to *The Constitution of Society,* Giddens produced an astonishing range of books. His analysis of warfare, its new technologies and globalization, as developed in *The Nation-State and Violence* (1985), has been highly influential in the disciplines of political science and international relations. *The Consequences of Modernity* (1990) was Giddens's response to postmodernism, in which he argued that the West and the developed industrial societies were entering conditions of "reflexive modernization." And in *Modernity and Self-Identity* (1991) and *The Transformation of Intimacy* (1992b), he addressed issues of the self, identity, intimacy, and sexuality in the context of social transformations sweeping the globe.

In 1996, Giddens left Cambridge University to become director of the London School of Economics and Political Science. As director of the LSE, not only has Giddens been much more directly involved with the shaping of higher education in Britain, but his writings have also become more politically focused. Before taking up the directorship, Giddens had tried, in his book *Beyond Left and Right* (1994), to reconnect sociology to public policy and to outline a radical political agenda beyond orthodox divisions of left and right. He continued this project in his best-seller *The Third Way* (1998). In 1999, Giddens gave the Reith Lectures on globalization and its political consequences, subsequently published as *Runaway World* (1999).

My aim in this chapter is to provide a brief overview of Giddens's writings in social and political theory. Given the broad sweep of his interests as well as his exceptional productivity, I have decided to concentrate on specific aspects of Giddens's work, namely (1) structuration theory, (2) modernity and modernization, and (3) his critique of radical politics. After examining Giddens's more substantive contributions to social theory, I shall consider some of the issues raised by his critics.

STRUCTURATION, MODERNITY, AND THE THIRD WAY

The Theory of Structuration

In a series of books, principally *New Rules of Sociological Method* (1976), *Central Problems in Social Theory* (1979), and *The Constitution of Society* (1984), Giddens sets out a highly original conceptualization of the relation between action and structure, agent and system, individual and society. The problem of the relation between action and social structure is one that lies at the heart of social theory and the philosophy of social science, and most social theorists have tended to stress one term at the expense of the other. In deterministic approaches, for example, social structure is accorded priority over action, as is evident in varieties of structuralism, systems theory, and structural sociology. In voluntaristic approaches, by contrast, attention is focused on individuals and the meanings attached to human action, of which the traditions of hermeneutics, phenomenology, and ordinary language philosophy are exemplary. Each of these contrasting approaches has its admirers and critics. However, Giddens argues that it is not possible to resolve the question of how the action of individual agents is related to the structural features of society by merely supplementing or augmenting one approach through reference to the other.

In an attempt to move beyond such dualism, Giddens borrowed the term *structuration* from French. The starting point of his analysis is not society as fixed and given, but rather the active flow of social life. In contrast to approaches that downgrade agency, Giddens argues that people are knowledgeable about the social structures they produce and reproduce in their conduct. Society, he argues, can be understood as a complex of recurrent practices that form institutions. For Giddens, the central task of social theory is to grasp how action is structured in everyday contexts of social practice, while simultaneously recognizing that the structural elements of action are reproduced by the performance of action. He thus proposes that the dualism of agency and structure should instead be understood as complementary terms of a duality, the 'duality of structure'. "By the duality of structure," writes Giddens, "I mean that social structures are both constituted by human agency, and yet at the same time are the very medium of this constitution."

Perhaps the most useful way to gain a purchase on the radical aspects of Giddens's social theory is by contrasting his conception of structure with the mainstream sociological literature. Sociologists have tended to conceptualize structure in terms of institutional constraint, often in a quasi-hydraulical or mechanical fashion, such that structure is likened to the biological workings of the body or the girders of a building. Giddens strongly rejects functionalist, biological, and empiricist analyses of structure. Following the "linguistic turn" in twentieth century social theory, Giddens critically draws upon structuralist and poststructuralist theory, specifically the relationship posited between language and speech in linguistics. He does this not because society is structured like a language (as structuralists have argued) but because he believes that language can be taken as exemplifying core aspects of social life. Language, according to Giddens, has a virtual existence; it "exists" outside time and space, and it is only present in its instantiations as speech or writing. By contrast, speech presupposes a subject and exists in time/space intersections. In Giddens's reading of structural linguistics, the subject draws from the rules of language in order to produce a phrase or sentence, and in so doing contributes to the reproduction of that language as a whole.

Giddens draws extensively from such a conception of the structures of language to account for structures of action. His theorem is that agents draw from structures to perform and carry out social interactions and in so doing contribute to the reproduction of institutions and structures. This analysis leads to a very specific conception of structure and social systems. "Structure," writes Giddens (1984: 26), "has no existence independent of the knowledge that agents have about what they do in their day-to-day activity."

Giddens's theoretical approach emphasizes that structures should be conceptualized as "rules and resources": The application of rules that comprise structure may be regarded as generating differential access to social, economic, cultural, and political resources. In *The Constitution of Society,* Giddens argues that the sense of "rule" most relevant to understanding social life is that which pertains to mathematical formulas. For instance, if the sequence is 2, 4, 6, 8, the formula is $x = n + 2$.

Understanding a formula, says Giddens, enables an agent to carry on in social life in a routine manner, to apply the rule in a range of different contexts. The same is true of bureaucratic rules, traffic rules, rules of football, rules of grammar, rules of social etiquette: To know a rule does not necessarily mean that one is able to explicitly formulate the principle, but it does mean that one can use the rule "to go on" in social life. "The rules and resources of social action," writes Giddens, "are at the same time the means of systems reproduction" (1984: 19). Systems reproduction, as Giddens conceives it, is complex and contradictory, involving structures, systems, and institutions. Social systems, for Giddens, are not equivalent with structures. Social systems are regularized patterns of interaction; such systems are in turn structured by rules and resources. Institutions are understood by Giddens as involving different modalities in and through which structuration occurs. Political institutions, for example, involve the generation of commands over people in relation to issues of authorization, signification, and legitimation; economic institutions, by contrast, involve the allocation of resources through processes of signification and legitimation.

To understand this recursive quality of social life, it is necessary also to consider Giddens's discussion of human agency and individual subjectivity. Action, according to Giddens, must be analytically distinguished from the "acts" of an individual. Whereas acts are discrete segments of individual doing, action refers to the continuous flow of people's social practices. On a general plane, Giddens advances a "stratification model" of the human subject comprising three levels of knowledge or motivation: *discursive consciousness, practical consciousness,* and the *unconscious.* He explains this stratification model of agency in *The Constitution of Society* as follows:

Human agents or actors—I use these terms interchangeably—have, as an inherent aspect of what they do, the capacity to understand what they do while they do it. The reflexive capacities of the human actor are characteristically involved in a continuous manner with the flow of day-to-day conduct in the contexts of social activity. But reflexivity operates only partly on a discursive level. What agents know about what they do, and why they do it—their knowledgeability *as* agents—is largely carried in practical consciousness. Practical consciousness consists of all the things which actors know tacitly about how to "go on" in the contexts of social life without being able to give them direct discursive expression. The significance of practical consciousness is a leading theme of the book, and it has to be distinguished from both consciousness (discursive consciousness) and the unconscious. (1984: xxii–xxiii)

Discursive consciousness thus refers to what agents are able to say, both to themselves and to others, about their own action; as Giddens repeatedly emphasizes, agents are knowledgeable about what they are doing, and this awareness often has a highly discursive component. *Practical consciousness* also refers to what actors know about their own actions, beliefs, and motivations, but it is practical in the sense that it cannot be expressed discursively; what cannot be put into words, Giddens says, following Wittgenstein, is what has to be done. Human beings know about their activities and the world in a sense that cannot be readily articulated; such practical stocks of knowledge are central, according to Giddens, to the project of social scientific research. Finally, the *unconscious,* says Giddens, is also a crucial feature of human motivation, and it is differentiated from discursive and practical consciousness by the barrier of repression.

While Giddens accords the unconscious a residual role in the reproduction of social life (as something that "erupts" at moments of stress or crisis), he nonetheless makes considerable use of psychoanalytical theory to theorize the routine patterning of social relations. Drawing from Freud, Lacan, and Erikson, Giddens argues that the emotional presence and absence of the primary caretaker (most usually, the mother) provides the foundation for a sense of what he terms "ontological security," as well as trust in the taken-for-granted, routine nature of social life. Indeed, the routine is accorded a central place in Giddens's social theory for (1) grasping the production and maintenance of ontological security and (2) comprehending the modes of socialization by which actors learn the implicit rules of how to go on in social life. To do this, Giddens draws from a vast array of sociological microtheorists, including Goffman and Garfinkel. His debt to ethnomethodology and phenomenology is reflected in much of the language of structuration theory, as is evident from his references to "skilled performances," "copresence," "seriality," "contextuality," "knowledgeability," and "mutual knowledge."

In the last few paragraphs, I have noted how Giddens approaches issues of human action, agency, and subjectivity. It is important to link these more subjective aspects of his social theory back to issues of social practices and structures to grasp his emphasis on duality in structuration theory. Agents, according to Giddens, draw on the rules and resources of structures, and in so doing they contribute to the systemic reproduction of institutions, systems, and structures. In studying social life, says Giddens, it is important to recognize the role of "methodological bracketing." He argues that the social sciences simultaneously pursue *institutional analysis*, in which the structural features of society are analyzed, and the *analysis of strategic conduct*, in which the manner in which actors carry on social interaction is studied. These different levels of analysis are central to social scientific research, and both are crucial to structuration theory. Connected to this, Giddens argues that the subjects of study of the social sciences are concept-using agents, individuals whose concepts enter into the manner in which their actions are constituted. He calls this intersection of the social world as constituted by lay actors, on the one hand, and the metalanguages created by social scientists, on the other, the "double hermeneutic."

Modernity and the Late Modern Age

In *The Consequences of Modernity* (1990) and *Modernity and Self-Identity* (1991), Giddens develops a comprehensive analysis of the complex relation between self and society in the late modern age. Rejecting Marx's equation of modernity with capitalism, and wary of Weber's portrait of the iron cage of bureaucracy, Giddens instead presents an image of modernity as a juggernaut. As with structuration theory, Giddens's approach to modernity involves considerable terminological innovation: "embedding and disembedding mechanisms," "symbolic tokens," "expert systems," "the dialectic of trust and risk," and, crucially, "reflexivity." Reflexivity, according to Giddens, should be conceived as a continuous flow of individual and collective "self-monitoring." "The reflexivity of modern social life," writes Giddens, "consists in the fact that social practices are constantly examined and reformed in the light of incoming information about those very practices, thus constitutively altering their character" (1990: 38). Elsewhere, Giddens (1991: 28) writes, "To live in the 'world' produced by high modernity has the feeling of riding a juggernaut. It is not just that more or less continuous and profound processes of change occur; rather, change does not consistently conform either to human expectation or to human control."

The experiential character of contemporary daily life is well grasped by two of Giddens's key concepts: *trust and risk* as interwoven with *abstract systems*. For Giddens, the relation between individual subjectivity and social contexts of action is a highly mobile one; and it is something that we make sense of and utilize through "abstract systems." *Abstract systems* are institutional domains of technical and social knowledge, they include systems of expertise of all kinds, from local forms of knowledge to science, technology, and mass communications. Giddens is underscoring much more than simply the impact of expertise on people's lives, far-reaching though that is. Rather, he extends the notion of expertise to cover "trust relations"—the personal and collective investment of active trust in social life. The psychological investment of trust contributes to the power of specialized, expert knowledge—indeed, it lies at the bedrock of our age of experts—and also plays a key role in the forging of a sense of security in day-to-day social life.

Trust and security are thus both a condition and outcome of social reflexivity. Giddens sees the reflexive appropriation of expert knowledge as fundamental in a globalizing, culturally cosmopolitan society. While a key aim may be the regularization of stability and order in our identities and in society, reflexive modernity is radically experimental, however; and it is constantly producing new types of incalculable risk and insecurity. This means that, whether we like it or not, we must recognize the ambivalence of a social universe of expanded reflexivity: there are no clear paths of individual or social development in the late modern age. On the contrary, human attempts at control of the social world are undertaken against a reflexive backdrop of a variety of other ways of doing things. Giddens offers the following overview, for example, in relation to global warming:

> Many experts consider that global warming is occurring and they may be right. The hypothesis is disputed by some, however, and it has even been suggested that the real trend, if there is one at all, is in the opposite direction, towards the cooling of the global climate. Probably the most that can be said with some surety is that we cannot be certain that global warming is *not* occurring. Yet such a conditional conclusion will yield not a precise calculation of risks but rather an array of "scenarios"—whose plausibility will be influenced, among other things, by how many people become convinced of the thesis of global warming and take action on that basis. In the social world, where institutional reflexivity has become a central constituent, the complexity of "scenarios" is even more marked. (1994: 59)

The complexity of "scenarios" is thus central to our engagement with the wider social world. Reflexivity, according to Giddens, influences the way in which these scenarios are constructed, perceived, coped with, and reacted to.

In *The Transformation of Intimacy* (1992b), Giddens connects the notion of reflexivity to sexuality, gender, and intimate relationships. With modernization and the decline of tradition, says Giddens, the sexual life of the human subject becomes a "project" that has to be managed and defined against the backdrop of new opportunities and risks—including, for example, artificial insemination, experiments in ectogenesis (the creation of human life without pregnancy), AIDS, and sexual harassment. Linking gender to new technologies, Giddens argues we live in an era of "plastic sexuality." "Plastic sexuality" (1992b: 2), he writes, "is decentered sexuality, freed from the needs of reproduction . . . and from the rule of the phallus, from the overweening importance of male sexual experience." Sexuality thus becomes open-ended, elaborated not through pre-given roles, but through reflexively forged relationships. The self today, as the rise of therapy testifies, is faced with profound dilemmas in respect of sexuality. "Who am I?" "What do I desire?" "What satisfactions do I want from sexual relations?"—these are core issues for the self, according to Giddens. This does not mean that sexual experience occurs without institutional constraint, however. Giddens contends that the development of modern institutions produces a "sequestration of experience"—sexual, existential, and moral—that squeezes to the sidelines core problems relating to sexuality, intimacy, mortality and death (see Elliott 1992).

Giddens, in other words, adopts an idealist language of autonomy, stressing as he does the creativity of action and the modernist drive to absolute self-realization, while remaining suspicious of intellectual traditions that prioritize subjects over objects, or actors over structures. This comes out very clearly in his work on the changing connections between marriage, the family, and self-identity. According to Giddens, individuals today actively engage with novel opportunities and dangers that arise as a consequence of dramatic transformations affecting self-identity, sexuality, and intimacy. For Giddens, divorce is undeniably a personal crisis, involving significant pain, loss, and grief. Yet many people, he argues, take positive steps to work through the emotional dilemmas generated by marriage breakdown. In addition to dealing with financial issues and matters affecting how children should be brought up, separation and divorce also call into play a reflexive emotional engagement with the self. Charting territory from the past (where things went wrong, missed opportunities, etc.) and for the future (alternative possibilities, chances for self-actualization, etc.) necessarily involves experimenting with a new sense of self. This can lead to emotional growth, new understandings of self, and strengthened intimacies. Against the conservative critique of marriage breakdown, Giddens sees the self opening out to constructive renewal. Remarriage and the changing nature of family life are crucial in this respect. As he develops this point:

> Many people, adults and children, now live in stepfamilies—not usually, as in previous eras, as a consequence of the death of a spouse, but because of the re-forming of marriage ties after divorce. A child in a stepfamily may have two mothers and fathers, two sets of brothers and sisters, together with other complex kin connections resulting from the multiple marriages of parents. Event the terminology is difficult: should a stepmother be called "mother" by the child, or called by her name? Negotiating such problems might be arduous and psychologically costly for all parties; yet opportunities for novel kinds of fulfilling social relations plainly also exist. One thing we can be sure of is that the changes involved here are not just external to the individual. These new forms of extended family ties have to be established by the very persons who find themselves most directly caught up in them. (1991: 13)

Marital separation, as portrayed by Giddens, implicates the self in an open project: tracing over the past, imagining the future, dealing with complex family problems, and experimenting with a new sense of identity. Further experimentation with marriage and intimate relationships will necessarily involve anxieties, risks, and opportunities. But, as Giddens emphasizes, the relation between self and society is a highly fluid one, involving negotiation, change, and development.

The manner in which current social practices shape future life outcomes is nowhere more in evidence than in the conjunction of divorce statistics, the reckoning of probability ratios for success or failure in intimate relationships, and the decision to get married. As Giddens rightly points out, statistics about marriage and divorce do not exist in a social vacuum; everyone, he says, is in some sense aware of how present gender uncertainties affect long-term relationships. When people marry or remarry today, according to Giddens, they do so against a societal backdrop of high divorce statistics, knowledge of which alters a person's understanding and conception of what marriage actually is. It is precisely this reflexive monitoring of relationships that, in turn, transforms expectations about, and aspirations for, marriage and intimacy. The relationship between self, society, and reflexivity is thus a highly dynamic one, involving the continual overturning of traditional ways of doing things.

The Third Way

In *Beyond Left and Right: The Future of Radical Politics* (1994), Giddens asserts that we live today in a radically damaged world, for which radical political remedies are required beyond the neoliberalism offered by the Right or reformist socialism offered by the Left. To this end, Giddens provides a detailed framework for the rethinking of radical politics. This framework touches on issues of tradition and social solidarity, of social movements, of the restructuring of democratic processes and the welfare state, and of the location of violence in world politics. Giddens's interpretation of the rise of radical politics can perhaps best be grasped by contrasting dominant discussions in the fields of critical theory and postmodernism. Theorists of the self-endangerment of modern politics, from Daniel Bell to Jürgen Habermas, characteristically focus on the loss of community produced by the invasion of personal and cultural life by the global capitalist system. Postmodernist social and political theorists, from Michel Foucault to Jean-François Lyotard, alternatively focus on an escalating pluralization of knowledge claims, concluding that there are no ordered paths to political development. Giddens's approach, by contrast, takes a radically different tack. He develops neither a lament for, nor celebration of, the ambivalences of contemporary political processes. Instead, Giddens asks, What happens when politics begins to reflect on itself? What happens when political activity, understanding its own successes and excesses, begins to reflect on its own institutional conditions?

At issue, says Giddens, are reflexivity and risk, both of which he isolates as central to transformations in society, culture, and politics. By reflexivity, as noted, Giddens refers to that circularity of knowledge and information promoted by mass communications in a globalizing, cosmopolitan world. Reflexivity functions as a means of regularly reordering and redefining what political activity is. Of central importance in this respect is the impact of globalization. Globalizing processes, says Giddens, radically intensify our personal and social awareness of risk, transforming local contexts into global consequences. Thus, the panic selling of shares on the Dow Jones has implications for the entire global economy, from local retail trade to the international division of labor. At the beginning of the twenty-first century, a world of intensified reflexivity is a world of people reflecting on the political consequences of human action, from the desolation of the rain forests to the widespread manufacture of weapons of mass destruction. In such social conditions, politics becomes radically experimental in character. People are increasingly aware of new types of incalculable risk and insecurity, and we must attempt to navigate the troubled waters of modern political culture. This means that, whether we like it or not, we are all engaged in a kind of continual reinvention of identity and politics, with no clear paths of development from one state of risk to another.

It is against this backdrop of transformations in risk, reflexivity, and globalization that Giddens develops a new framework for radical politics. The core dimensions of Giddens's blueprint for the restructuring of radical political thought include the following claims:

- We live today in a posttraditional social order. This does not mean, as many cultural critics and postmodernists claim, that tradition disappears. On the contrary, in a globalizing, culturally cosmopolitan society, traditions are forced into the open for public discussion and debate. Reasons or explanations are increasingly required for the preservation of tradition, and this should be understood as one of the key elements in the reinvention of social solidarity. The new social movements, such as those concerned with ecology, peace, or human rights, are examples of groups refashioning tradition (the call to conserve and protect "nature") in the building of social solidarities. The opposite of this can be seen, says Giddens, in the rise of fundamentalism, which forecloses questions of public debate and is "nothing other than tradition defended in the traditional way."
- Radical forms of democratization, fueled by reflexivity, are at work in politics, from the interpersonal to the global levels. But the issue of democratization cannot be confined only to the formal political sphere, since these processes also expose the limits of liberal political democracy itself. As the American sociologist Daniel Bell put this some years ago, the nation-state has become too small to tackle global problems and too large to handle local ones. Instead, Giddens speaks of a "democratizing of democracy," by which he means that all areas of personal and political life are increasingly ordered through dialogue rather than preestablished power relations. The mechanisms of such dialogic democracy are already set in process, from the transformation of gender and parent–child relations through to the development of social movements and self-help groups. The rise of psychotherapy and psychoanalysis is also cast in a favorable political light by Giddens. Democ-

ratizing influences such as these also influence the more traditional sphere of institutional politics as well.

- The welfare state requires further radical forms of restructuring, and this needs to be done in relation to wider issues of global poverty. Here Giddens urges the reconstruction of welfare away from the traditional "top down dispensation of benefits" in favor of what he terms "positive welfare." Welfare that is positive is primarily concerned with promoting autonomy in relation to personal and collective responsibilities, and it focuses centrally on gender imbalances as much as class deprivations.
- The prospects for global justice begin to emerge in relation to a "postscarcity order." This is a complex idea, but it is central to Giddens's political theory. Giddens is not suggesting that politics has entered an age in which scarcity has been eliminated. On the contrary, he argues that there will always be scarcities of goods and resources. Rather, a postscarcity society is a society in which "scarcity" itself comes under close reflexive scrutiny. Coping with the negative consequences of industrialism, says Giddens, has led to a radical reappraisal of the capitalistic drive for continuous accumulation. This broadening of political goals beyond the narrowly economic is reflected today in the pursuit of "responsible growth." Several key social transformations are central here. The entry of women into the paid labor force, the restructuring of gender and intimacy, the rise of individualization as opposed to egoism, and the ecological crisis: these developments have all contributed to a shift away from secularized Puritanism toward social solidarity and obligation.

TOWARD A CRITIQUE OF GIDDENS

Having briefly discussed Giddens's principal contributions to social theory, I want now to consider some of the major criticisms of his work. For some critics, Giddens's social-theoretical project is cast so wide that his writings might be likened to a vast theoretical supermarket, in which a variety of unusual commodities (Merleau-Ponty, Gadamer, Hagerstrand, Garfinkel) are stocked beside better-known brand names (Marx, Freud, Weber, Durkheim). Some commentators see Giddens's theoretical eclecticism as unhelpful, while others criticize his appropriation of particular traditions of thought. Roy Boyne (1991), for instance, sharply criticizes Giddens's appropriation of structuralist and poststructuralist theory, claiming that he "systematically misrepresents" French social theory.

In what follows, I shall leave to one side this type of criticism, since I think that hermeneutic issues about Giddens's interpretation of theorists like Foucault, Lacan, and Derrida are largely beside the point. The more interesting questions about Giddens's work are those that concentrate on his project of formulating a general social theory. What perhaps is especially interesting is that—

notwithstanding Giddens's claim to have inaugurated a "duality" for the subject/ object binary—most critiques of his work tend to concentrate on either the subjective or social-institutional shortcomings of his analysis.

In several celebrated critiques, Margaret Archer (1982, 1990) argues not only that it is undesirable to amalgamate agency with structure but that it is necessary to treat structure and agency as analytically distinct to deal with core methodological and substantive problems in the social sciences. At the heart of Archer's critique of Giddens is an anxiety about his claim that structures have no existence independent of the knowledge that human subjects have about what they do in their daily lives. She argues that Giddens's structuration theory fails to accord sufficient ontological status to the preexistence of social forms, specifically the impact of social distributions of populations on human action. Archer juxtaposes to Giddens a morphogenetic theory that focuses on the dialectical interplay between agency and the emergent properties of social systems.

Similarly, Nicos Mouzelis argues that, while the notion of structuration is appropriate to routine social practices where agents carry out their actions without undue levels of reflection, there are other forms of social life that require that structure and agency be kept apart. Theoretical reflection on the social world, for example, involves dualism, in Mouzelis's eyes, since there is a shift from the individual to the collective level, and this necessarily depends on a distancing of our immediate, everyday lives from broader social structures.

In an especially sharp critique of Giddens's structuration theory, John B. Thompson (1989) questions the analytical value of (1) the notion of rules and resources for grasping social structure and (2) the conceptualization of structural constraint as modeled on certain linguistic and grammatical forms. According to Thompson, Giddens's account of rules and resources is vague and misleading. Linguistic and grammatical rules, says Thompson, are important forms of constraint on human action; however, they are not the only forms of constraint in social life; indeed, when considering social constraint, the core issue is to understand how an agent's range of alternatives is limited.

Thompson acknowledges that Giddens goes some distance in accounting for this by distinguishing between structure, system, and institutions. But again he questions Giddens's account of the transformational properties of structures and suggests there is confusion here between structural and institutional constraint. A worker at the Ford Motor Company, notes Thompson, can be said to contribute to the reproduction of the institution and thus also said to contribute to the reproduction of capitalism as a structure, to the extent that the workers pursue their everyday employment activities. However, it is also possible that workers might undertake activities that threaten or transform the institution, but without similarly transforming their structural conditions. "Every act of production and reproduction," writes Thompson (1989: 70), "may also be a potential act of transformation, as Giddens rightly insists; but the extent to which an action transforms an institution does not coincide with the extent to which social structure is thereby transformed."

Other critics have likewise targeted Giddens's conceptualization of subjectivity, agency, and the agent. Bryan S. Turner, for example, finds Giddens's theory of the human agent lacking a sufficient account of embodiment (Turner 1992). Alan Sica has suggested that, notwithstanding his commitment to macro social theory, Giddens's borrowings from Garfinkel, Goffman, Erikson, and others indicate an awareness that a theory of the subject and its complex darkness has been central to the project of contemporary social theory. "Giddens reinvolves himself with 'the subjective'," writes Sica (1989: 48),

> because he knows that a general theory of action will surely fail that does not come to terms with it. But he fondly thinks, it seems, that by inventing a new vocabulary, by bringing in the ubiquitous 'duality of structure' or 'reflexive rationalization of conduct', he can make good his escape from both the calcified Marxism without a subject (Althusser) or sloppy-hearted Parsonism, which is all norms, values and wishes.

Sica's argument here rests on a particular sociological reading of the relations between the reflexive monitoring of action, the routinization of day-to-day social processes, and the material conditions in which all activities are located and undertaken. There is a sense, for Sica, in which Giddens tries to outflank both Althusserian Marxism and Parsonian sociology, only to find that the crippling dualism of subjectivity and objectivity reappears in his beloved sociological upgrading of the routine (whatever is done habitually). On this view, Giddens's ethnomethodological imperialism produces not only a risky suppression of the material conditions structuring routinized activities but also cancels those unconscious or symbolic dimensions of human experience untrammeled by routine or convention.

There is something intriguingly divided about Giddens's self-actualizing "subject of routinization," who is at once structured and structuring, commanding and contextual, a post-Freudian master coolly keeping the unconscious contained within the realm of the habitual while all the time remaining unquestionably in ethnomethodological control. Yet these polarities have less to do with Giddens's fundamental concept of routinization as such; rather, sociological problems arise—for reasons I shall explore subsequently—as a consequence of the manner in which Giddens attempts to force an ontological division between discursive and practical consciousness, on the one side, and the unconscious dimensions of subjectivity or agency, on the other.

For the moment, however, let us stay with Sica's complaint that Giddens's vision of a routinized subject is disturbingly ungrounded in sociostructural or moral-normative concerns. There can be little doubt that Giddens makes the concept of routinization central to the constitution and reproduction of history and consciousness. "Routine," writes Giddens (1984: 60) "is integral both to the continuity of the personality of the agent, as he or she moves along the paths of daily activities, and to the institutions of society, which *are* such only through their continued reproduction." This is not an expression of sociological determinism (in the sense that all action is preprogrammed) or political conservatism; there is no logical reason why reflexively constituted processes of social reproduction demand an acceptance of *particular* habitual practices. Moreover, Giddens's more recent political writings advancing a "third way" further indicate aspects of his discontent with late capitalist societies. Rather, Giddens's grounding of ontological security in routinization suggests that both existing and alternative (or oppositional) forms of life demand some sort of motivational commitment to the integration of habitual practices across space and time.

Where Giddens's sociology of routinization is problematic is not its privileging of the capabilities of actors to "go on" in the contexts of social life without being necessarily able to give them direct discursive expression, but in its assumption that practical consciousness brackets, limits, and contains unconscious representation and repressed desire. For Giddens, the repetition of activities that are undertaken in like manner day after day provides the grounding for what he terms "ontological security," protecting against the unwanted eruption of anxiety. Predictable routines keep the unconscious at bay. Yet anyone with a psychoanalytic ear reading of Giddens's sociology of routinization is likely to feel unsympathetic to such a characterization of the nature of the unconscious. Concentrating mainly on the notion of repression leads Giddens to give sociological expression to the widespread cultural fantasy that the fracturing effects of the unconscious must be limited, held in check. But even in the terms of his own stratification model, one has only to raise a few psychoanalytically inspired questions to see the problems here. What kind of good is it to practical consciousness to bracket anxiety at the level of the unconscious? Does such bracketing lead to autonomy of action, guarantee it, as it were? What of Freud's speaking up for unconscious passion, for the strangeness and otherness of emotional life, a life not dominated by system or custom?

Given a routinized frame for the playing out of identities at the level of practical consciousness, Giddens's structuration theory—I want to suggest—clashes with psychoanalytic constructions of subjectivity in terms of fantasy and repressed desire. Freudian and post-Freudian theorists have used a variety of strategies to connect psychoanalytic thought to the current ambivalences and evasions of culture and politics. Of core importance in this connection is the multiplicity of unconscious ties and attachments as manifested in the self's relations with others; in contrast to traditional understandings of the individual as self-identical and rational, the individual is revealed in psychoanalysis to exhibit a range of subjective identifications available in fantasy. The notion of multiple subjective identifications, as experienced in unconscious fantasy, is potentially troubling to Giddens's self-monitoring reflexive individual—primarily because it threatens a range of conceptual oppositions on which his work rests, including active/passive, knowledge/desire, and mind/body.

From this angle, we can begin to grasp why Giddens's appropriation of psychoanalysis for social theory is less than satisfactory. For one thing, Giddens's whole vocabulary of self-organization—"bracketing anxiety," "ontological security," and "emotional inoculation"—has a very different intent from that advanced in psychoanalytic theory. For Giddens, individuals must be capable of trust, relatedness, and routine to go about day-to-day social life successfully. Once these emotional capacities are secured, the individual is deemed to have met the basic requirements for generating self-coherence and a degree of autonomy. Yet psychoanalytic theory radically problematizes whether the self can ever be "normalized" in this way.

Consider Winnicott, for example. Winnicott stresses the fractured and divided nature of all self-experience—a product of unconscious sexuality itself. In Winnicott's theory, the self is never free from the task of relating inner and outer worlds; significantly, the self is always subject to dissolution through unconscious fragmentation and dread. Yet Giddens can offer no account of this. Instead, the realm of the unconscious is portrayed by him as "bracketed" by social routine. What this standpoint fails to acknowledge is that social routine may be constituted to its roots by unacknowledged desires; social routines may involve pathological, obsessional, or narcissistic emotional forces. Consider here Giddens's analysis of changing patterns effecting intimacy and marriage. Women and men, we can agree with Giddens, pursue intimate relationships today against a cultural backdrop of dramatic transformations governing sexuality, love, marriage, the family, and work. Many embrace these social changes wholeheartedly; others may have mixed impressions; some no doubt try to carry on by ignoring current shifts in gender thinking and practice. Yet these social and sexual issues undoubtedly press in on everyone as private matters and interpersonal crises. Giddens is surely right, then, to tie self and society ineluctably together around our reflexive discontent over sexuality and gender. But however aware of the current historical moment we may try to be, we are all linked to specific emotional pasts and prior generational histories—and this is where Giddens's work runs into difficulty, as he seems to downplay the degree to which the influence of emotion, memory, and desire can limit or conflict with our conscious attempts to order our lives and make sense of the world in more reflective terms. A person who has suffered emotional abandonment by a parent in childhood, for example, might display a quite defensive emotional need to embrace, or equally to deny, intimacy; such needs and desires, while not automatically in conflict with reflexive knowledge of the self and world, do not reduce to the language of social practices.

At this point, I need to enter some immediate qualifications to the criticisms I have made earlier. Surely I have failed to consider adequately, it might be said, Giddens's ongoing interest in psychoanalysis as a rich discourse on the self for social theory, as well as his many references to the role of unconscious forces in social relations. It is true that Giddens is unusual within the discipline of sociology for displaying an interest in things emotional and psychosexual. In his 1979 volume, *Central Problems in Social Theory,* he drew from Lacan's Freud in positing a theory of socialization and the unconscious. By the time of *The Constitution of Society* in 1984, Giddens had dropped Lacan in favor of Erikson, focusing particularly on the latter's work on anxiety and trust. From Erikson, Giddens was able to elaborate what he termed "a modified version of ego psychology" (1984: xxiii). Come the 1990s and Erikson was less displaced than added to with the insights of Winnicott, Balint, and Kohut. The shift from a concern with subjecthood to sexuality in *The Transformation of Intimacy* involved further conceptual reworkings, inspired by the psychoanalytic departures of Janine Chasseguet-Smirgel, Hans Leowald, and Jessica Benjamin, among others.

What can be gleaned from all this? For many critics, Giddens's appropriation of psychoanalysis for social theory may seem maddeningly eclectic: this paper by Lacan, that book by Erikson, this concept of Winnicott's, and so forth. To be sure, the tension between a restricted and expanded theory of the unconscious in social relations is sometimes obvious enough in Giddens's corpus; there is, it must be acknowledged, a considerable difference between the Giddens of *The Constitution of Society,* for whom routinization brackets repressed desire, and the Giddens of *Modernity and Self-Identity,* for whom self-interrogation of affect is crucial to personal and cultural experimentation in late modernity. That said, however, it seems to me that Giddens's appropriations of concepts from various psychoanalytic texts have one thing in common, namely an insistence that our practical know-how—our knowing how to "go on" in social life—is quite at odds with the realm of the disruptive, creative unconscious. There is a sense, at least as a first approximation, in which Culture cancels out Nature for Giddens; or, to put the matter somewhat differently, that the repetitions of sociality will subdue the archaic transgressions of the unconscious.

Part of the problem here, as might be expected, depends on one's definition of the unconscious. Like Erikson and Marcuse before him, Giddens's version of the unconscious is one centered on organic tensions, libidinal strivings, asocial desires. This notion of the unconscious as an unruly force, a kind of animal instinct waiting to erupt, is brought out clearly in *The Constitution of Society:* "Routinization is vital to the psychological mechanisms whereby a sense of trust or ontological security is sustained in the daily activities of social life. Carried primarily in practical consciousness, routine drives a wedge between the potentially explosive content of the unconscious and the reflexive monitoring of action which agents display" (1984: xxiii).

What, exactly, is the potentially explosive content of the unconscious as represented by Giddens? Anxiety mostly, of which it is the function of routinization and trust to bracket out. Yet there are, of course, other ways of understanding the unconscious. British psychoanalysis has, for example, been much more interested in depression than in anxiety, and hence it is interesting to wonder about what the connections between depression and routinization might look like through the lens of Giddens's social theory. Similarly, the idea of an unconscious of provocative, enigmatic "messages" (derived from the psychic force field of primary others) has gained considerable attention in recent French psychoanalysis (see, e.g., Laplanche 1999), and again we might ponder the relations between routine, repetitive social practices and perplexing enigmatic messages in the unconscious.

In pointing to these other psychoanalytic viewpoints, my intention is not to insist on certain versions of Freudian theory over others—though some of Giddens's critics have done just that. Ian Craib (1992: 171), for example, argues that Giddens's model of the subject is experientially and psychodynamically reductive, the core of which he attributes to Giddens's "misuse or misinterpretation of psychoanalysis." Craib notes that Giddens limits the reach of Freud in an attempt to bring sociological precision to his dialectical model of consciousness, preconsciousness, and the unconscious; Giddens argues, for instance, that regressive psychic functioning is generally initiated only in moments of societal stress. The result is that Giddens's conception of the person lacks complexity of desires, contradictions of experience, and a sense of internal division.

This argument is interesting, but it carries wider implications than Craib perhaps realizes. The issue is not how well or badly Giddens reads Freud; my point is that Giddens's circumscription of the functioning of the unconscious carries substantive implications for his theorem of the duality of structure. Giddens adopts the novel view that structural rules and resources have no existence independent of the memory traces of subjects. If this argument is to be sustained, what is required is a much more detailed account of the unconscious representations and affects that underpin and condition practical and discursive consciousness as these relate to, and draw from, structure (see Elliott 1994, 1996). If the unconscious, as Freud relentlessly insisted, is unaware of contradiction, time or closure, then it is surely misguided to speak of the bracketing of repressed desire in the routine activities of everyday life. One can no more bracket or limit the unconscious than one can successfully institutionalize psychoanalysis—though this clearly hasn't prevented people from trying.

The location of these aspects of the internal world as opposed to the cognitive elements of the knowledgeability of social actors is, however, an essential problematic for Giddens—or, at least, this is so for the Giddens of *Central Problems in Social Theory* at any rate. "The proposition that all social agents," he writes (1979: 5),

> are knowledgeable about the social systems which they constitute and reproduce in their action is a logically necessary feature of the conception of the duality of structure. But it is one that needs to be carefully elucidated. There are various modes in which such knowledge may figure in practical social conduct. One is in unconscious sources of cognition: there seems no reason to deny that knowledge exists on the level of the unconscious.

But if "unconscious sources of cognition" are pivotal and inspirational to self-knowledge, as Giddens suggests, then what does the social theorist think he or she is containing or limiting when asserting the bracketing of anxiety in and through routine? In what sense might it be possible to assert instead an affinity between the unconscious and routine? Not bracketing, but mixing?

Just as Nietzsche famously contended that we are "artists in our dreams," it might be said that—thanks to the creative indeterminacy of unconscious representation—we are all imaginative artists of our daily practical sociologies. This is, in effect, a version of psychoanalysis recast for social theory that positions the unconscious imagination in a relation of dynamism as it is played out between practical and discursive consciousness. If in performing the daily work of our practical sociologies—family interaction, work, leisure pursuits, and so forth—we engage in the recursive building up of (virtual) structures in the constitutive practice of social reproduction and transformation, then it is also the case that the unending work of self-monitoring (of ourselves and others) is constituted to its roots by the fantasmatic dimensions of the unconscious. Yet Giddens's social theory does not sufficiently grasp that the routinization of our practical sociologies is effectively interwoven with a deeply inventive unconsciousness. As Charles Lemert aptly develops this point:

> Giddens's unconscious is a reservoir of memory, a resource. Freud's is the internal Other, a force aggressively resistant to the conscious mind (and, thus, the internal Other of civilisation itself). Giddens cannot go so far as Freud because that far would wreck the theory of modern structures. If virtual structures exhibit their properties only in instances of practices and "memory traces" guiding an agent's conduct, then social memory must be "for," not "against," modern consciousness. In this delicate theoretical distinction, the fundamental fact of differences must be denied. (1995: 154)

This summing up, with its emphasis on the lineaments of the otherness of the unconscious, can be accepted fully. The recovery of the subject that Giddens has so brilliantly undertaken in the aftermath of its poststructuralist decentering should not be taken up in such a manner as to render self-identity equivalent to a taming or habituation of the creative contours of the unconscious imagination. A critical appraisal of the imaginative constitution of our social practice is not possible if social theory succumbs to the very sociopolitical tendencies of denial and displacement of the unconscious depths of being that is its task to theorize. To do so would go against the spirit and seriousness of Giddens's imaginative social theory.

3

Jacques Lacan as Social Theorist

"The unconscious is structured like a language"; "A letter always arrives at its destination"; "The unconscious is the discourse of the Other"; "There is no such thing as a sexual relationship." These slogans emanate from the most original, brilliant, and controversial figure in French psychoanalysis, Jacques Lacan. Among psychoanalysts of the post-Freudian era, it is Lacan who has produced the most outrage in discussions of subjectivity, sexual desire, and culture and who has most powerfully asserted the interdisciplinary power of psychoanalysis in theoretical and empirical research.

Many things have been said of Lacan, including that he was eccentric, that he had an inadequate clinical knowledge of psychoanalysis, and also that his complex, dense reading of Freud has been widely misunderstood. Scandalously, he introduced the practice of short analytic sessions—often consisting of no more than a few minutes—and was consequently expelled from the International Psychoanalytical Association. So, too, he caused an intellectual uproar in France in the early 1970s during a television interview that sought to introduce contemporary psychoanalysis to a mass audience, when he arrogantly announced, "I always speak the truth." The political irony of this was that, in his theoretical papers at least, Lacan ceaselessly argued that it is impossible to be in possession of "the truth." The belief that any other person, or political ideal, or ideological position, holds the answer to our personal problems, says Lacan, is itself an illusion—thus the paradoxes surrounding Lacan's absolute theoretical certainty, on the one hand, and his unrelenting deconstruction of the self, on the other. For it is as if this self-proclaimed master of contemporary theory was relying on the authority of Freud to proclaim the impossibility of authority itself.

Jacques Lacan was born in 1901 in France, the year after Sigmund Freud's foundational *The Interpretation of Dreams* was published. Lacan was educated at the Collège Stanislas, and, after completing his secondary education, he studied medicine in Paris. He went on to do his clinical training in psychiatry under the supervision of Gaetan Gatian de Clérambault. He published his first articles while he trained as a psychiatrist, and these were mostly on psychiatric and neurological topics. In 1932, Lacan published his doctoral thesis, "Paranoid Psychosis and Its Relation to the Personality," a copy of which he sent to Freud. As a psychoanalyst, Lacan was highly unconventional; his fascination with Freud and psychoanalysis was matched by his passion for philosophy, literature, and the arts. His public seminars at the Hospital Sainte-Anne were a mixture of psychoanalytic theory, continental philosophy, and surrealism; the seminars were increasingly well attended, mostly by an eclectic mix of students and professionals. In the 1960s, Lacan moved his seminar to the École Normale Supérieure, as well as founded his own psychoanalytic organization, the École Freudienne de Paris. In addition to his work as a practicing psychoanalyst, Lacan wrote many papers on a range of theoretical issues. As the influence of his ideas spread, he traveled to the United States to give lectures at Johns Hopkins University, Yale University, and the Massachusetts Institute of Technology. He died in Paris in 1981, at the age of eighty.

Believing himself to be following in Freud's footsteps, Lacan sought to revolutionize the temperate Freudianism of his time, to rescue psychoanalysis from its institutionalized conservative and conformist tendencies, and to reinscribe and resituate psychic meanings and processes within broader social systems and historical structures. He was widely acclaimed for his philosophical interpretation of Freud. No one would question the assertion that Lacan, along with his structuralist and poststructuralist contemporaries such as Lévi-Strauss, Foucault, Barthes, and Derrida, was one of the major French theorists of the postwar era. His writings, principally his magisterial nine-hundred-page *Écrits,* which was published in France in 1966, as well as his published seminars, are notorious for their complexity and difficulty. Indeed, Lacan's style is often infuriatingly obscure, cryptic, and elusive.

Important intellectual reasons can be offered for the complexity of Lacan's language, however. For one thing, in fashioning a difficult form of thought or discourse, Lacan wanted to be true to his object of study: the psyche and its relation to human subjectivity. For another, he sought to fashion a psychoanalytic language that would not submit easily to normalization (which he thought had been Freud's fate at the hands of American psychoanalysis); he sought a language that could not easily be flattened.

Lacan's work is thus quite different in scope from that of other psychoanalytic innovators, such as Melanie Klein, D. W. Winnicott, and Wilfred Bion. While he kept abreast of developments in mainstream psychoanalysis (e.g., he borrowed from Klein's account of the paranoid position, in formulating his idea of the ego as an agent of misrecognition), Lacan primarily developed a "return to Freud" that sought to exceed the confines of psychology and a reductive clinical understanding of psychoanalysis. In widening the frontiers of Freudian theory, Lacan drew from many varied sources: from his encounter with the surrealists; his friendships with Georges Bataille, Alexandre Koyré, and Alexandre Kojève introduced him to European philosophy, and in turn he borrowed, and reworked, philosophical notions from Hegel, Husserl, Nietzsche, and Heidegger; his reading of the linguistic departures of Ferdinand de Saussure and Roman Jakobson led to the privileging of structures and the decentering of the subject; and his encounter with the structural anthropology of Lévi-Strauss added to his enlarged conception of the Oedipus complex and the triangular structure of the individual's relation to society and history.

The importance of Lacan's thought for contemporary social theory is considerable and varied, and it requires some comment before proceeding further. Lacan was a psychoanalyst, not a social theorist. To some, therefore, it might seem odd that a chapter is devoted to him in a book that is primarily concerned with contemporary social theory. Yet I shall propose, in what follows, that Lacan should indeed be considered a major social theorist, a theorist who developed a systematic approach to the study of the relation between self and society. Lacan's importance consists in certain key themes and problematics that he has helped bring to prominence in social theory—including the status of the imaginary in personal and social life, the symbolic ordering of social relations, the fracturing effects of the unconscious upon social order, and the phallocentric structuring of sexual subjectivity in contemporary culture.

LACANIAN PSYCHOANALYSIS AND SOCIAL THEORY

Lacan's "Return to Freud"

Perhaps the most central preoccupation of Lacan's interpretation of Freudian psychoanalysis is the primacy accorded to the unconscious in the human subject's relations with others. Freud's discovery of the repressed unconscious, which contradicted the unitary rational subject, and hence the belief that the ego was master in its own house, was of great importance to Lacan, as indicated by his skeptical and mostly negative comments about American ego-psychology and its negation of the spirit of subversion of psychoanalysis. The theoretical downgrading of the unconscious at the hands of the American ego-psychologists and of Anna Freud's followers was, according to Lacan, an attempt to adapt psychoanalysis to the cultural conformism of the present epoch. By translating Freud's maxim on the task of psychoanalysis, "Wo Es war, soll Ich werden," to fit with the ideals of enlightenment reason—that is, that the unconscious is to be made conscious—the American model presented an idealistic and deceptive view that the patient might free herself from all constraint. In contrast, Lacan showed little interest in issues of adaptation or with debates about mental health. He instead challenged the defenders of adaptational psychoanalysis by translating Freud's sentence as "Where it was, the I must be," thus granting primacy to the unconscious. The unconscious, Lacan argued, precedes "I."

Informing this reading of Freud was Lacan's structural recasting of the psyche, consisting of three terms or orders: the *imaginary,* the *symbolic,* and the *real.* Lacan included in the category of the imaginary the paradoxes, illusions, and deceptions of the optical image; narcissism and its connection with doubles; as well as the death drive and anxieties of fragmentation and disintegration. The category of the symbolic included all the reworkings of theory he had undertaken through an engagement with structural linguistics, including the prominence he accorded to language in founding the unconscious, symbolic spacing through difference, and the primacy of the signifier. The order of the real was derived from Freud's discussion of psychical reality and, while redefined several times throughout Lacan's career, was equated with that which resists mirror play and all attempts at symbolization. Let us now turn to consider Lacan's account of the psyche in more detail.

The Mirror Stage and Misrecognition

There are two, essentially contrasting, conceptions of the genesis of the ego in Freud's writings. The first conception equates the ego as a representative of reality testing, making it responsible for the control of unconscious drives and passion. Freud elaborated this conception in the early part of his career, and in it the ego is understood as a product of the gradual differentiation of the unconscious-preconscious-conscious system. The second conception, detailed by Freud after his introduction of the concept of narcissism in the metapsychological papers of 1915, locates the genesis of the ego in terms of projection and identification. It is this second conception of the ego that Lacan adopts, focusing on the ego's structuring by means of representations derived from the other.

In his paper "The Mirror Stage as Formative of the Function of the I" (1949), Lacan advances the thesis of the self-deception of the ego by considering the infant identifying with a mirror image of a complete unified body. Following closely Freud's proposition that the ego is fundamentally narcissistic in character, as well as his insight that a period of self-love precedes the object love initiated through the Oedipus complex, Lacan notes that the infant is initially unable to differentiate between its own body and the outside world. The key moment of this pre-Oedipal state of being is that of fragmentation, of an endless array of part objects, all of which collide with multiplex drives and passions. The infant's drafting of a distinction between itself and the outside between the age of six and eighteen months, says Lacan, takes place within the paradoxes and illusions of the visual field, or what he calls the mirror stage. As a metaphorical and structural concept, the mirror provides the subject with relief from the experience of fragmentation, by granting an illusory sense of bodily unity through its reflecting surface. As Lacan (1977: 1–2) develops this:

[U]nable as yet to walk, or even to stand up, and held tightly as he is by some support, human or artificial . . . he nevertheless overcomes in a flutter of jubilant activity, the obstruction of his support and, fixing his attitude in a slightly leaning-forward position, in order to hold it in his gaze, brings back an instantaneous aspect of the image.

Note that Lacan stresses that the image is cast within the field of optics: it is in and through a *reflecting surface* that the subject narcissistically invests its self-image. This contrasts radically with other psychoanalytic conceptions of mirroring, such as the work of Winnicott, who views early interchanges between self and others as crucial to the founding of a "true" self. It also contrasts with the ideas of other social theorists of intersubjectivity, such as Cooley, who wrote of a "looking glass self" that exists in relation to the gaze of others.

Lacan situates the constitution of the ego in a line of fiction. The ego is created as defensive armor to support the psyche against its otherwise terrifying experiences of fragmentation and dread. The capture of the self or "I" by the subject's reflection in the mirror is inseparable from what Lacan terms misrecognition of its own truth (*miconnaissance*). The mirror stage is profoundly imaginary in character, argues Lacan, because the consoling image of self-unity presented in the mirror is diametrically opposed to the multiplicity of drives and desires experienced by the child. In a word, the mirror *lies*. This process of misrecognition, Lacan writes (1977: 2), "situates the agency of the ego, before its social determination, in a fictional direction, which will always remain irreducible for the individual alone, or rather, which will only rejoin the coming-into-being of the subject asymptotically, whatever the success of the dialectical syntheses by which he must resolve his discordance with his own reality."

In his later writings on this nature of the imaginary, Lacan looks in further detail at the heterogeneous flux of unconscious desire, on which the mirror stage confers a primordial misrecognition of self-unity. During the *premirror* period, according to Lacan, the human body is experienced as a series of fragmented organs, part-objects, dispositions, and needs. Lacking any defined center of self, objects pass continually into the flux of unconscious imagination, and desire slides around a libidinal plenitude generated in relation to part-objects. These earliest experiences of fragmentation center around part-objects that, paradoxically, can only exist as *lacking objects*—what Lacan calls *objet petit a*. It is important to distinguish here what Lacan means by the *objet a* from the definition of part-objects referred to in object-relations theory and Kleinian psychoanalysis. Unlike these Anglo-American perspectives that attribute a pregiven subjective capacity to human subjects to endow part-objects (breast, penis, feces) with meaning, Lacan's *objet a* refers to part-objects that play a *constituting* role in the structuration of the psyche. The *objet a* refers to the introjection of certain primordial images and signs that always *escape* the knowledge of the human subject. These part-objects refer to any part of the body whatsoever (gaze, lips, voice, imaginary phallus) that *fails* to be mirrored or symbolized. Structured by the inescapable lack or destitution of the Real Order, the central point for Lacan is that such zones of the body always escape the full imaginary and symbolic articulations of the subject. "These objects," writes Lacan, "have one common feature in my elaboration of them—they have no specular images, or in other words, alterity. . . . It is what enables them to be the 'stuffing' or rather the lining, though not in any sense the reverse, of the very subject that one takes to be the subject of consciousness."

The idea that "lacking" part-objects generate imaginary identifications might appear maddeningly vague or abstract. Yet Lacan had good theoretical reasons for introducing the notion of the *objet a*. If, as Lacan claims, the imaginary always inflects the other person as a mirror, then the question arises as to how people construct particular identities, meanings, significations. That is, the question arises as to how the imaginary plays a role in the formation of the human subject's ego ideals. The central difficulty with Lacan's early looping of self and other through mirror identifications is that it makes the imaginary operate in a rather unspecific and ahistorical manner. Thus, the introduction of the *objet a* at the heart of human subjectivity allows for a more complex and differentiated account of the unconscious relays that affect imagination. In short, the *objet a* provides a perspective on the constitution of psychic reality. Through an in-mixing of body, desire, and signifiers the *objet a* inscribes a particular subjective style and *causes* certain imaginary fantasies that cover over that gap or lack that is taken by Lacan to be at the center of human subjectivity. Accordingly, it is because the human subject first experiences its body in bits and pieces—as fragmentation, loss, and lack—that she or he is forever prevented from establishing an identity as "complete" or "whole." For Lacan, this is the fundamental trajectory that desire will follow in all human social relationships. "The mirror stage," he notes, "is a drama whose internal thrust is precipitated from insufficiency to anticipation . . . [and] the armour of an alienating identity . . . will mark with its rigid structure the subject's entire mental development."

Lacan sets out these relationships of otherness in the structuration of the psyche in his so-called L-Schema graph (see figure 3.1). This graph illustrates Lacan's thesis of the alienation of the human subject's desire, connecting it to the dialectic of intersubjective relations. In particular, the graph focuses on the oscillating intersections between the "Imaginary Order," of the desired object and the ego, and the "Symbolic Order," the place of the subject and the Other, designated by Lacan as language or the unconscious.

Language, Symbolic Order and the Unconscious

Having argued that the ego is a paranoid structure, an agent of misconstruction and misrecognition, Lacan set out to show that the subject is also divided through insertion into a symbolic order of positions in relation to other subjects. Through

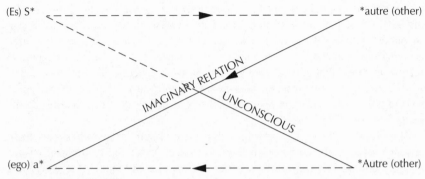

Figure 3.1.   L-Schema

Note: The effect of subjectivity in the L-Schema is located entirely within the place of the Other. S denotes the unconscious subject of speech (as the space of the subject of desire). The *Other (Autre)* is the impact of language itself. The *a* and *other* designate the ego and imaginary object of desire, respectively.

an engagement with Ferdinand de Saussure's *Course in General Linguistics* and Claude Lévi-Strauss's *The Elementary Structures of Kinship*, Lacan arrived at a structuralist theory of the subject in which the concepts of signifier, system, otherness, and difference figure prominently. The central texts in which he elaborates this antihumanist or structural-scientific conception of psychoanalysis are "The Field and Function of Speech and Language in Psychoanalysis" (1953) and "The Agency of the Letter in the Unconscious, or Reason since Freud" (1957).

In setting out his idea that the human subject, and hence by implication culture and society, is dominated by the primacy of language, Lacan drew from and refashioned Saussure's theory of the arbitrary nature of the linguistic sign. The importance that Saussure placed on the status of oppositions—not on things themselves but on the relationship between things—appealed to Lacan's psychoanalytic and structuralist sensibilities. Saussure, as well as the analysis of language developed by Roman Jakobson, provided Lacan with the means to bridge his theoretical concerns with both symbolic production and the formal organization of desire. He argued in his seminar, following Saussure, that the linguistic sign is composed of two parts: the signifier (the acoustic component or linguistic mark) and the signified (the conceptual element). In line with structuralist thought, Lacan argued that the relationship between signifiers and signifieds is arbitrary. The meaning of signifiers—'man', for example—is defined by difference, in this case by the signifier 'woman'. However, where Saussure placed the signified over the signifier, Lacan inverts the formula, putting the signified under the signifier, to which he ascribed primacy in the life of the psyche, subject, and society. All is determined for Lacan by the movement of signifiers. In fact, the position of each of us as individual subjects is determined by our place in the system of signifiers; our lives are negotiated in and against a plane of enunciation.

The signifier represents the subject for Lacan; the primacy of the signifier in the constitution of the subject indicates the rooting of the unconscious in language. The idea that language might be a product of the unconscious was widespread among many analysts, and indeed Lacan continually affirmed in his writings and seminars that the importance he placed on language was in keeping with the spirit of Freud's corpus. However, Lacan's structuralist elaboration of Saussure is, in fact, a radical conceptual departure from the Freudian conception of the unconscious. Whereas Freud sees connections between the psychic systems of unconscious representation (fantasy) and conscious thought (language), Lacan views subjectivity itself as constituted to its roots in language. This linguistification of the unconscious has important ramifications, making this psychic stratum not something that is internal to the subject (as with, say, a bodily heart or kidney), but rather an intersubjective space of communication, with language constantly sinking or fading into the gaps that separate signifier from signifier. The unconscious, writes Lacan, represents "the sum of the effects of the parole on a subject, at the level where the subject constitutes itself from the effects of the signifier" (Lacan quoted in Ragland-Sullivan 1986: 106). Or, in Lacan's infamous slogan: "The unconscious is structured like a language."

If the unconscious is structured like a language, as a chain of signifiers, the apparent stability of the mirror image of the subject is alienated twice over. First, the subject is alienated through the mirrored deceptions of the imaginary order, in which the ego is organized into a paranoid structure; second, the person is constituted as an *I* in the symbolic order, an order or law indifferent to the desires and emotions of individual subjects. Language is thus the vehicle of speech for the subject and a function of the symbolic order, order in which the individual is *subjected* to received social meanings, logic, and differentiation. It is this conception of the function of the symbol that paves the way for Lacan's incorporation of Lévi-Strauss's structural anthropology. Drawing on Lévi-Strauss's conception of the unconscious as a symbolic system of underlying relations that order social life, Lacan argues that the rules of matrimonial exchange are founded by a preferential order of kinship that is constitutive of the social system:

> The marriage tie is governed by an order of preference whose law concerning the kinship names is, like language, imperative for the group in its forms, but unconscious in its structure. . . . The primordial Law is therefore that which in regulating marriage ties superimposes the kingdom of culture on that of a nature abandoned to the law of mating. . . . This law, then, is revealed clearly enough as identical with an order of language. For without kinship nominations, no power is capable of instituting the order of preferences and taboos that bind and weave the yarn of lineage through succeeding generations. (1977: 66)

This primordial Law to which Lacan refers is the Freudian Oedipus complex, now rewritten in linguistic terms. What Lacan terms *nom-du-père* (name-of-the-father) is the cornerstone of his structural revision of the Oedipus complex. For Lacan, as for Freud, the father intrudes into the imaginary, blissful union of the child–mother dyad in a symbolic capacity, as the representative of the wider cultural network and the social taboo on incest. It is, above all, the *exteriority* of this process that Lacan underlines. Broadly speaking, Lacan is not arguing that each individual father forbids the mother–infant unity. Rather, he suggests the "paternal metaphor" intrudes into the child's narcissistically structured ego to refer her or him to what is outside, to what has the force of the law—namely, language.

In identifying these structuring symbolic mechanisms of the unconscious, Lacan advances a conception of the *determination* of the human subject by the Symbolic Order. In *Écrits* Lacan characterizes this social determination in the following manner: "Symbols in fact envelop the life of man in a network so total that they join together, before he comes into the world, those who are going to engender him 'by flesh and blood'; so total that they will bring to his birth . . . the shape of his destiny" (68). Or, more succinctly, that the Symbolic Order "cannot be conceived of as constituted by man, but as constituting him" (68). Such a treatment of the structuring symbolic properties of subjectivity bears a close affinity, of course, with Lévi-Strauss's (1970: 12) infamous contention that structuralism "claims to show, not how men think in myths, but how myths operate in men's minds without their being aware of the fact." But Lacan's adoption of the methodological principles of structuralism was neither uncritical nor uniform. Indeed, as early as the mid-1950s, throughout a series of articles and lectures, he had already forged a powerful critique of the objectivist claims of structuralism. Against Lévi-Strauss's conception of the unconscious as a "category of collective thought," Lacan argues, "it isn't a matter of positing a communal soul somewhere . . . the symbolic function has absolutely nothing to do with a para-animal formation, a totality which would make of the whole of humanity a kind of large animal—for in the end, that's what the collective unconscious is" (Lacan 1998b). Rather, Lacan's repeated stress on the symbolic mutations of unconscious desire, and his appreciation of the intricacies of human recognition, always prevented him from participating in the structuralist attempt to bracket the subject from social analysis. Thus, to conceptualize the trajectories of the Symbolic Order on subjectivity—without reducing the individual to a mere epiphenomenon—Lacan introduces the term "the Other."

Of all Lacan's ideas, the term "the Other" is perhaps the most ambiguous. The concept plays, however, a crucial role in Lacan's account of the structuration of the psyche. Generally speaking, the Other designates that which is *beyond* subjective intention—hence the unconscious/language. As Lacan remarks: "The presence of the unconscious, being situated in the place of the Other, is to be sought for in discourse, and its enunciation" (quoted in Dews 1987: 82). Or, as he states aphoristically: "the unconscious is the discourse of the Other." As such, there is a fundamental separation in Lacan's work between the Other (language/ the unconscious) and the other (person) of imaginary identifications. Lacan argues that, in all subjective interactions, the individual subject searches for a confirming image or reflection of her or his own self-identity through reactions from the other person. But given the specular traps and lures of the Imaginary Order, as previously discussed, the identifications forged through such involvement are said to result in fundamental subjective misrecognitions. With the introduction of the concept of the Symbolic Order, however, Lacan argues that mutual recognition is absolutely unobtainable since the Other introduces an uncertainty, an interminable shifting, into language. As Lacan formulates this tragic ontology: "Language is constituted in such a way as to found us in the Other, while radically preventing us from understanding him."

LACANIAN THEORY AND ITS OTHERS: CRITICAL COMMENTS

The political pessimism of Lacan's doctrines—the distorting traps of the imaginary; the symbolic determination of the subject; the lack or failure of desire—has proved attractive to many social theorists and cultural analysts. His portrayal of the ego as a paranoid structure has served as a balance against conservative and liberal theories that construct the self at the center of rational psychological functioning. Lacan, by contrast, stresses that the self is always alienated from its own history, is constituted in and through otherness, and is inserted into a symbolic order as a decentered subject. The theme of otherness in particular is something that runs deep in contemporary social thought, and Lacan's reflections on the strangeness that mediates subjectivity and culture have been highly influential across the social sciences and the humanities. However, Lacan's "return to Freud" has also come under fire by many social theorists and cultural commentators. In this section, I shall consider the case for and against Lacan in social theory (see also Macey 1988; Elliott and Spezzano 2000; Elliott 2002).

Lacanian and Post-Lacanian Social Theory

In the early 1930s, two maidservants of humble origins viciously murdered their wealthy employers in the town of Le Mans in northwestern France. The celebrated crime of the Papin sisters both shocked and gripped the French public and press; it was reported as a tale of class hatred, of social tension, of hysteria and madness. On the day of the crime, a power failure had prevented Christine Papin from carrying out her household duties, for which she was firmly rebuked by her employer, Mme Lancelin. The sisters thereupon lashed out and attacked the Lancelins, gouging out their victims' eyes and cutting up their bodies. Jacques Lacan, fascinated by the case of the Papin sisters, suggested that while the crime was undertaken against a backdrop of rising social, economic, racial, and national hatreds, another—more structural—psychic force was at work: that of paranoid delusion and alienation. "Lacan," writes Elizabeth Roudinesco (1997: 63–64) in her biography of the French psychoanalyst,

> set out to show that only paranoia could explain the mystery of the sisters' act. The episode of insanity seemed to arise out of a seemingly everyday incident: a power failure. But this incident might well have had an unconscious significance for the Papin sisters. Lacan suggested it stood for the silence that had long existed between the mistresses and the maids: no current could flow between the employers and their servants because they didn't speak to one another. Thus the crime triggered by the power failure was a violent acting out of a *non-dit:* something unspoken, of whose meaning the chief actors in the drama were unaware.

Although many years prior to the formalization of his psychoanalytical account of the imaginary, symbolic, and real orders, Lacan presented the crime of the Papin sisters primarily in terms of an interweaving of language, symbolism, the unconscious, and paranoid alienation.

Lacan, as his reflections on the case of the Papin sisters illustrate, was profoundly interested in the links between the individual and society. Yet however deeply engaged by the connections between psychoanalysis, philosophy, and social theory, Lacan failed to develop an account of the relevance of his theories to social life in any detailed fashion. As a psychoanalyst, he was preoccupied by other (clinical and institutional) issues. On the other hand, he was aware of (and followed with great interest) the many attempts by others to bring Lacanian theory to bear on issues of pressing social, cultural, and political importance.

The Marxist Louis Althusser, a friend of Lacan's, was among the first social theorists to argue for the importance of Lacanian theory to the development of a theory of ideology. By bridging Marxist and Lacanian theory, Althusser sought to challenge traditional conceptions of ideology as a set of false beliefs or illusions. For Althusser, the view that social practices are real, while the ideas and beliefs that sustain them are simply false illusions, mistakenly assumes that ideology is imaginary in only a passive sense, as a weak copy of the structures of our social practice. In breaking from the imaginary/real opposition of traditional Marxism, where the former stands as a sort of ethereal medium that veils real political and economic structures, Althusser argues that the imaginary is embodied in the relations to the real that are organized and sustained through ideology. Ideology is the *imaginary relation* of individuals to their real conditions of social existence. This imaginary dimension of ideology, which Althusser develops from Lacan's Freud, is not understood as some kind of private space internal to individuals. Rather, Althusser emphasizes that the imaginary dimensions of ideology exist on the "outside" but are continually woven through us as an effect of subjective positioning. He defines this process as follows:

> All ideology represents in its necessarily imaginary distortion is not the existing relations of production (and the other relations that derive from them), but above all the

(imaginary) relationship of individuals to the relations of production and the relations that derive from them. What is represented in ideology is therefore not the system of real relations which govern the existence of individuals, but the imaginary relation of these individuals to the real relations in which they live. (1984: 38–39)

On this view, then, ideology is the social cement of human society. It positions human subjects at a place where ideological meanings are constituted and thereby structures the real organization of social relations. It establishes, in sum, the unconscious dimensions by which subjects come to "live out" their real relation to society.

Althusser, commonly regarded as the founder of applied Lacanian doctrine, promoted a structuralist approach to issues of subjectivity, agency, and ideology in the social sciences. Consideration of the status of subjectivity, and especially the notion of the decentering of the subject, became widespread across disciplines concerned with the study of human activity. In the writings of Pierre Machery, Etienne Balibar, Stuart Hall, Fredric Jameson, Paul Hirst, and Barry Hindess, to name only a few, the Lacanian/Althusserian framework figured prominently in addressing key political issues such as nationalism, race, ethnicity, and class. Debate over the specular structure of ideology raised important issues concerning the creative capabilities of human subjects. To what extent Lacanian theory dissolved the subject in social analysis generated considerable controversy in social theory. Some argued that the decentering of the subject is formally equivalent to its disappearance, a conceptual move that mirrors the decline of the individual brought about by contemporary social changes (see, e.g., Giddens 1979). Others argued that the subject is not desubjectivized in Lacanian theory in such a thoroughgoing manner.

Lacan's influence is also strongly evident in the study of culture, especially popular culture. Cultural and media studies throughout the 1980s and 1990s have indicated a considerable Lacanian debt, specifically in the field of cinema studies. The writings of Stephen Heath, Christian Metz, Laura Mulvey, and Teresa De Lauretis, among others, have drawn from Lacanian theory to analyze the complex, contradictory ways in which spectator–subject positions are constituted, as well as rearticulated, in relation to symbolic systems.

Perhaps the most vibrant deployment of Lacanian theory for the analysis of popular culture can be found in the writings of the Slovenian critic Slavoj Zizek (1989, 1991). Seeking to extend Lacanian criticism beyond such notions as the symbolic positioning of the subject, Zizek relates the imaginary and symbolic fields to Lacan's order of the real to produce a highly original account of the traumatic and disruptive aspects of human subjectivity. In Zizek, the real is portrayed as that which erupts at the edge of the mirror, as a leftover of the symbolic order, a leftover that returns to derail intersubjective draftings of identity construction and cultural forms.

The most fruitful area of engagement with Lacan's Freud, however, has occurred in feminist studies. Many feminists have turned to Lacanian theory to advance political debate on issues of subjectivity, gender, and sexual difference. Here there is a key stress on the role of symbolic forms in the constitution of the self and thus of gender. The symbolic order, language, the Name-of-the-Father, the phallus as transcendental signifier: these are the signature concepts through which Lacanian and post-Lacanian feminists analyze asymmetrical power relations of gender and sexuality. "There is no woman," says Lacan (1975), "but excluded from the value of words." What Lacan means by this pessimistic reading of gender relationships is that, in patriarchal societies, femininity always remains on the outside of language and power. In contemporary culture, the phallus comes to be identified with the penis and hence with male power. Woman functions in the symbolic order of language as excluded Other, lack, negativity. Lurking within this apparently rigid, phallocentric organization of sexual difference, however, is something discerned by Lacan to be more fluid and ambivalent. Since human subjects are split at the core, radically divided between the narcissistic traps of the imaginary and the unconscious ruptures of the symbolic order, so, too, gender determination is always open to displacement. In short, if femininity is constituted in relation to otherness, this is an otherness that threatens to outstrip the foundations of sexual difference.

It will be apparent that there are two dominant, and competing, strands in Lacan's psychoanalytic interpretation of sexual difference. The first stresses the symbolic determination of the subject; the second highlights the fracturing effects of the unconscious on phallic organizations of language and culture. Not surprisingly, it is also possible to discern these different emphases of Lacan's approach to sexual difference in much feminist social theory.

An emphasis on the symbolic determination of the subject, for example, is strongly evident in Juliet Mitchell's pathbreaking book, *Psychoanalysis and Feminism* (1974). Arguing that feminism must found its utopic vision upon a full examination of the most distressing and painful elements of gender relations, Mitchell deftly situates the relevance of Lacan's Freud in relation to social theory. "If psychoanalysis is phallocentric," writes Mitchell (1984: 274) in a subsequent book of essays, *Women: The Longest Revolution*, "it is because the human social order that it perceives refracted through the individual human subject is patrocentric. To date, the father stands in the position of the third term that must break the asocial dyadic unit of mother and child." Of course, everything hangs on the projected time frame of "to date"; certainly, Mitchell's work has been sharply criticized for its deterministic and ahistorical approach to issues of gender power.

By contrast, in the writings of Julia Kristeva, Luce Irigaray, and Hélène Cixous, it is possible to discern a more critical stance toward Lacan's deterministic account of the symbolic positioning of gendered subjectivity. Indeed, this brand of feminism might be described as "neo-Lacanian" or "post-Lacanian," primarily because a more positive image of femininity is evoked. As Cixous (1980: 262) takes aim at Lacan, "What's a desire originating from lack? A pretty meagre desire." By contrast, the vital feminist task is to explore and valorize women's difference from men in order to go beyond the repressive confines of phallocentric culture. In the work of Irigaray and Cixous, this has involved a reconsideration of the affective dimensions of female sexual pleasure—in which Lacan's writings and seminars have figured as both inspiration and limitation. In the writings of Kristeva, the importance of Lacan's thought consists primarily in certain major themes that she draws from and reworks—themes including the narcissistic lures of the imaginary, the centrality of language to gender spacing through difference, and the mutations of the symbolic order.

Critique of Lacan

Notwithstanding Lacan's considerable contributions to contemporary social theory, his rereading of Freud has failed to generate the revolution in philosophical understanding of problems of subjectivity, intersubjectivity, and culture that once was routinely asserted by Lacanian-orientated social theorists. There are three core respects, I argue, in which Lacan's psychoanalytic thought is particularly deficient, especially when considered in the light of the typical preoccupations of social theory with the relations between self and society.

First, while Lacan's conception of the imaginary is of great interest to social theory, it is associated too closely with the logic of the specular (see Elliott 1999: chapter 4); the idea that the imaginary is only constituted when the self is reflected as an object fails to grasp that it is the psyche self that represents, figures, invests, and identifies with this specular image. How, after all, does the small infant come to (mis)recognize itself in the mirror? How, exactly, does the individual subject cash in on this conferring of an ideal self, however brittle or illusory? These difficulties are especially well illuminated in Cornelius Castoriadis's critique of Lacan. Rejecting the standpoint that the imaginary is born from a specular image that is somehow "already there," Castoriadis rather contends that the production of images and forms actually *is* the work of the imaginary. In his words:

> The imaginary does not come from the image in the mirror or from the gaze of the other. Instead, the "mirror" itself and its possibility, and the other as mirror, are the works of the imaginary, which is creation *ex nihilo*. Those who speak of the "imaginary," understanding by this the "specular," the reflection of the "fictive," do no more than repeat, usually without realizing it, the affirmation which has for all time chained them to the underground of the famous cave: it is necessary that this world be an image *of* something. (1987: 3)

For Castoriadis, the argument that the ego is constituted through a misrecognition of its reflected image fundamentally ignores the point that it is the psyche that *invests* the "mirror" with desire. The problem with Lacan's position is that surely for an individual to begin to recognize its reflected image in the "mirror," it must *already* possess the imaginary capacities for identification and representation, or what Freud named psychical reality. In the end, Castoriadis argues, Lacan's theory palpably cannot account for the psychical processes by which mirror images are *created* and *formed*. That is, Lacan's account of specular identity fails to address how it comes about that the other as mirror is perceived as real—how the reflected object is rendered intelligible to the subject.

In his various seminars and writings, Lacan indicated that he was aware of these criticisms of his account of the nature of the Imaginary Order. As Dews (1987) notes, it was precisely the question of the *individuality* of the subject that prompted Lacan to develop the notion of the *objet petit a*—the object of desire in unconscious fantasy. In *The Four Fundamental Concepts of Psychoanalysis*, Lacan (1979: 103) argues that the "*objet a* is something from which the subject has separated itself, in the form of an organ. It functions as the symbol of a lack, that is to say as the phallus, not as such, but in so far as it is lacking." The *objet a* represents for Lacan that lost or lacking aspect of self that the "subject of the unconscious" forever tries to recapture through fantasies of wholeness. More specifically, Lacan argues that a part of the body must be psychically separated from the subject in order to avoid complete absorption into the Symbolic Order, into the radical "otherness" of language. Such part-objects are constituted through an introjection of fragmented and fragmenting images, textures, sounds. The presence of the *objet a*, of an unconscious part of the subject as signifier, is thus said to guarantee the existence and individuality of the subject. In effect, this is a repressed signifier to which the subject can always *cling* when threatened with the radical "otherness" of language.

The concept of the *objet petit a* has been much debated in contemporary social theory and modern European thought, with many Lacanians asserting that the structural positioning of these part-objects provides a route out of the aporias of specular identity discussed in the foregoing paragraphs. Constituted from an interplay of "lack" and desire, yet subjectively framed prior to the mirror stage, it has been argued by some critics that Lacan's *objet petit a* offers a nonreflexive theory of the constitution of the human subject. Dews (1987), for example, argues that Lacan's theorization of the *objet a* is crucial to transcending the limits of specular identity, since the formation of such part-objects occurs prior to the mirror phase in the life of the infant and is accordingly *nonspecularizable*. For Dews, the *objet a* is necessarily unconscious. As that which is constitutively repressed, the *objet a* structures the center point of our unique individuality. Such part-objects account for why we are driven to hunt for particular (lost) meanings and signifiers throughout life. Yet there are still immense psychodynamic and conceptual problems with this doctrine. Exactly how part-objects that are "lacking" come to be implanted within the roots of psychic life is insufficiently explored by Lacan. Certainly, little indication is given in Lacan's work as to how lacking objects may induce the unconscious imagination to construct certain representations and images. Part of the difficulty here, I have argued previously (Elliott 1999, 2002), is that Lacan's formulation seeks to nail down an external trigger that sets off a reordering of the psyche—outlined variously as the mirror stage, the *objet a*, or, indeed, structure itself. But rather than lack, absence, gap, and object-loss functioning as pregiven phenomena, my argument is that such representational forms and affecting dynamics can only come into existence for the human subject *through* unconscious imagination.

Second, there are major substantive and political problems with Lacan's contention that the unconscious/conscious dualism should be conceptualized as a linguistic relation. Many critics, including Paul Ricoeur, Jean-François Lyotard, and Jean Laplanche, have argued the Freudian point against Lacan that the unconscious is resistant to ordered syntax. Against this linguistification of the psyche, we need to return to Freud's account of the unconscious, a realm of the psyche that he notes "is not simply more careless, more irrational, more forgetful and more incomplete than waking thought; it is completely different from it qualitatively and for that reason not immediately comparable with it. It [the unconscious] does not think, calculate or judge in any way at all; it restricts itself to giving things a new form" (1900: 507). This "new form" of which Freud speaks, and explicitly contrasts with waking thought and language, concerns representation: the flux of desires and fantasies in which things strange and unknown make themselves felt at the level of psychic functioning.

Third, the politics of Lacanianism has often been criticized for its determinism and pessimism (see Castoriadis 1984a, 1984b; Frosh 1987; Elliott 2002). Certainly, Lacan's structuralist leanings led him to underscore the symbolic determination of the subject. "Symbols," he writes (1977: 68), "envelop the life of man in a network so total that they join together, before he comes into the world, those who are going to engender him "'by flesh and blood'"; so total that they will bring to his birth . . . the shape of his destiny." Lacan's view that the subject enters a symbolic order that is prestructured linguistically, and in which the law appears terroristic, creates immense difficulties for theorizing human agency and the creative dimensions of subjective and intersubjective life. Whereas Freud, in his own decentering of the ego, at least posits the subject's prospects for critical self-reflection and autonomy, Lacan sees the self as a complete distortion, a defensive structure. According to Lacan, the structure of human knowledge is delusional through and through, with the imaginary order offering a misleading promise of self-unity on the one side, and the symbolic and real orders operating antagonistically on the other. As Castoriadis and others have noted, however, there are major epistemological difficulties with Lacan's account, including the central issue of paranoid delusion and its infinite regress. For if the imaginary is a specular trap, the law omnipotent, and the symbolic order a mask for lack and loss, how exactly is the subject to know when something of value or substance has ever been found? How is a meaningful relationship with the outside world to be forged, let alone transformed (as with the practice of psychoanalysis)? And what of the theorist or social scientist? Are all claims to knowledge punctured by the illusory traps of the imaginary and its hall of mirrors? What of Lacan's discourse? If truth is inconceivable, communication paradoxical and endlessly problematic, and general social theories authoritarian, how to assess the master's pronouncements? Of course, this is precisely why Lacan formulated his theorems in such cryptic and elusive terms: to give full vent to the skidding signifiers of the unconscious. But there must be serious reservations about such claims, primarily because issues of self-actualization and critical self-reflection remain unaddressed in Lacan's work.

POSTSCRIPT: DERRIDA ON LACAN'S FREUD

In his powerful critique of French Lacanian psychoanalysis set out in *Resistances of Psychoanalysis,* Jacques Derrida recalls the circumstances of his initial meeting with Lacan in 1966 at Johns Hopkins University in Baltimore. A key moment in contemporary French intellectual history, their encounter was marked by anxiousness, driven by intellectual competition and the struggle for academic fame. Here it is worth quoting Derrida at some length:

> I only met Lacan twice, though I crossed paths with him a third time, long after, at a cocktail party. I don't know if that means we were together, one *with* the other, but in any case these two encounters did not take place at the home of (*apud*) one or the other but at a third party's, first abroad, in 1966 in the United States, to which both of us had been for the first time exported. . . . So, to start over, when I met Lacan in Baltimore for the first time, in 1966—we were introduced to each other by Renée Girard—his first words, uttered in a friendly sigh, were: "So we had to wait to come here, and abroad, in order to meet each other!" Here, I remark, perhaps because of the problem of destinerrance that it is waiting for us and perhaps because of Baltimore's mortal name (Baltimore: dance or trance and terror), Baltimore the city of Poe, whose grave I looked for in vain during those days, although I was able to visit his house on that occasion (I went *chez* Poe in 1966), perhaps then because of this mortal name of Baltimore, I remark that the only two times we met and spoke briefly one *with* the other, it was a question of death between us, and first of all from Lacan's mouth. (Derrida 1998: 49–50)

One might be forgiven for thinking that Derrida is merely cute to be suggestive about anxiety staged under the death drive: hinting at the horrifying, passionate sense we have of cities and space (the *terror* of Baltimore), as well as our often destructive unconscious assumptions about others (the meeting of the philosopher and psychoanalyst already had death inscribed in it).

And the "question of death" from the mouth of Lacan? Well, for those well versed in the deconstructionist examination of texts, it will surely not come as any surprise to learn that the question concerned one of reading—or of what Derrideans might term the problematic of "the trace." "In Baltimore," writes Derrida, "Lacan talked to me about how he thought he would be read, particularly by me, after he was dead." So Lacan was worried—or, at least, anxious enough to raise this as a matter for conversation—about how he would be read after his death and worried in particular about what the trace of his "return to Freud" would look like in the hands of Derrida's deconstruction. As it transpires, Lacan was indeed right to be concerned about how his less shrewd acolytes on both sides of the Atlantic would interpret his "return to Freud"—as the history of post-Lacanianism graphically demonstrates. Derrida himself notes as much:

> I consider it an act of cultural resistance to pay homage publicly to a difficult form of thought, discourse, or writing, one which does not submit easily to normalization by the media, by academics, or by publishers, one which rebels against the restoration currently underway, against the philosophical or theoretical non-conformism in general (let us not even mention literature) that flattens and levels everything around us, in the attempt to make one forget what the Lacan era was, along with the future and the promise of his thought, thereby erasing the *name* of Lacan. (Derrida 1998: 45–46)

As it happens, Lacan also had good reason to be worried about how Derrida would read him. This is evident from Derrida's book title *Resistances of Psychoanalysis,* as I shall subsequently argue. Yet it is also clear from prior readings of Lacan's work that Derrida has performed. In "The Purveyor of Truth," Derrida's celebrated critique of Lacan's seminar on Poe's "The Purloined Letter," he argues that Lacan's specular theory of identity screens from view the strangeness and otherness that disrupt the narcissistic, mirrorlike formation of subjectivities; in this sense, Lacan's paper on the mirror stage can be descontructed as an allegory of the truth of psychoanalysis itself.

But to what extent can we trace forward—as Lacan was apparently trying to do in Baltimore; as opposed to tracing backward, or after "the event," as might deconstructionists—our anxieties about all these things? *"The (pure) trace is differance,"* wrote Derrida in *Of Grammatology.* As Derrida (1967: 62) continues:

> It does not depend on any sensible plenitude, audible or visible, phonic or graphic. It is, on the contrary, the condition of such a plenitude. Although it *does not exist,* although it is never a *being-present* outside of all plenitude, its possibility is by rights anterior to all but one calls sign (signified/signifier, content/expression, etc.), concept or operation, motor or sensory. This differance is therefore not more sensible than intelligible.

If for Derrida the trace involves ways of attempting to remember an ever-receding "original" event, one that remains forever out of reach of the effects it produces in the present, then it might be said that Lacan couldn't have provided a better prospective tracing of his anxieties. Consider, for example, Derrida's deconstruction of Lacan in *Resistances of Psychoanalysis*. In a fluently condensed analysis, Derrida deconstructs Lacan's texts and teachings within the broader frame of poststructural linguistics. He questions, in effect, what we have come to know of Lacanian psychoanalysis by pointing to its multiplex existence as seminars, tape-recorded archives, texts, transcripts, quotations, and slogans. He thus argues that it is impossible to speak of "Lacan in general—who does not exist." In developing this viewpoint, Derrida insists on the power of resistance. There is an unavoidable ambiguity, he says, between Lacanian theory and that to which it lays claim—the thought of Lacan. But if resistance is understood as structural limit, not in the psychological but rather the rhetorical sense, where exactly does this leave psychoanalysis?

An engrossing critique of psychoanalysis, a confessional memoir, a tale of intellectual influences, a history of the great twentieth-century love affair with Freudian thought—such is Derrida's *Resistances of Psychoanalysis,* a work that (more than anything else Derrida has written) raises the level of debate over the relationship between psychoanalysis and deconstruction several notches. Returning to classical psychoanalytical theory, Derrida finds "resistance" at the heart of Freud's ideas, including the unconscious, repression, and the Oedipus complex. He understands resistance not in the psychoanalytic sense of repression or defense but rather in terms of a linguistic distortion or failure, of something that resists the identity of author and meaning. In a kind of lifting of psychoanalysis to the second power, Derrida contends that resistance arises from the structure of psychoanalysis itself. In short, Freud's dream machine is, for Derrida, continually on the brink of bringing itself undone.

Derrida contends that psychoanalysis is itself inscribed in a logic of difference. Freud's legacy is best approached as a product of numerous texts, histories, institutions, and processes of inscription. There is no such thing as psychoanalysis in general—only various theorists, concepts, quotations, teachings, schools, and factions, all of which exist as socially structured differences. This seems to me an interesting and useful angle on the place of psychoanalysis as a discourse and practice within our culture. The scope of psychoanalytic theory is extremely wide today, ranging from classical to postmodern approaches in therapeutic settings, and with an equally broad range of theory (object-relational, clinician post-Lacanian) that circulate within the social sciences and the humanities.

However, there are limitations to Derrida's critique of Lacan as well as his deconstructionist recycling of Freud. To say of a particular school of psychoanalysis that its structure arises in and through "difference" is interesting only up to a point. Why, for example, did Lacanian theory fail for so many years to establish its legitimacy in Anglo-American psychoanalysis? Why, for example, is Slavoj Zizek's reading of Lacan so popular in the academy at the current time, and why is it preferred over Derrida's Freud? Derrida is unable to address these issues satisfactorily, I believe, since they require an examination in depth of the political context in which psychoanalytic theory operates. Derrida himself has hardly been noted for his political and institutional as opposed to his linguistic and discursive critiques. From this angle, the Lacanian deconstruction and reconstruction of Freudian psychoanalysis is probably the more suggestive for contemporary social theory.

4

Subjectivity, Culture, Autonomy: Cornelius Castoriadis

In the last fifteen or so years, a number of commentators have argued for the importance and relevance of Cornelius Castoriadis's writings to contemporary debates in modern European thought and the philosophy of the social sciences (Thompson 1984; Rorty 1991; Whitebook 1995; Lambropoulos 1997). Despite these philosophical confrontations, however, Castoriadis's contribution to social theory has yet to be adequately understood, discussed, and developed. In this chapter I shall highlight certain aspects of Castoriadis's mature writings in the light of conceptual controversies concerning relations between human subjectivity, contemporary culture, and political autonomy. My discussion of Castoriadis's remarkable work will proceed from an analysis of his writings that are well known in the English-speaking world, principally *Crossroads in the Labyrinth* (Castoriadis 1984a) and *The Imaginary Institution of Society* (Castoriadis 1987) but also his late writings that are not yet known well: *World in Fragments* (Castoriadis 1997) and *The Castoriadis Reader* (Curtis 1997), as well as the French publications *Figures du Pensable* (Castoriadis 1999a) and *Sur le Politique de Platon* (Castoriadis 1999b).

I also develop the claim that Castoriadis can now be regarded as a classic figure in social theory. Alongside Jürgen Habermas or Pierre Bourdieu, Anthony Giddens or Julia Kristeva, Castoriadis deserves to be entered as a major theorist of contemporary culture and the crisis it is undergoing. Indeed, it is arguable that Castoriadis is the most formidably brilliant theorist of the complex relations between the individual and society to have emerged in postwar Europe. But the more important change that Castoriadis's mature writings bring is a deeper appreciation of the extent to which interdisciplinary issues intrude into the tasks of social scientists. For one of the main themes of his writings is that the social sciences must recognize, as they have failed to do hitherto, the imaginative and creative capacities of human beings in their dealings with the social world. In his late writings, Castoriadis develops both a social theory dedicated to revealing the objective relations that constitute and underpin social life, and a psychoanalytic excavation of creation and imagination in the psyche, personality, and human nature itself.

My discussion in what follows is divided into three sections. In the first section I begin by situating Castoriadis's writings on society and history within the tradition of classical social theory, indicating a few of the respects in which his early social thought has been modified by his late writings, as well as the extent to which his thinking both conforms to, and departs from, the history of classical social thought.

The second section discusses Castoriadis's theory of radical imagination and his associated notion of the social imaginary. As many key problems to do with subjectivity, imagination, and reflective self-understanding, as well as processes of institutionalization and modernization, have been traced out in critical exchanges between Castoriadis and the German critical theorist Jürgen Habermas, I shall use these dialogues as a basis for situating Castoriadis's proposals for the critique of self and society.

In the third section I offer some critical reflections on the core arguments advanced by Castoriadis. Three central areas, I shall suggest, make Castoriadis's theoretical innovations important for the history of social thought: (1) his analysis of the mediation of psyche and society, (2) his views on culture, and (3) his interpretation of autonomy.

THE CONTEXT OF CASTORIADIS'S SOCIAL THEORY

The aim of this chapter is to elucidate some of the connections between Castoriadis's mature writings and his contributions to the social sciences and social theory. As a preface, it will be useful to briefly situate Castoriadis's work in relation to the tradition of classical social thought.

Castoriadis died in Paris on 26 December 1997, shortly after the publication of *World in Fragments,* aged seventy-five. Throughout his half-century of writings, he was both dauntingly prolific and amazingly versatile, able to leap in a sentence from Hegel to Handel, equally at home with the writings of a Fichte or Freud, and passionate about social movements, especially environmentalism. He wore many professional hats. So many, in fact, that he gives new meaning to the term *multidisciplinary.* Economist, social theorist, philosopher, psychoanalyst, political radical: Castoriadis was an intellectual jack-of-all-trades and master of many. He had moved from Athens to France in 1945 when, as a young wartime Greek communist, his life was threatened by fascists. He undertook postgraduate studies in Paris and subsequently worked for many years as a professional economist at the Organization of Economic Co-operation and Development. Intensely political, he was for a time a member of the Fourth International.

After a political falling out in 1949, he cofounded the noncommunist revolutionary group, Socialisme ou Barbarie, with his friend and coauthor Claude Lefort. A journal bearing the group's name soon appeared thereafter, and it continued to be published throughout the 1950s and early 1960s. During this period, Castoriadis developed his reputation as a first-rate political theorist. In his journal writings, he repudiated the Soviet Union, developed a powerful critique of bureaucratic capitalism, and suggested the Left needed to support workers' uprising in Eastern Europe (Singer 1979). His views on the crisis of Western society, in particular, significantly influenced the May 1968 student–worker rebellion in France. The political highs and lows of May 1968 led Castoriadis to reconsider the depth of commitment needed to bring about social change geared to the realization of new values.

Provoked by the simultaneous power and failure of this social upheaval, he left his post at the OECD in 1970 and began training as a psychoanalyst. The encounter with Freud was to prove decisive for his future thinking. In Freud, Castoriadis found a means to correct the misfires of Marx's economically reductionist approach to identity and culture. Like many before him who attempted to marry Marx and Freud, such as Wilhelm Reich or Herbert Marcuse, he argued that we must listen to our dreams and desires if our social struggles are to usher in genuine change.

In the early part of his career, Castoriadis had developed his social thought against the backdrop of Marxism. He had long been critical of the deterministic framework elaborated by Marx, though he would not develop the full implications of these views until later. For some years, he sought to reaffirm the liberationist emphasis of Marxist principles against watered-down instrumentalized Marxism. This stance accounts, in large part, for the widespread view of Castoriadis's work as "too Marxist" (Rorty 1991). However, it had become increasingly apparent to Castoriadis, after emerging evidence of exploitative relations in Russia and Eastern Europe, that the Marxian legacy was fundamentally flawed; in several celebrated critiques, he argued that Marx's social theory was profoundly misguided, as it rested on a deterministic conception of history and a scientistic understanding of social change. In addition to Marx, Weber also loomed large in Castoriadis's social theory, though often in a disguised fashion. Like Weber, Castoriadis is concerned to trace connections between rational action and social rationalization—what Castoriadis terms "pseudo-rational mastery." But unlike Weber, Castoriadis argued that polarities such as "subjectivity" and "objectivity," and "rationality" and "irrationality," cannot satisfactorily elucidate the conditions of history and social transformation.

Castoriadis's central theoretical innovation rather is that history *is* radical imagination, the eruption of the new that did not exist in any prior form. "Each Society," writes Castoriadis in the opening chapter of *World in Fragments*, "is a construction, a constitution, a creation of a world, of its own world." In this sentence, Castoriadis defines the core of his social theory: to acknowledge the irreducible creativity of society and history. Human creation, imagination, and autonomy are the central themes through which Castoriadis attempts to rethink the relations between self and society. In his writings, he mediates the persistent misunderstanding of the imaginary and imagination in traditional philosophical and sociological discourses. He examines the classical ontology underpinning conceptions of the imagination, mainly in Aristotle but also in Kant and Hegel. The nub of the problem, according to Castoriadis, is that philosophy has too often assumed that the imaginary is a mere copy, a reflection of the outside world. Rejecting this standpoint, he argues that human imagination is what actually renders possible a relation of minds and worlds. "The imaginary," he writes, "is the subject's whole creation of a world for itself." The impact of psychoanalysis—or, at least, Castoriadis's interpretation of Freud—runs deep here. Castoriadis's Freud is not the gloomy prophet of repression and repetition but rather the high priest of imagination. The dream, desire, wish, pleasure, fantasy: these are for Castoriadis at the core of our social process and political institutions. His theory of the radical imaginary is not only profoundly innovative (stretching the term *imagination* well beyond the narrow meaning accorded to it by Jacques Lacan in French theory), but it opens a path of research as to the social process of radical creation and cultural innovation. Castoriadis's psychoanalytic concern with imagination, its conditions of possibility and consequences, thus has to be understood as an outcome of a lifelong preoccupation with issues of both social reproduction and political transformation.

It has been said that Castoriadis's work represents a shift toward "post-Marxist theorizing" (Arnason and Beilharz 1997: vi). Thus expressed, this is a misleading statement. Judged in terms of neo-Marxist models, Castoriadis certainly rejected the view that Marx's social analysis could be easily amended or updated; his work shows, in fact, the fundamentally unsound ground on which the thought of Marx was built. Not so much post-Marxist as Marxism transcended. Yet the same could equally be said of Castoriadis's relation to Freud. While it is undoubtedly the case that Castoriadis turned increasingly to Freud in his late writings, his conception of radical imagination profoundly outstrips the Freudian conceptualization of fantasy and desire. Castoriadis was, in fact, highly critical of the naturalistic and objectivistic tendencies in Freud's thought.

THE CASTORIADIS-HABERMAS EXCHANGE

During the late 1980s and early 1990s, Castoriadis entered into several theoretical exchanges with Habermas. These exchanges were prompted by Habermas's sharp critique of Castoriadis in *The Philosophical Discourse of Modernity*, where the former claimed that the latter failed to break with the dead-ends of the philosophy of consciousness centered on the subject and, moreover, granted too much privilege to subjectivist concerns over objective social contradictions. In response, Castoriadis was similarly critical of Habermas, primarily on the grounds of the latter's alleged false equation of "intersubjectivity" with "the social-historical," and for squeezing imagination to the sidelines in an excessively rationalistic account of the human subject.

In his lectures on modernity, Habermas argued that thinkers such as Heidegger, Foucault, and Derrida were correct to reject the philosophy of consciousness but incorrect for drawing the conclusions they do. Habermas contended that proclamations about the "death of the subject" and "end of history" were fundamentally misguided; modernity, he argues, is not so much a discredited as an incomplete project. After having dismissed the general tenets of structuralist and poststructuralist thought, Habermas addressed Castoriadis's theory of the imaginary institution of society. His critique of Castoriadis is primarily concerned with the ontological status of creation in the mediation of the relationship between the individual and society (Habermas 1987b: 327–35). That is, Habermas contends that Castoriadis downgrades epistemological issues in favor of reworking conceptions of human being and social doing, with particular emphasis on the creation of meaning. Philosophical problems concerning the explication of meaning, being, and praxis, in Habermas's appraisal, form the starting point for Castoriadis's social theory and political philosophy.

According to Habermas, Castoriadis develops his perspective from the writings of Aristotle, drawing especially on the Aristotelian notion of praxis in interpreting the advancement of autonomy in both the life-world and social systems. As he puts this, "Castoriadis (like Aristotle) finds the characteristics of an unabridged praxis in instances of political, artistic, medical, and educational practice. . . . [P]raxis aims at promoting autonomy, from which, at the same time, it itself issues" (Habermas 1987a: 328). According to Habermas, Castoriadis connects this Aristotelian concept of praxis with the domain of the social and political by explicitly theorizing the role of imagination in the creation *ex nihilo* of figures, forms, and worlds. The constitution and reproduction of society for Castoriadis are in a very general sense an outcome of imaginary representations that are active and creative. New meanings are continually brought into existence, and are subsequently reproduced, displaced, or transfigured, as each society creates a world of its own. "Social process," writes Habermas of Castoriadis's idea of the imaginary institution, "is the generation of radically different patterns, a demiurge setting itself to work, the continuous creation of new types embodied in ever different exemplary ways—in short, the self-positing and ontological genesis of ever new 'worlds'" (Habermas 1987a: 329).

In Habermas's eyes, Castoriadis has reached this social-theoretical point of departure through a fusion of the late Heidegger with the early Fichte, a fusion that enables a theorization of the self-positing of world interpretations. Yet whatever the advantages in grasping the various forms in which Being/being creates a world for itself and of its own, it remains the case that, for Habermas, Castoriadis's thesis of the ontological genesis of ever new "worlds" prevents an adequate understanding of the dimension of intersubjectivty in self-understanding and institutionalized society—of which I will say more shortly.

Such a limitation is perhaps nowhere more obvious, says Habermas, than in Castoriadis's reinterpretation of Freud, specifically his account of imaginary signification. Habermas glosses what Castoriadis terms the "monadic core of the psyche" as a radical wildness of inner nature, of an "isolated consciousness" that must somehow be colonized and controlled by the socially institutionalized world in the course of the socialization process. This description of Castoriadis's approach brings to mind, of course, the Freudian emphasis on the necessities of society against the pleasures of sexuality—an element of the Freudian narrative of which Castoriadis is, in fact, profoundly suspicious. Yet Habermas himself is not especially alarmed with what he takes to be Castoriadis's adoption of the Freudian drama of the pleasure and reality principles. For psychoanalysis, on Habermas's own reckoning, can be viewed as a depth hermeneutic capable of reclaiming the apparently irrational. Rather, it is Castoriadis's insistence on the radical otherness of the unconscious, as an entity not subservient to language, that Habermas finds unconvincing. The main charge he makes against Castoriadis is that, in placing the world-constituting medium of the unconscious imagination prior to language, Castoriadis ultimately falls victim to a psychoanalytically formulated version of subjectivism. In treating the imagination as the prime focus of social-theoretical analysis, Castoriadis tends to skirt issues concerned with institutions, large-scale organizations, ideology, and power. Indeed, Habermas thinks that Castoriadis veers so much to the subjectivist side of the equation that he can have no effective means of making contact with society at all. "Castoriadis," writes Habermas, "cannot provide us with a figure for the mediation between the individual and society. . . . Intrapsychic conflicts are not internally linked with social ones; instead, psyche and society stand in a kind of metaphysical opposition to one another" (1987a: 329). Against this conceptual backdrop, Habermas charges Castoriadis with reproducing a "metaphysical opposition" between the individual subject and social structure.

Clearly, Castoriadis's theory of the monadic core of the psyche does not make much sense to Habermas in the light of the "linguistic turn"—that is, the shift from the philosophy of consciousness to the philosophy of intersubjectivty, and in particular Habermas's account of communicative rationality. In short, Habermas finds Castoriadis's account of the imaginary, at once psychic and social, unsatisfactory since it is glaringly at odds with an intersubjective emphasis on the primacy of language in the constitution and conditioning of the psyche and the socially institutionalized world. Habermas regards Castoriadis's stress on the imaginary fabrication of the social as effacing many of the core concepts of social theory—society, capitalism, modernity. He thinks that Castoriadis's downgrading of "society" in favor of the social properties generated by *imaginaire radical* constitutes a break with the themes of institutional orders and structural forms advanced by Marx and Weber. But nowhere does Habermas recognize Castoriadis's novel insight that the significance of radical or social imaginaries is that they introduce new mediations between self, society, and culture. This strongly suggests that imaginary significations express, and are expressed in, the heterogeneity of social doings and cultural activities which they inform. The radical imaginary is the medium whereby social life is constituted *as* meaningful by human subjects.

Let me now turn to Castoriadis's response to Habermas. Castoriadis has raised various philosophical issues about Habermas's work in more than one place. I shall concentrate only on comments that he develops in "Done and to Be Done," an essay in which Castoriadis responds to various critics about his work (in Curtis 1997: 361–417). Castoriadis says that several persistent misunderstandings about his approach to social theory have arisen from "the strange notion that I have taken up Aristotle's idea of praxis—an idea launched by Habermas." In a witty and polemical response, Castoriadis contends that Habermas seems unable to "read a contemporary author except as if he had to be copying ancient ones" (Curtis 1997: 398). (As for Habermas's projection of Heidegger into Castoriadis's work, Castoriadis comments that his use of the term "imagination" is wholly different from "the *Lebenswelt* of Husserl and Heidegger") (Castoriadis 1997: 181).

The reader is then sent on a theoretical adventure, the point of which is to emphasize that Castoriadis's theory of the subject is not Cartesian, as well as that his approach to the question of autonomy involves a radical break with Aristotle's idea of praxis. In the Aristotelian conception, Castoriadis concurs with Habermas, praxis appertains to human activity that has its ends in itself. Yet, in Castoriadis's version of praxis, autonomous activity cannot have its ends in itself, since that activity aims at self-transformation. That is, the self is treated as an "object" of reflective and deliberative activity. It is this emphasis on a certain transformation of the subject as *human object* that leads Castoriadis into a sustained engagement with deliberative and reflective subjectivity, with the work of Freud, and, ultimately, with the theory of the imaginary institution as such.

One major reason given by Castoriadis for the misunderstandings that pervade Habermas's critique of his work is that Habermas tends to identify the psyche with the socialized individual, reducing the former to the latter. As Castoriadis writes:

> It is said that my conception would render the mediation between individual and society impossible. But it is not a matter of establishing such a "mediation." The individual is of the social, it is total fragment of the world as it is each time instituted. It is a matter of elucidating, as far as possible, the fact that the psyche is (though never fully) socialized. (Curtis 1997: 377)

In other words, what Habermas calls the 'individual', as the designation of the singular human being, is for Castoriadis nothing other than society itself—an introjection of its successive strata of socialization, its codes and perspectives, its ontological coordinates and pragmatic presuppositions. This point is of the utmost significance for grasping the conceptual differences between Castoriadis and Habermas. Orthodox social and political theory tends to operate with a defective view of the singular human being, and it is this reductiveness that for Castoriadis is reiterated by Habermas in his elaboration (following Mead) of the socialization process.

By contrast, Castoriadis asserts that the living being can most profitably be regarded as endowed with imagination (nonfunctional imagination), discerned in the workings of unconscious representational pleasure and central to the psychic capacity for deliberate and reflective activity in personal and social life. This means revising our understanding of the process of socialization and the social individual. The social individual for Castoriadis arises as an intermixing of the psychic and social imaginaries, an intermixing fundamental to the psyche's capacity for sublimation as well as society's institutionalization of representations and practices for the psyche to invest in and sublimate. If there is an opposition operating here, it is not the individual and society, but rather the psyche and society—a relation that for Castoriadis is contradictory, tensional, conflictual.

The objections that Habermas levels against Castoriadis regarding the mediation of self and society can be reversed, Castoriadis adds, by criticisms of the manner in which Habermas himself interprets the linguistic intermixing of the unconscious and society to forge a preestablished harmony. In criticizing Habermas, Castoriadis directs attention to the failure of any linguistic reformulation of the Freudian unconscious to capture the energetic and affective marks of this stratum of the psyche. "The psyche," writes Castoriadis, "is not socializable without remainder—nor is the Unconscious translatable, without remainder, into language. The reduction of the Unconscious to language (where Lacan and Habermas curiously meet in agreement) is alien to the thing itself (and obviously also to Freud's thought: 'in the Unconscious there are only representations of things, not representations of words')" (Curtis 1997: 376).

The approach to language and the unconscious that Castoriadis advances is undoubtedly one at odds with certain dominant paradigms in contemporary philosophy and social theory. From Saussure to Derrida, contemporary theory develops by way of a shift from ideas of 'representation' and 'mentation', and from the notion that the mind "represents" the world and therefore provides a foundation for knowledge, and toward the study of language and the analysis of discursive practices. This move away from representational theories of the subject might seem, at first glance, to render Castoriadis's stress on imagination and the imaginary outdated or redundant. However, it is important to stress that in using the term *representation,* Castoriadis does not mean the "imitation" or "copying" of a world in the mind of the subject. For one thing, Castoriadis insists that the imaginary is not a mere reflection, a specular image of a preconstituted domain. On the contrary, he defines the imaginary as "the capacity to posit that which is not, to see in something that which is not there." Against the reductive scopic account of the imaginary posited by Lacan, Castoriadis defines the radical/social imaginary not as the creation of images in the mind or in society but rather in terms of the *signifiable.* As he remarks, "one of the gross inadequacies of Lacan's conception of the imagination is his fixation on the scopic. For me, if one is speaking of stages that are worked out, the imagination par excellence is the imagination of the musical composer. . . . Suddenly, figures surge forth that are not in the least visual. They are essentially auditory and kinetic—for there is also rhythm" (Castoriadis 1997: 182).

The "surging forth" of figures in the radical imagination, involving as it does the fundamental creativity and alterity of the subject and the social-historical sphere, takes us to the heart of Castoriadis's critique of the deterministic character of social theory and philosophy. Castoriadis proposes the term *ensemblistic-identitarian (la logique ensembliste-identitaire)* to capture the logic of ordered relations in all social activity (see the development of these concepts in Castoriadis 1984 and 1987).

By the term *ensemblistic-identitarian,* Castoriadis draws attention to the role of self-enclosed systems in the production and remaking of social life, of the various operations, strategies, and practices that can be undertaken and performed within the logic of set theory. For example, he views the structuralist understanding of language as a self-enclosed system of binary oppositions as essentially ensemblist, in so far as structuralist linguistics reduces language to an ontology of determinacy. Such a concern with the internal structure of language, says Castoriadis, can have no proper grasp of the creative fabrication of language at both the individual and societal levels. The core of Castoriadis's argument lies then in establishing a new and comprehensive term for the analysis of subjectivity and the social-historical world in which signification escapes the logic of ensemblist organizations.

To designate this *something* that escapes from the systems logic of parts and wholes, he refers to the 'magmas'. Castoriadis reserves for magmas that realm of signification that always escapes a logically structured whole, the leftover of meanings in terms of their relations to referents, the representational and affective flux of the imaginative stratum. The magmas function principally in the imaginary domain. Its logic prefers chaos to organization, groundlessness to structure, the affective to the cognitive, desire to rationality.

EVALUATION AND CRITIQUE

The theoretical exchange between Castoriadis and Habermas is instructive in that it brings to the fore a range of issues and concerns that seem now to have surfaced strongly in various versions of social theory. Many social analysts, especially those drawing from traditions as diverse as action theory, psychoanalysis, or hermeneutics, would no doubt welcome the stress that Castoriadis places on human creation and radical imagination in the constitution and reproduction of self and society. Rejecting a view of human agents and social structures as discrete, such a standpoint underlines that cultural and symbolic signification is always mediated through an interpreting self. For those practitioners of social theory drawn to styles of thought such as poststructuralism, postmodernism, or systems theory, however, it is likely that Castoriadis's theory of the imaginary institution of society might be regarded as perhaps too subjectivist or voluntaristic. The subjectivity of the individual agent, it might be argued, is elevated in Castoriadis's work over and above the objective structures of society, domains of power, or scripts of cultural life. Whatever the precise intellectual stock market fortunes of Habermas's theory of communicative action in the academy at the present time, it seems likely that such practitioners would concur with Habermas's judgment that Castoriadis is unable to come to grips with issues concerning structural or system constraints over human subjectivity and intersubjective relations. In what follows, I shall discuss some of the major contributions of, as well as substantial problems with, Castoriadis's social theory under three headings: his analysis of the mediation of psyche and society, his assessment of the crisis of the culture, and his discussion of autonomy and the autonomous society.

The Mediation of Psyche and Society

Castoriadis's ideas on the intermixing of the psychic and social imaginaries are among his most innovative and important, and many of his formulations will remain, I suspect, of enduring interest to social theorists. In Castoriadis's view, the interweaving of the psychic and social imaginaries depends on the entrance of the psyche into society and culture, and specifically on how processes of socialization and sublimation impose upon the unconscious. From the outset, according to Castoriadis, there is a psychical monad, closed in upon its own imaginary pleasures. This monad is subsequently broken apart during a violent triadic phase (which, psychoanalytically speaking, involves the Oedipal drama and various processes of sublimation), the result of which is the fabrication of the 'social individual'. Perhaps the most important feature here is his assertion that the psyche must renounce the imaginary all-powerfulness of primary narcissism and, in turn, recognize the self as a limited being in a world of other people. Castoriadis's account of this process is primarily Lacanian in its theoretical orientation. He argues that it is the function of the symbolic father to break the imaginary dyad of infant–mother; paternal prohibition—or the "violent break-up of the psychical monad"—at one stroke leads to a repression of radical imagination and instantiates received social meanings and the social imaginary. "The *infans,*" writes Castoriadis, "is faced with the need to cease believing that the breast is its object, that the mother is at its disposal, that it forms an exclusive couple with the mother; it must recognize that the mother (this is Lacan's contribution toward restoring the meaning of the Oedipus complex in Freud's work) desires someone else" (Castoriadis 1997: 187). The violent breakup of the monadic self-enclosure of the imagination unfolds through the violence of disappointment (the symbolic intervention of the father underlines that the child is not *everything* for its mother) and the pain of failure (the infant does not actually *create* the world). While adhering to the Freudian and Lacanian view that takes the father or phallus as the starting point for comprehending the process of individuation, Castoriadis's position also accords some weight to the revisionist position of object-relational theorists that maternal identification is also central. According to Castoriadis, it is the mother, or the person who takes the mother's place, that helps usher in the breakup of the psychic monad through referring the child to other desires and other cultural representations. Here Castoriadis refers to the crucial role of "society's maternal ambassador" in the internalization of the social imaginary. This is not only a psychoanalytic narrative, however. There is another side to the socialization of the psyche, and this has to do with the reproduction of institutions and social imaginary significations. These broader, cultural significations are crucial to the shared meanings of intersubjectivity and history. "Socialization," writes Castoriadis, "is the process whereby the psyche is forced to abandon (never fully) its pristine solipsistic meaning for the shared meanings provided by society" (in Curtis 1997: 330).

Yet if Castoriadis argues that Lacan's structuralist interpretation of the Oedipus complex goes some distance in recovering the deeper social-historical significance of the repression of desire, he is at the same time scathing of the more general features of Lacan's "return to Freud." Never one to hide his contempt for the academic posturing and solemn silliness of the jargon of poststructuralism, Castoriadis publicly broke with Lacan in the late 1960s and wrote several powerful critiques of Lacanianism as theory and as practice. In one particularly blistering attack, he dubbed Lacanianism a "monstrosity" (Castoriadis 1984: 46–115). He criticized Lacan's structuralist tendencies and lampooned the master's clinical practice of short therapy sessions. His critique of Lacan's paper "The Mirror Stage as Formative of the Function of the I" is especially interesting and important, and it serves to distinguish Castoriadis's highly original theoretical position concerning the connections between creativity, signification, and culture from that of Lacan. This critique was particularly prominent in *The Imaginary Institution of Society* and *Crossroads in the Labyrinth*. Examining Lacan's argument that ego formation in the mirror phase is premised upon narcissistic misrecognition, Castoriadis turns his psychoanalytical attention to the question of representation in the problem of accepting difference and otherness. According to Castoriadis, if the subject-to-be (mis)recognizes its reflected image in the 'mirror'—or mirroring other—this is so because it must already possess certain imaginary capacities for representation and identification. As Castoriadis (1987: 3) writes:

> The imaginary does not come from the image in the mirror or from the gaze of the other. Instead, the 'mirror' itself and its possibility, and the other as mirror, are the works of the imaginary, which is creation *ex nihilo*. Those who speak of the 'imaginary', understanding by this the 'specular', the reflection of the 'fictive', do no more than repeat, usually without realizing it, the affirmation which has for all time chained them to the underground of the famous cave: it is necessary that this world be an image *of* something.

In contrast to Lacan, Castoriadis proposes that the fabrication, and thus ownership, of our desire and representation arises from the profoundly creative dimension of the imaginary register—the precondition for the 'mirror' itself, its myriad reflections, and possible distortions.

These limitations inherent in Lacan's logic of the specular, says Castoriadis, are fundamentally related to an ambiguity or displacement in Freudian psychoanalysis concerning the creative power and depth of the unconscious imagination. For while Freud's writings pointed toward a philosophical understanding of the role of imagination and creativity in the constitution of the psyche and society, he also retained an unswerving commitment to positivistic science in which mental representation and desire were explained in mechanistic terms (Castoriadis 1995). For Castoriadis, Freud's commitment to a positivistic version of science and objectivistic terminology of an unconscious mechanics is simply shifted up a gear in Lacan's protostructuralist formulations on the intermixing of language and desire.

Actually, Castoriadis makes the Freudian point against Lacan that the unconscious is resistant to ordered syntax. For Castoriadis, the repressed unconscious is best approached as a primary realm of representational forms, drives and affects. On this basis, he rejects Lacan's dictum that "the unconscious is structured like a language." Such a viewpoint, says Castoriadis, suppresses the radical implications of Freud's discovery of the unconscious through structuralizing desire, reducing passion and creativity to a binary code of signifiers.

What are the consequences of these differences between Lacan and Castoriadis on the imaginary domain for the analysis of self and society? Having had a dramatic impact on debates about the decentering of the subject, Lacan's account of the mirror stage of identity formation has generally been understood in pessimistic terms within theory-construction and research in the social sciences and humanities (Frosh 1987: chapter 5; Elliott 1999: chapter 5). With respect to the specular traps generated by the imaginary, for example, the focus of much Lacanian orientated social theory has been on the ubiquity of ideological illusion. Critical tones vary somewhat in this respect, from Althusser's interpellated subject or cultural dope through to Zizek's preideological subject of lack; in most crucial

respects, though, these interventions encourage a conception of passive subjectivity (Althusser 1984; Zizek 1989). By contrast, the virtue of Castoriadis's theory
of radical imagination is that it offers a more differentiated view of the subject's
imaginary capacities for self-representation and reflection, particularly as these
capacities extend to issues of social domination on the one hand and resistance
and autonomy on the other. The importance of Castoriadis's approach lies in the
attention it pays to the dual nature of radical imagination: omnipotence and illusion, on the one side, and the decentering of omnipotence as necessary to participation within the social imaginary, on the other. Such elements do not separate
out in forced divisions. They are elaborated in personal and social life in complex
and often contradictory ways, with dangers of regression always present.

Having noted Castoriadis's major differences from Lacan, what I want to do
in the remainder of this section is to think about the implications of Castoriadis's
account of radical imagination and unconscious representation in the light of
debates about difference and otherness. There are important conceptual difficulties, in my view, with Castoriadis's formulation of the breakup of the monadic
self-enclosure of the imagination, difficulties that relate to the mediations
between the psyche and society. Now Castoriadis, following Freud, rightly pin-
points primary narcissism and hallucinatory wish fulfillment as the defining features of the unconscious imagination. What is problematic, however, is his
particular formulation of a "psychic monad" disconnected from its time–space
environment of significant other persons. Various questions can be raised in this
connection. How does the psychic monad, exactly, open itself onto other worlds?
How does the psychic imaginary, self-enclosed upon unconscious representational pleasure, communicate with anything outside itself?

These questions are nowhere satisfactorily answered by Castoriadis. Apart
from one or two passing comments about the premature birth of the human infant
and hence the integral role of others in the child's development, Castoriadis
offers little in the way of a systematic discussion of the *infant's psychic processes*
that lead into encounters with otherness, relationships, learning, and socialization. To the put the matter slightly differently, his account of the socialization of
the psyche operates on a mostly metatheoretical level. He does, from time to
time, refer to other psychoanalytical doctrines, including Kleinian and Lacanian
theory, but only sparingly and in quite abstract terms. This failure to engage in
any detail with the empirical or clinical findings of contemporary psychoanalysis
might again be traced back to Castoriadis's preoccupation with developing a philosophical elucidation of human imagination. However, since a good deal of Castoriadis's writing consists of speculation about the unconscious imagination and
its constitution, an engagement with the more substantive claims of contemporary psychoanalysis and critical psychology is surely required. How do infants,
for example, come to relate inner and outer worlds in play? How much is cultural
experience interwoven with the fantasy projections of our inner lives? One path
of research to follow here is the British psychoanalyst, D. W. Winnicott, who

insists that transitional space is essential to the constitutional bridging of inner and outer in both play and culture (Winnicott 1971). Again, however, it is difficult to know how to trace out notions like transitional or liminal space from Castoriadis's starting point of monadic isolation.

The analytical issues connected with the interrelations of subjectivity and intersubjectivity, as these are raised in the Castoriadis–Habermas exchange, concern the duality of identity/otherness in the mediation between psyche and society. If we continue to view these issues through the standpoints developed by Castoriadis or Habermas, it would appear that we can only develop a theoretically sophisticated account of the mediation of the psyche and society by either beginning with the monadic isolation of the psyche and tracing how unconscious representations become linked to an extrapsychic reality or, alternatively, by beginning with modes of communication and mapping various displacements and deformations of language at the level of the unconscious. The second approach is that which is adopted by Habermas (and also Lacan), and it is a position that strikes me as fundamentally mistaken—since the conscious/unconscious relation cannot adequately be conceived as a linguistic one. I thus prefer to stay closer to the first approach, the path developed by Freud and extended by Castoriadis. However, in what follows I shall seek to link this first formulation with aspects of the second. Contemporary research concerning the character of human subjectivity, and especially the newborn infant, suggests that the psyche's capacity to produce unconscious representations from the earliest days of life is not separated off from the time–space environments of significant other persons in the manner that classical Freudian theory supposes and for which Castoriadis provides a particularly robust philosophical justification.

The issues raised here go far beyond what could be covered in the space of this chapter, and hence I am only able to touch on some of the more compelling changes in recent theorizing about the newborn infant and its emerging psychic structure. In both object-relational and structural-psychoanalytical approaches, there has been a broad shift away from the triadic, Oedipal phase to the pre-Oedipal phase of psychic development as a means of engaging with issues of representation, affect and desire. This research focuses on the earliest and most primitive phases of psychic functioning of the infant and emphasizes the role of the mother in a very different manner from Freud and Castoriadis. The relation between the subject-to-be (infant) and other (mother) is revalued as essentially creative in form, and in which the constitution of psychic structure depends on various affective exchanges and communicative dialogues. Critical and feminist psychoanalysis, in particular, stresses that the mother and maternal body play a more constitutive role in subjectivity and emotional life (see, e.g., Irigaray 1993). From this feminist perspective, it is possible to theorize a different position on the psychic underpinnings of representation and the web of identifications that connect the subject-to-be to the sociosymbolic network (see Benjamin 1998). The use of the symbolic father or phallus to conceptualize the emergence of individuation in the Freudian and Lacanian standpoints is understood as resting on a masculinist inability, at once conceptual and political, to represent the mother as both a containing and sexual subject within the child's psychic world. As Irigaray has notably argued, it is the failure to represent the umbilicus—in both psychoanalytic theory and the general culture—as a symbol of connection with, and separation from, the mother that leads to the continuing dominance of the phallus in contemporary theory.

This revaluing in contemporary psychoanalysis of the intersubjective sphere as concerns the development of mind also incorporates a recognition that the creation and play of subjectivities structure a potential space within which a web of psychic and sociosymbolic identifications can unfold. This intersubjective recasting of the relation of desire to the subject-to-be differentiates the work of psychoanalytic feminists like Jessica Benjamin from that of Habermas's highly cognitive and linguistic version of intersubjectivity. Technically speaking, it is also a perspective that is radically different from the work of neo-Lacanians, such as Jean Laplanche, who have developed intersubjective accounts of Freudian theory by stressing that sexuality and repressed desire are inscribed into the child's psychic world from the outside, the sociosymbolic network (see Laplanche 1987). This viewpoint, that the child imbibes what parents unknowingly express of their own fantasies and fears concerning sexuality, is limited in its understanding of the psychodynamics of intersubjectivity since it makes the subject-to-be a passive recipient of the Other. In this connection, Benjamin's stress on mutuality and recognition in the child–mother dyad is to be preferred, in my opinion, to the understanding offered by neo-Lacanians.

What relational analysts such as Benjamin fail to explicitly theorize, however, are the sources of psychic creativity and of representation that allow the subject-to-be to gather meaning and make something of the intersubjective field for itself. This is where Castoriadis's formulations on radical imagination are perhaps most pertinent to recent debates about intersubjectivity. In these debates there is a strong emphasis on the interweaving of internal mental space and the space of otherness in the registration of preself and preobject relations, an interweaving that is viewed as preparatory for the constitution of subjectivity as well as the field of intersubjectivity. In the work of Kristeva, this emerges as part of an attempt to rework the psychoanalytic understanding of the child–mother dyad, giving of course special attention to prelinguistic forms of interaction, such as tones, rhythms and silences, which she describes as semiotic (Kristeva 1984). In the work of Anzieu, it is a discussion of the archaeology of a 'skin ego', of a "preverbal writing made up of traces upon the skin" (Anzieu 1989: 57). In the work of Tustin, it is a series of claims about the nature of sensory impressions of autistic shapes in affective framings of warmth, coldness and textures (Tustin 1980; 1984: 279–90). In the work of Ogden, it is an excavation of the primitive edge of experience, with special attention to the binding of surfaces including both the human body and nonhuman substances (Ogden 1989). There is also research in psychology which suggests that interaction between the psyche and its environment starts prior to birth and that from the moment of birth the infant is engaged in creative and active communications with the world (among other authors, see Stern 1985; Chamberlain 1987).

What these approaches suggest is that interiority and exteriority, as framings for the earliest and most primitive forms of subjectivity and intersubjectivity, interweave in the process of projective identification with the pre-Oedipal maternal body. The psyche, as Castoriadis rightly emphasizes, should still be granted a determining and creative role in accounting for the formation of representations, drives, and affects on which layers of subjectivity and intersubjectivity are based. However, these approaches also highlight major difficulties with Castoriadis's position, namely the thesis of the monadic self-enclosure of the imagination. In post-Lacanian and post-Kleinian developments, imagination is also accorded a constitutive and constituting role. However, *pace* Castoriadis, the imagination is seen as constituting and constituted through both psychic and material space, such that elaborations of preself and preobject relations are bound up with others and with the material environment.

Analysis of Culture

The crisis of Western societies, the dominance of technoscience, postmodernism as generalized conformism, the crumbling apart of social imaginary significations: these are some of the central motifs of Castoriadis's engagement with the contemporary crisis of culture and its conditions. One of his main lines of argument is that the capacity of contemporary society to posit itself as *self-representation* is becoming increasingly empty, self-contradictory and flattened out. As he remarks in an essay of 1982, "The Crisis of Western Societies," "[T]here is a crisis of social imaginary significations, that these significations no longer provide individuals with the norms, values, bearings, and motivations that would permit them both to make society function and to maintain themselves, somehow or other, in a livable state of 'equilibrium' (the 'everyday unhappiness' Freud contrasted with neurotic misery)" (in Curtis 1997: 262). Social life, says Castoriadis, has become increasingly superficial and incoherent, communal relationships increasingly sterile and brittle. Underlying this is the thesis of the privatization and depoliticization of modern culture. Privatization, according to Castoriadis, involves a kind of closure of individuals, a closure that leads subjects to view themselves as creative agents of social life. He explains this in terms of a shift from the battle cry of liberalism, "The State is evil," to the cynical and ego-centered battle cry of postmodernist culture, "Society is evil." People now live their lives as an "odious chore," without collective prospects or projects, conforming only to the fashionable precepts of individualism and retail therapy.

Castoriadis's conception of our current cultural crisis shares much in common with the arguments of other social theorists—such as Marcuse's critique of "one-

dimensional society" and Lasch's appraisal of the "culture of narcissism"—who
see an increasing unification and homogeneity of the social field. Yet despite
some occasional qualifications, Castoriadis's treatment of the new cultural conformity is developed in only the broadest and most general terms; as a result, this
aspect of his work often seems inadequate. Very often he concentrates on the
theme of depoliticization. Apart, however, from stressing the breakdown of traditional party loyalties and the fragmentation of political interests, he has relatively
little to say about newly emerging forms of civic engagement beyond the formal
political sphere (including those involving citizen initiative groups, gender relations, and the politicization of interpersonal relationships). Part of the difficulty
here, I think, stems from Castoriadis's tendency to equate politics with the state
and the formal political system. (For a perceptive discussion of this problem in
contemporary social and political theory, see Beck 1997.)

Elsewhere in his writings, Castoriadis (1999b) locates the new social conformity more within the cultural sphere and asserts that the psychic underpinnings of
privatization and apathy are reproduced by the hundreds of millions of TV view-
ers all over the world absorbing daily inanities. But this, too, is surely unconvincing and in fact contradicts much recent research in cultural studies concerning
new forms of media interaction and the changing character of the public sphere.
(For further discussion on this point, see Thompson 1995: chapters 3 and 7; Stevenson 1995.)

These criticisms can be pressed further. Not only is much of Castoriadis's critique of the crisis of modern societies inadequate, but his reflections on cultural
conformity and homogeneity seem to contradict the social-theoretical emphasis
that he places on human creation elsewhere in his writings. Castoriadis maintains
that the irrationalities of capitalist rationalization have atrophied imagination and
spontaneity, yet there is something rather weak and disturbing about his arguments on this point. "As concerns substantive culture, the era of great modern
creativity," Castoriadis generalizes, "reached its end around 1930" (Curtis 1997:
264). In the same manner that Adorno adopted a dismissive and elitist view of
popular culture (and in the process violated the theoretical possibilities opened
by his philosophy of 'negative dialectics'), Castoriadis fails to confront the development of new cultural directions, such as certain kinds of music and cinema and
their expression of alternative, hybrid, and dissident forms of subjectivity and
identity. Instead, issues concerning cultural production in the wake of, say, new
communication technologies are simply bypassed in favor of confused and general claims about the disintegration of cultural creativity.

One result of such an orientation is that multifarious cultural spaces and aesthetic styles—from the literary innovations of Beckett to the musical departures
of Bowie—are simply consigned to oblivion. Much the same applies to some of
his arguments about identity. "The typical contemporary man," writes Castoriadis from an Olympian height, "acts as if he were submitting to the society . . .
he is ever ready to blame all evils on" (Curtis 1997: 263). Seemingly unaware of

the rise of the politics of difference, and specifically differences relating to gender and sexuality, Castoriadis attributes a general sameness to human subjectivity and in the process offers a universal masculinist formulation ("typical contemporary man"). Although there are perhaps good reasons for taking at least some of what he says about the nature of modern rationality's relationship to identity conformity very seriously, the more general point is that Castoriadis's theory of the social imaginary suggests that the relations between subjectivity and social regulation are far more heterogeneous than he has formulated them in the foregoing speculations. He tends, in short, to treat the analysis of culture and cultural production as derivative from degraded social conditions (and hence without aesthetic value), even though his theoretical studies suggest that these issues are much more complicated.

Where Castoriadis displays a more interesting and penetrating political vision is in his comprehensive survey of the dominance of technoscience and its unlimited expansion in contemporary cultural life. Reading Castoriadis's analysis of some of the principal forms and transformations of technoscientific rationality helps to illuminate some of the connections which exist between fantasy, symbolic systems, and political domination, and his general approach contains many suggestive insights and observations. Castoriadis regards the apparently progressive advances of technoscience as involving the rationalization of politics; the roots of this cultural urge for the "technological fix" are to be found in the unfurling of the irrational and the regressive, in the fantasy of being all-powerful, and in the institutionalization of omnipotent thinking. This is especially clear as concerns violence in modern societies, most notably the technoindustrialization of war. According to Castoriadis, the impersonal mastery of expert-organizational knowledge is a psychically closed system of fantasmatic illusion. For this reason, technoscientific logic leads to the illogical, constituting a pseudorational realm in which means and ends become unconnected. In "Dead End?" Castoriadis (1991a: 249) writes:

> Who among the proponents of technoscience today really knows where they want to go—not from the standpoint of "pure knowledge" but with regard both to the kind of society they would wish to live in and to the paths that will take them there? . . . This path—quite paradoxically, considering the amount of money and effort being expended—is less and less that of the *desirable* in any sense, and more and more that of the simply *doable*. We do not try to do what 'would be necessary' or what we judge 'desirable'. More and more, we do what we can, we work on what is deemed doable in the approximate short term. . . . What is technically feasible will be done regardless. Likewise, embryo transplants, in vitro fertilization, fetal surgery, and so on, have been put into practice as soon as the respective techniques were mastered. At present, many years later, questions about these techniques are not even really discussed.

Castoriadis sees the contradictions and failures of technoscience everywhere, from scientific research concerning DNA and the genetic code to the destruction of tropical forests and disturbances in the Earth's biosphere. The imaginary, ideological dimension of technoscience lies predominantly in its quasi-omni-scient, quasi-omnipotent assurance of social and political progress; technoscience thereby effaces the possibility of reasoned, reflective debate in political society and thus abandons the public domain to financial, managerial, and bureaucratic oligarchies.

In outlining an overall conception of rationality as dominated by techno-science, Castoriadis connects social theory directly with issues of pressing politi-cal concern to everyone. From developments in genetic engineering to the proliferation of nuclear weapons, Castoriadis tackles issues that many social the-orists choose to overlook. Repeating themes from the writings of Weber and Ellul, he sees technical forms of knowledge as producing high degrees of ratio-nalization in modern societies, which in turn produces loss of meaning and the waning of formal participation *qua* political society. However, Castoriadis char-acteristically asserts that it is the imaginary domain of technical knowledge that has been unsatisfactorily grasped to date by social theorists. Technoscience, says Castoriadis, is *fantasmatic*. The development of multinational capitalism, he argues, unleashes omnipotent fantasies and illusions, concealing its own social practice and political bids for power by taking flight in "pseudo-rational mas-tery." In short, Castoriadis uncovers phenomena in late capitalism that, far from leading toward mastery and control of the social world, threaten global peace and security. The domain of technoscience is, for Castoriadis, a defensive sham, premised on a regressive and unexamined social-historical tendency of omnipo-tent domination, the driving forces of which he conceptualizes along axes of psy-chic repetition, the narcissistic disavowal of reality, and collective hallucinations and phantoms.

Interpretation of Autonomy

Of the issues raised earlier, there remains that of individual autonomy and the autonomous society. The notion of autonomy is, of course, a radically contested one, a notion that today carries a plethora of meanings for different people. It is this very diversity in understandings of freedom that Castoriadis thinks produc-tive for grasping the marks of the autonomous condition. In so far as the modern obsession with self and self-realization brings to the fore the possibility of dis-cerning some alternatives to the given social order, Castoriadis turns again to psy-choanalysis as a means of furnishing an account of contemporary impulses for personal and political autonomy. According to Castoriadis, the psychoanalytic cure is a little like the realization of political autonomy. Just as psychoanalysis aims at helping the individual to become capable of self-reflective deliberation, so, too, the emancipatory project of democracy seeks to foster collective decision making and reasoned judgments.

Such a parallel between psychoanalysis and politics is, it might be said, not exactly new. Several decades ago, Habermas, in his pathbreaking *Knowledge and Human Interests,* argued that the psychoanalytic model clarifies how political knowledge might be related to social change. For Habermas, Freud's therapeutic maxim—"where id was, there ego shall be"—means the realization of self-control, the renunciation of passion (Habermas 1971). Castoriadis, however, emphatically rejects such a standpoint. As he writes, "[T]here can be no human being whose Unconscious is conquered by the Conscious, whose drives are fully permeated and controlled by rational considerations, who has stopped fantasizing and dreaming." Human imagination, creation, and autonomy are, for Castoriadis, inextricably intertwined. Turning Freud's maxim against itself, he argues that passion is bound up with everything we do. Quite unlike Habermas, Castoriadis (1999a) thinks that more passion, not less, is essential to reflective, deliberative politics. According to Castoriadis, it is not just that society needs coherent meanings and values to function effectively. For the meanings by which people live are imaginary constructions as well as rational organizations, and behind the social world lies the emotional domain. Unless this is recognized, he says, any attempt to develop a critical theory of society is likely to be defective.

These and other characteristics of our personal and social practice bring us to the core of human autonomy: *ontological opening.* "Autonomy," writes Castoriadis, "is not closure but, rather opening: ontological opening, the possibility of going beyond the informational, cognitive, and organizational closure characteristic of self-constituting, but *heteronomous* beings" (Curtis 1997: 310, 316). The principle that the possibility of challenging established significations and institutions is central to the attainment of autonomy is reflective of a broader movement in history, a movement away from tradition and the sacred and toward the contingency of the social. This amounts to saying that a conception of society has emerged historically which recognizes that there can be no supracollective guarantee of meaning; the end of foundationalism involves an acceptance of the fact that meaning and its actualization always presuppose a social context. As Castoriadis explains: "if autonomous society is that society which self-institutes itself [*s'auto-institue*] explicitly and lucidly, the one that knows that it itself posits its institutions and significations, this means that it knows as well that they have no source other than its own instituting and signification-giving activity, no extrasocial 'guarantee.'"

Many aspects of these arguments are, in my view, convincing. For one thing, Castoriadis shows that, while social theory has tended to lapse into either subjectivism or objectivism on the exploration of the autonomous condition, the actual projects of personal and collective autonomy actually presuppose one another. If the struggle for autonomy in modern societies is one that involves a radical putting into question of the social world itself, this is so because of the existence of individuals with rationally and emotionally articulated capacities for self-interrogation and self-reflection. A related theme of Castoriadis's is that the process of autonomy is necessarily open-ended. This open-ended process of engagement

with the autonomy of the self and the Other is situated in the context of ambivalence, uncertainty, and the realm of conflicting scenarios. "We have to create the
good," writes Castoriadis, "under imperfectly known and uncertain conditions.
The project of autonomy is end and guide, it does not resolve for us effectively
actual situations" (Curtis 1997: 400).

There is an important difference between Castoriadis's reflections on the open-
ended nature of the autonomous condition and those versions of critical theory
in which utopianism is disconnected from institutionally immanent possibilities
of the given social order. The latter versions of critical theory have been
described by critic Terry Eagleton as a form of "bad utopianism," in which alternative value positions are "parachuted in from some ontological outer space."
By contrast, Eagleton terms "good utopianism" that which "seeks somehow to
anchor what is desirable in what is actual" (Eagleton 1991: 131). Castoriadis
clearly holds to the Marxian doctrine that we must attempt to discover paths for
desired social change in the structural contradictions of capitalist modernity; by
emancipation, Castoriadis refers to that shift from power-driven heteronomy to
critical self-reflection. Most important, however, Castoriadis's framework for the
project of autonomy underwrites the contingency of the social. The process of
autonomy for Castoriadis requires individuals and groups to live without moral
or ethical guarantees, with the awareness that the search for personal and political
autonomy is shot through with ambivalence and uncertainty, while also acknowledging that the search for autonomy may quickly be overshadowed by the
impulse to domination and oppression.

There are, however, some important theoretical and substantive difficulties
with Castoriadis's position. In the first place, Castoriadis's elucidation of Freud
and psychoanalysis does not adequately resolve how the psychological production of autonomy relates to the movement and realization of collective autonomy.
That is, he does not demonstrate the various challenges, paradoxes, and reintegra-
tions that are involved in newly constituted relations between self-reflection and
self-transformation, on the one hand, and the transfiguration of social domination
or power, on the other. Castoriadis justifies his concentration on the transformation of psychic identities and affective bonds on the grounds that the political
challenge is to find new ways of realizing and expanding personal empowerment,
in so far as this leads into transformed relations between individuals at various
levels of social and political life. Critics, however, have not been slow to point
out the omission from Castoriadis's writings concerning specific divisions
between races, genders, and classes and of how these might be transformed
through a politics of radical imagination (Thompson 1984: 36–38). Certainly, it
is difficult to see how domination in the sense of psychic repetition or closure
has much similarity to the problems of social organization and long-term processes of political change. To carry this discussion further, it remains to be shown
what kinds of connection, dialogue, translation, and transformation are necessary
to bring about conditions for psychic autonomy (involving multiple positionings

and assimilations of self and other) and novel questionings and interrogations of the domination sustained in the power relations between groups and collectivities.

However, even if we accept that autonomy involves the challenging of individual and social significations, it remains to be shown exactly what kind of demystifying interrogations are being carried out in contemporary societies, and how such knowledges might be concretely related to processes of social transformation. Castoriadis contrasts archaic societies, which he describes as cognitively, informationally, and organizationally closed, with modern societies, which in his view promote challenges to established institutions and significations. The culture of critical discourse that processes of modernization and detraditionalization promote is analyzed with great skill by Castoriadis, yet his account of the ideological differentiation of contemporary social formations is vague. How, exactly, might the resurgence of ideological movements such as Christian Evangelicalism in the United States, Islamic fundamentalism in the Middle East, or revolutionary nationalism in the Third World be explained in terms of the modes of signification that Castoriadis argues are increasingly dominant in the contemporary era?

The notion of reflexivity, particularly as formulated by Anthony Giddens (1990, 1991), might be useful in this context. But the way to develop such an approach is unlikely to follow from Castoriadis's work alone since, as I have argued, his emphasis on the "project of autonomy" links human imagination to the social field only at the cost of displacing the ideological and the political. I think that this displacement is especially problematic in Castoriadis's writings because of the hiatus between his theoretical insistence on creativity, imagination, and the possibility of challenging established significations and institutions, on the one hand, and his substantive analysis of the loss of meanings and values in contemporary culture, on the other. This hiatus, I have suggested, creates immense difficulties for Castoriadis's pessimistic reading of our current cultural condition, but it also creates problems as concerns his interpretation of autonomy.

CONCLUSION

In this chapter I have examined Castoriadis's approach to issues concerning human subjectivity, contemporary culture, and autonomy. Throughout I have tried to analyze some of the key strengths and weaknesses of his views. Castoriadis is right, I have suggested, to be critical of the deterministic elements of intersubjective and structural approaches to mediations between the psyche and society. His attempt to develop a systematic perspective on the fundamental and irreducible creativity in the radical imagination of the individual and in the institution of the social-historical sphere will become, I think, an emboldening reference point for the future development of social theory.

On a more specific level, Castoriadis's account of the breakup of the psychic monad is, as I have argued, beset with difficulties. These difficulties stem, in large part, from his disconnection of the unconscious imagination from the time–space environments of significant other persons in the life of the infant. Yet his account of the monadic self-enclosure of the imagination, while flawed in the ways I have suggested, also contains some powerfully analytical points of departure. My argument, in this connection, has been that Castoriadis's thesis of radical imagination needs to be grounded in a broader theory of affective and interpersonal life, and reconnected to post-Kleinian and post-Lacanian psychoanalysis.

Turning my attention to the analysis of culture, I argued that Castoriadis's emphasis on the waning of political imagination has led him to overemphasize homogeneity and to underplay the impact of social and cultural conflict. However, his critical analyses of technoscience will, I believe, stand the test of time and will nourish the continuing debate about the links between individual subjectivity, cultural fantasy and political domination.

Finally, I suggested that his views on autonomy are of especial interest to social theory. For Castoriadis's theorizing here captures with great richness and originality the role of ambivalence and uncertainty in the search for human autonomy. While Castoriadis's views on autonomy might be contested in many respects, I believe that it is only through further inquiry into the radical imagination of the individual and the social imaginary of society that illumination of alternative political futures will begin to unravel.

5

Habermas, Kristeva, and Global Transformations in the Public Sphere

In his provocative essay "Why Europe Needs a Constitution," Jürgen Habermas develops an account of the core challenges—economic, political, cultural, moral—facing the European Union (EU) as a consequence of globalization and transnational financial markets. According to Habermas, analysis and critique of European networks of interaction have, for the most part, tended to center on economic matters—for instance, debates on monetary union and global consumer capitalism. Habermas, by contrast, elaborates a less economistic view of the EU as a transnational institution. "The economic advantages of European unification are valid as arguments for further construction of the EU," writes Habermas (2001c: 9), "only if they can appeal to a cultural power of attraction extending far beyond material gains alone." For Habermas, it is clear that what bridges economy and culture, materialism and the political, is social solidarity, which in his conception operates as "deliberative discourse" within democratic procedures promoting rationally grounded agreements. Only in the context of European deliberative democracy, where a plurality of national publics congeals to transform classical international law into some kind of cosmopolitan order, will cultural resources for the advancement of social identity flourish. "Economic justifications," notes Habermas (2001c: 8), "must at the very least be combined with ideas of a different kind—let us say, an interest in an affective attachment to a particular ethos: in other words, the attraction of a specific way of life."

Appropriately enough for an author concerned with the cultivation of a postnationalist political system and the fostering of unconstrained public debate, Habermas directs our attention toward globalization and the changed conditions of culture. He argues forcefully against fashionable pronouncements of the death of history; against the backdrop of Sarajevo, Chechnya, and the globalization of terrorism, such prophecies have proved spectacularly inept. He further observes that cultural identities are increasingly constituted against the backdrop of painful memories—of nationalist ideology, ethical lapse, the horrors of recent European history. For Habermas, the advancement of "postconventional," "postparticularist" forms of identity, society, and culture is directly tied to a learning process mobilizing the self-understanding of citizens. As he develops this (2001c: 21):

> What forms the common core of a European identity is the character of the painful learning process it has gone through, as much as its results. It is the lasting memory of nationalist excess and moral abyss that lends to our present commitments the quality of a peculiar achievement. This historical background should ease the transition to a postnational democracy based on the mutual recognition of the differences between strong and proud national cultures. Neither 'assimilation' nor 'coexistence'—in the sense of a pale modus vivendi—are appropriate terms for our history of learning how to construct new and ever more sophisticated forms of a 'solidarity among strangers'. Today, moreover, the European nation-states are being brought together by the challenges which they all face equally. All are in the process of becoming countries of immigration and multicultural societies. All are exposed to an economic and cultural globalization that awakes memories of a shared history of conflict and reconciliation—and of a comparatively low threshold of tolerance toward exclusion.

Today's proliferation of socially structured differences—economic, ethnic, racial, sexual, cultural, political, and religious—is stabilized through societal members seeking "solidarity among strangers."

There is nothing necessarily sentimental or nostalgic about this doctrine. If Habermas speaks of "the common core of a European identity," it is because, as for the former German chancellor Helmut Kohl, there are encouraging signs concerning more active and participatory forms of democratic government within the emerging political framework beyond the nation-state. Habermas is particularly insistent that a range of issues—concerning, for instance, the activities of transnational corporations, the proliferation of nuclear weapons, and problems of pollution and environmental degradation—cut across territorial boundaries and cannot be satisfactorily dealt with by national governments. As he puts this (2001c: 18):

> A European-wide public sphere must not be imagined as the projection of a familiar design from the national onto the European level. It will rather emerge from the mutual opening of existing national universes to one another, yielding to an interpenetration of mutually translated national communications. There is no need for a stratified public communication, each layer of which would correspond, one by one, to a different "floor" of the multilevel political system. The agenda of European institutions will be included in each of a plurality of national publics, if these are interrelated in the right way.

But what this "plurality of national publics" founds itself *on* would seem a good deal more ambiguous. This is perhaps why Habermas stresses that national publics must be "inter-related in the right way"—if cosmopolitanism is to adequately discharge the political burdens that his theory of deliberative democracy sets. After all, to root the postnational global society in the sharing of political culture, moral norms and discursive will formation is, in one sense, to recognize the alarmingly fragile and precarious nature of political power and popular consent.

Habermas's conception of a postnational constellation has generated a great deal of disagreement and dispute in political theory, especially among pluralists and communitarians (see, e.g., Cook 2001). Yet his provocative political program has not received the consideration it deserves in the literature of recent critical social theory, especially from writers influenced by the currents of poststructuralism and postmodernism. From a poststructuralist or postmodernist angle, Habermas's work looks somewhat out of date. Indeed, to some postmodern theorists, his project appears as a last-ditch attempt to maintain the scaffolding of Enlightenment reason. In the eyes of such critics, Habermas's universal pragmatics—the belief in the "force of the better argument," the ideal speech situation, and so forth—is itself shaped by a modernist desire for conceptual closure, certainty, and control.

That this has been the predominant reaction among postmodernists is unfortunate, as there are interesting questions to pursue here. How, for example, might Habermas's account of "the common core of European identity" look from a non-European vantage point? In what ways might the new European values of which Habermas speaks end up, in practice, as non-self-identical? Is there division between publicness as identity and publicness as hybridity? And what, exactly, does the regeneration of European subjectivity exclude—what cultural differences get displaced, what psychic damage sustained in the framing of a common culture? What happens to "strangeness" in the founding of "solidarity among strangers"?

In this chapter, I discuss some of the themes of Habermas's most recent and politically forceful work. In the first section I shall describe the main features of Habermas's social-theoretical contribution with regard to the contemporary political scene, paying especially close attention to the arguments he develops in *The Postnational Constellation*. Then I shall examine arguments advanced by the French feminist and psychoanalyst Julia Kristeva on the psychic and political consequences of globalization. Both social theorists, in quite different ways, have wrestled with the question of globalization in transforming national and cultural identities; in the final sections, I will emphasize those strands of Kristeva's theoretical orientation that, I believe, enhance and deepen the terms of the debate raging over global culture and European identity. Specifically I am concerned with the question of the cultural regeneration of the European subject but also with the dangers that cosmopolitan, globalized culture presents to other, nondiscursive forms of political identification.

HABERMAS, CRITICAL THEORY, AND POLITICS

Habermas, by any reckoning, is a giant of the academic world: a leading figure in European critical theory and philosophy, and one of the finest writers on culture and society of the twentieth century. His analytical rigor and his interest in language and communication, as a means to understanding the power of rationality in everyday life, have set him in a class apart. Priding himself on his intellectual roots in Frankfurt School philosophy, Habermas remains in many respects a sociologist in the grand tradition, an architect of macrotheory. Against the postmodernist tide, he is perhaps the most influential contemporary advocate for a full-blooded universalism in political and moral affairs. Language, rationality, and communication are key themes of his writing, and he insists that the heritage of Enlightenment reason is no mere projection of local tradition, preference or power.

In 1994, after nearly half a century working in German academia, Habermas retired from his post as professor of philosophy and sociology at the University of Frankfurt. Notwithstanding retirement, his academic output has perhaps been more astonishing than ever, as an overview of recent English translations would suggest: *The Past as Future* (1994), *A Berlin Republic* (1997a), *Between Facts and Norms* (1997b), *On the Pragmatics of Social Interaction* (2001b), *The Postnational Constellation* (2001c), *The Liberating Power of Symbols* (2001a), *The Future of Human Nature* (2002), and *Truth and Justification* (2003). Wrapping sociology, politics and philosophy ineluctably together, these works represent an extraordinary confrontation with the entire discourse of the social sciences and humanities. In fact, it is hard to think of a writer who equals Habermas in terms of breadth, originality and variety. He is the author of half a dozen masterpieces—*The Structural Transformation of the Public Sphere* (1962), *Theory and Practice* (1963), *Knowledge and Human Interests* (1968), *Legitimation Crisis* (1973), *The Philosophical Discourse of Modernity* (1987b), and *Between Facts and Norms* (1997b).

His magnum opus, *The Theory of Communicative Action* (1991a, 1991b), is a sprawling work that traces the concept of rationality from the widest possible sources. Briefly, Habermas's faith is that language is always oriented by and toward mutual agreement and consensus. This can be shown, he argues, in our most basic human capacities for speaking, hearing, reasoning, and arguing. In every act of speech, however shaped by power interests, validity claims are raised and reciprocally recognized: that what we say makes sense and is true, that we are sincere in saying it, and that there is a performative appropriateness to the saying of it. In a philosophical move anticipated by the American pragmatist

C. S. Peirce, Habermas projects from this model of language a theory of truth, defined as that which we ultimately come to rationally agree about through communicative dialogue. It is from our capacity for communicative reason that Habermas claims to discern a normative image of the political values of freedom, equality, mutuality, and ethical responsibility.

The book had an enormous impact, and I suspect the reason for this partly derived from the challenge that Habermas laid down to deconstruction and postmodern theory. While *The Theory of Communicative Action* might be so conceptually dense that few can claim to have fully grasped it, the work nonetheless expressed a voice of sober dissent and of unmistakable philosophical authority. For those questioning the radical chic of postmodernism, Habermas (more than anyone else) provided the terms of reference.

The relationship between communicative action, intersubjectivity, and rationality was subsequently further explored by Habermas in *Postmetaphysical Thinking*. Developing arguments outlined in *The Theory of Communicative Action,* Habermas in this work continued his preoccupation with tracing the conditions of rational decision making in the life-world and of specifying the intersubjective dimensions of subjectivity, meaning, and truth. *Postmetaphysical Thinking* demonstrated an attempt to come to grips with an extraordinary variety of standpoints and theorists, ranging from Kant, Humboldt, and Kierkegaard to Rawls, Derrida, and Beck. Throughout, Habermas sought to appraise social analysis in the light of our inherited conceptions of reason and the rational subject. But he did so in a manner that confronted head-on issues that he has often been accused of neglecting, especially the individual, otherness and difference.

Perhaps the central article in this connection is "Individuation through Socialisation: On George Herbert Mead's Theory of Subjectivity." The theory of the human subject, Habermas argues, has always had as its main focus reflection: reflection on the world of objects of which a subject is conscious. This is true from mirror models of self-consciousness to be found in German idealism through to the self-reflexively steered personality systems theorized by Beck in contemporary sociology.

By contrast, the theory of intersubjective communication, as elaborated from Humboldt to Mead, captures the cognitive, expressive relations established *between* human subjects. Intersubjectivity, Habermas says, is what makes an instituted relation-to-self possible. Individuals draw from, and project conceptions of self into, intersubjective contexts and thus establish a relation to the norm of a universal community of speakers. But how should we understand the relations between the supposition of a universal community and the concrete individual? Habermas argues that a universalization of norms *presumes* individual differences in concrete forms of life. He writes:

[T]he transitory unity that is generated in the porous and refracted intersubjectivity of a linguistically mediated consensus not only the deports but furthers and accelerates the pluralization of forms of life and the individualization of life styles. More discourses means more contradictions and difference. The more abstract the agreements become, the more diverse the disagreements with which we can *non-violently* live.

Greater universalization thus underwrites the individual, otherness, and difference.

In addition to his academic influence, Habermas is also of course a celebrated public intellectual. I am perhaps not alone in thinking that Habermas's political essays are considerably easier to read than plowing through his sociological and philosophical reflections, and this is nowhere more evident that in *The Postnational Constellation.* For one thing, he drops the cumbersome vocabulary of "universal pragmatics," "systems reproduction," and "ideal speech situation." With a real sense of public engagement, the reader gains a firm appreciation of how Habermas's social theory applies to current political realities. If there is a central theme to *The Postnational Constellation,* it concerns global transformations. The study of globalization has a deservedly special status in the social sciences, and Habermas examines how the current phase of globalization is transforming nationhood, the role of the state, and the bases of democratic legitimacy.

Razor sharp in political critique, *The Postnational Constellation* takes few hostages. Is the nation-state under threat from the global economy? Of course it is. Should renewed forms of nationalism be used to advance antiglobalization? Under no circumstances. (Habermas has been a vocal critic of attempts to tighten the Federal Republic's liberal immigration and asylum laws.) Can globalization promote transnational political institutions? Perhaps, but there is no guarantee about how democratic legitimacy will be handled in a postnational world.

Against the backdrop of these political challenges and opportunities that we face collectively in the new millennium, Habermas assesses the prospects for, and perils of, democratic political structures and the extension of forms and processes of collective will formation across territorial borders. There are a number of distinctive elements to the analysis he sets out in *The Postnational Constellation,* and it is worth briefly dwelling on these for a moment. First, Habermas argues that the disempowering consequences of globalization for national governments are increasingly evident. He writes (2001a: 80):

> The fiscal basis for social policies has steadily dwindled, while the state has increasingly lost its capacity to steer the economy via macroeconomic policy. Moreover, the integrational force of nationality as a way of life is diminishing, along with the relatively homogeneous basis of civil solidarity. As nation-states increasingly lose their capacity for action and the stability of their collective identities, they will find it more and more difficult to meet the need for self-legitimation.

Second, he contends that the moral and political challenges facing the European Union cannot be met by adapting a policy of laissez-faire, much less by embracing neoliberal or postmodern theories of globalization processes. "Under the changed conditions of the postnational constellation," he writes (Habermas 2001a: 81):

> the nation-state is not going to regain its old strength by retreating into its shell. Neo-nationalist protectionism cannot explain how a world society is supposed to be divided back up into pieces, unless through a global politics which, right or wrong, it insists is a chimera. A politics of self-liquidation—letting the state simply merge into postnational networks—is just as unconvincing. And postmodern neoliberalism cannot explain how the deficits in steering competencies and legitimation that emerge at the national level can be compensated at the supranational level without new forms of political regulation.

Third, Habermas argues that the prospects for transnational political institutions are better than ever before, but so too that our need to achieve global solidarity has never been greater. Again, he stresses that European Union institutions can significantly contribute to the furtherance of democratic political communication, and in this connection he questions the political claims advanced by Euroskeptics, Market Europeans, and Eurofederalists. The growth of transnational or transboundary problems for national political communities can only partly be addressed by bureaucratic initiatives and market dynamics; we are compelled, says Habermas, to recognize both the intensity and extensity of globalizing forces, with all the radical challenges this presents for democratic political thought.

Finally, he argues in favor of popular processes of collective will formation at the global level. In short, he suggests that social solidarity, which has for so long been stabilized at the level of nation-states, must be shifted up a gear in order to produce a cosmopolitan sense of shared commitments and shared responsibilities. Such a radicalization of democracy, comments Habermas, is not necessarily abstract; the flowering of culturally cosmopolitan sentiments of belonging, inclusion, and shared interests is already emerging from the weakening of the nation-state. In terms of the debate over Europe, Habermas wishes to speak up for

> a pan-European political public sphere that presupposes a European civil society, complete with interest groups, non-governmental organisation, citizens' movements, and so forth. Transnational mass media can only construct this multivocal communicative context if, as is already the case in smaller countries, national education systems provide the basis of a common language—even if in most cases it is a foreign language. The normative impulses that first set these different processes in motion from their scattered national sites will themselves only come about through overlapping projects or a common political culture. (103)

It is perhaps not difficult to discern parallels between Habermas's call for cosmopolitan global government and his early, pathbreaking arguments concerning political transformations of publicness, as set out in *The Structural Transforma-tion of the Public Sphere* (1962). An emphasis on the rapid expansion of political participation within the bourgeois public sphere was an essential aspect of Haber-mas's early social and political thought, particularly the democratic initiatives leading to new forms of public life beyond the sphere of the state. The historical emergence of a bourgeois public sphere in the eighteenth century, as represented by Habermas, signified emergent individuation, autonomy, and enlightenment—even though he acknowledged the political form of such a "public" did not last for long. It is clear, at least in the context of the arguments developed in his essay "The Postnational Constellation and the Future of Democracy," that Habermas still sets ultimate political value on public participation and the widest reaching democratization of decision-making processes. Only popular processes of com-munication and practical discourse, reflecting the impress of collective will for-mation, will adequately generate forms of cosmopolitan solidarity geared to the pluralization of democracy emerging at the level of transnational or global social policies. Crucially, moreover, it is clear that Habermas views such democratiza-tion as central to the advancement of modernity, especially in terms of the devel-opment of postconventional learning patterns in the realms of society, personality, and culture. As he puts this:

> The artificial conditions in which national consciousness arose argue against the defeatist assumption that a form of civic solidarity among strangers can only be gen-erated within the confines of the nation. If this form of collective identity was due to a highly abstractive leap from the local and dynastic to national and then to demo-cratic consciousness, why shouldn't this learning process be able to continue? (2001a: 102)

Habermas's political tracts have in turn a historical ground. From the ashes of World War II, West Germany was charged with the task of growing a liberal polit-ical culture only *after* the Allied powers had imposed the basic law that provided for democratic institutions. This accounts, in large part, for Habermas's ongoing concern with democratic legitimization and liberal constitutionalism. "There can be no poetry after Auschwitz," wrote Habermas's mentor Theodor Adorno. Yet it is reflection on the incomprehensible Nazi death camps that leads Habermas to insist that the unified Federal Republic of Germany must anchor itself centrally in respect for universal human, civil, and political rights. Viewed through a post-modern lens, this view may hardly seem radical. As if anticipating this response, Habermas positions himself directly at odds with the bulk of modern European thought. He writes (2001a: 45): "From Horkheimer and Adorno to Baudrillard, from Heidegger to Foucault and Derrida, the totalitarian features of the age have also embedded themselves into the very structure of its critical diagnosis. And this raises the question of whether these negativistic interpretations, by remaining transfixed by the gruesomeness of the century, might be missing the reverse side of all these catastrophes." This reverse side, for Habermas, is represented in the great political innovations of popular sovereignty, democratic procedures, legally enforceable human rights, and the vital solidarity that has bound people together pursuing political projects, from peace and ecological concerns to feminist issues.

For those nostalgic for some critical rigor in the evaluation of contemporary society and politics, the arguments developed by Habermas in *The Postnational Constellation* will surely be indispensable for years to come. The politically committed fashion in which he connects the dominant motifs of critical theory to our world in the new millennium accounts for his huge influence in a range of fields—from law and international relations to politics and history. That said, I cannot see Habermas's reworking of European culture and identity around the theme of global public spheres appeasing his critics. For many, Habermas's writings remain stubbornly abstract, speculative, or utopian. His critical theory is too academicist and thus open to the charge of intellectualism. I partly agree, if only for the reason that it is not easy to see how democratic ideals can be projected from the allegedly universal structures of language. Nor is it easy to see, for that matter, how Habermas's stress on participation in rational debate can cope with problems arising from the exclusionary character of the public sphere— exclusions on grounds of, say, identity, gender, or ethnicity (see Fraser 1989).

Some other commentators are especially critical of Habermas's reconceptualization of the normative dimension of the public sphere in terms of the theory of communicative action. "Habermas's social theory," comments Max Pensky (1999: 222), "is largely silent concerning the culturally specific forms of reaction, aversion, legitimation and accommodation that arise as strategies to compensate for the loss of traditional meaning in modern societies." But what, exactly, comprises the emotional undercurrent, at once individual and collective, that underpins that which Pensky designates as a compensation for loss? Might it be argued, for example, that the intricate ties between emotional loss and culturally specific forms of symbolic expression influence and shape the development of democratic institutions and practices as much, if not more, than the cognitive reflective learning processes that Habermas privileges? To quote Pensky again (1999: 222): "All traditions that retain a meaning-giving force in a postconventional social milieu do so either as a result of some half-way successful processes of collective self-reflection or as the result of a failed or missing discourse, by structural failure or strategic manipulation." Pensky only hints here at what might be missing in Habermas's dense conceptual proposals (structural failure, strategic manipulation), though this might be extended to include the point that what is lacking or missing is precisely a social theory of unconscious forces. That is, the democratic aspects of collective will formation are severely constrained or even crippled by an overestimation of purely formal procedures, moral norms, and rational consensus. I shall return to this line of argumentation later in the chapter.

Habermas's arguments, sketched briefly here, have the social-theoretical merit of highlighting the broader political significance of globalization processes to the social challenges facing the European Union in particular and to the future of democracy in general. In what follows, however, I shall raise some questions about Habermas's work, paying particularly close attention to his understanding of social transformation in the public sphere. To do this, I shall draw, in a partial and selective manner, from the writings of the European feminist psychoanalyst Julia Kristeva. To many this may seem an unlikely point of comparison. However, I hope to clearly demonstrate that Kristeva's theorization of identity and culture within the framework of the public sphere provides for a more subtle, reflexive model of social transformation than does that offered by Habermas.

Though there are various points of conceptual and political difference between Kristeva and Habermas, there are two central issues that I shall confront in what follows. The first is Kristeva's heavy stress on the internal world of human subjectivity, of suppressed desires, unnameable urges, semiotic ruptures, melancholic longings. Kristeva's stress on unconscious fantasy, and the fantasmatic dimensions of culture in particular, contrasts sharply with Habermas's excessively rationalist, cognitive conceptualization of individuality and his model of communicative action. I shall argue that not only analytical attention to the affective dimensions of subjectivity and social relations significantly complicates Habermas's theory of public discourse and its transformation, but that such a focus is vital if social theorists are to develop an emotionally literate understanding of the complex relations between politics and the passions.

The second issue concerns Kristeva's "agnostic" conception of public space, and in particular her emphasis on social forces of nonidentity or difference as well as political moments of displacement, rupture, and dislocation in history. Such a stress provides for a very different understanding of the public sphere and public space than that developed by Habermas. For it is a view that puts public space not as a process for the dialogic "founding" of truth but as creative narrativization that cannot but reflect the painful truth of maladies of the soul.

MALADIES OF THE SOUL: THE POETIC LANGUAGE OF JULIA KRISTEVA

"The political discourse which is dominant in the human sciences in universities everywhere is too narrow," Julia Kristeva once commented. The challenge facing today's intellectual, according to Kristeva, is to grasp the political without reduction to "mere politics." That typically rarefied formulation from one of the leaders of French feminism is vintage Kristeva, ironically disdainful of humdrum political realism while at the same time militantly committed to the power of utopian visions. In her supple, civilized intelligence, sensuous language, and poetic cast of mind, Kristeva is one of the most distinguished contemporary heirs of the tradition of radical Freudian criticism, which flows through Herbert Marcuse and Erich Fromm to Jacques Lacan and Louis Althusser and on to such modern-day luminaries as the postcolonial theorist Homi Bhabha and the feminist critic Judith Butler.

Kristeva is a writer for her times. An exile from Bulgaria, she was born in 1941 and was educated by French nuns. Working briefly as a journalist in the 1960s and studying linguistics with Lucian Goldman and Roland Barthes in Paris, she in time became immersed in the Parisian intellectual scene—becoming a key member of the radical group Tel Quel. In much of her autobiographical writing, Kristeva has reflected on being overpowered by a melancholic longing for her homeland. She has tended to present herself as a marginal woman whose exile gives her clarity and independence of thought.

It was this personal interest in exile, melancholia, and memory's creation that led Kristeva to undergo psychoanalytic training with the French psychoanalyst Jacques Lacan, and most of her work since has been an intriguing cross of private biography and cultural history. Indeed, her impressive body of works stands up to comparison with any of her famous philosophical contemporaries, from Jacques Derrida and Gilles Deleuze to Hélène Cixous and Catherine Clement.

To shift from the theoretical and sociopolitical reflections of Habermas to those of Kristeva requires a significant adjustment in conceptual tone and cultural orientation. For one thing, their temperaments and dispositions contrast radically. Habermas is a systematic theory builder, an author of dry, turgid sociological constructs, and a public intellectual engaged with global political issues of the day. Kristeva, by contrast, is a psychoanalyst and feminist, a writer who has twinned the poetic and the clinical to fashion powerful studies of the changing terrain of subjectivity, the psyche, affect, representation, and the aesthetic. For another, their philosophical backgrounds diverge sharply. While Habermas was deeply influenced by the Frankfurt School (he was Theodor Adorno's assistant at the Institute for Social Research), Kristeva comes out of structuralist linguistics and psychoanalysis as reinterpreted by Lacan. From one angle, then, Kristeva is a marvelous example of the European mandarin denouncing the repressive structures of Western rationality that Habermas vehemently critiques in *The Philosophical Discourse of Modernity*. (Though Habermas attacks poststructuralism as represented in the writings of Heidegger, Foucault, and Derrida in *Philosophical Discourse*, interestingly he does not mention Kristeva at all.)

From another angle, however, there are certain parallels between Habermas and Kristeva, especially as concerns theorizing about the complex relations between intersubjective communication and the transformation of public political life. Kristeva's account of public space and the process of social transformation, like Habermas's version, is one essentially that grants privilege to the intersubjective structuring of identity and culture. (Because of this shared emphasis on intersubjectivity, both Habermas and Kristeva, at various points in their careers, have criticized monological accounts of human subjectivity and the "philosophy of consciousness.") Like Habermas, Kristeva views the process of globalization as producing intense psychic turmoil. She sees the contemporary world system as inflicting various forms of suffering on individuals and cultures; one consequence of this, she argues, has been that people have lost access to symbolic discourse and have retreated inwards. This turn to empty narcissistic satisfaction she describes as "new maladies of the soul"; at the present time, more individuals than ever before have retreated to privatism, to a denial of community and public engagement. Such denial of the connection between the self and others reflects a deadening of public discourse, a jamming of dialogue.

Political power, for Kristeva as for Habermas, has come to implant itself in subjectivity itself. The maladies of the soul, one might say, are constituted to their roots by the colonization of the life-world, and from this angle it seems probable that Kristeva might concur with Habermas's political judgment that liberal-democratic states distort and violate "the internal organisation of speech" through the never-ending imposition of functionalist imperatives on human subjects. The complication that Kristeva stresses as a coda to Habermas, however, is the internal world of the individual as well as the fantasmatic dimensions of culture. This complication is politically urgent, says Kristeva, because channels of communication between subjects or citizens and the public political sphere involve forms of human connection other than language. It is here, as we will see, that Kristeva introduces repressed desire, or what she terms "unnameable urges," into her political argument. In contrast to Habermas's excessively cognitive or rationalist account of dialogue, Kristeva emphasizes the centrality of unconscious, nondiscursive, or semiotic components of meaning within the public political sphere.

Like Habermas, Kristeva stresses the importance of individuation and critical self-reflection as embedded in interconnected public spheres. A reflexive sense of shared responsibilities and shared commitments to political participation and cultural inclusion is vital if the democratic process is to secure a basis for legitimacy in our age of pervasive globalization, and from this angle Kristeva emphasizes the attitudes and feelings of citizens as of core importance to critical social theory. The dynamic of globalization, for Kristeva as for Habermas, is not just an economic matter, but nor is it reducible to political forms involving decision-making techniques, administrative practices, and electoral routines. For globalization is also a question of everyday practices, lived identities and relationships, cultural values and moral attitudes, and the transformation of structures of subjectivity. Thus, the political and cultural challenges to European society and to European subjectivity encompass for Kristeva not only the intersubjective forms through which the historical past influences the contemporary political scene (what Habermas terms "painful learning processes") but also a recognition of the split, fractured delicacy of the psyche and human subjectivity itself.

What role does culture have to play in an enlightened political context? The political philosopher who best meets Kristeva's criteria is Hannah Arendt. For

Kristeva, what is intriguing in Arendt's political thinking is her unflagging commitment to language, and especially to poetry as an indispensable medium for the institution and flowering of civil society. Language, poetry, the aesthetic: such symbolic forms permit the public sphere to operate as a discursive space reflecting both shared interests and conflicting agendas. This is an idea that Kristeva finds provocative, and she approvingly notes that Arendt thought poetry "the most human of the arts." Indeed, Arendt routinely invoked poets and writers to support her philosophical conjectures—from Rilke and Yeats to Auden and Valéry, but also Robert Lowell, Randall Jarrell and Emily Dickinson. In the hands of Arendt, says Kristeva, poetry is no longer defined as the opposite of the public, political, or discursive.

The same could be said for Kristeva, of course. Although the similarity of her theoretical project to Arendt's is not explicitly spelled out, it persistently shadows her writings. Like Arendt, Kristeva rejects the orthodox division of politics between left and right as superficial, and she instead urges a shift in orientation from political rationalism to the poetic sublime. In this context, Kristeva sees artistic creation and literary form as possible containers for unspoken experience, in particular giving symbolic expression to the semiotic. It is in the cultural products of the artist or the writer, says Kristeva, that the semiotic may impress itself on symbolic structures, thus threatening established meaning—and she has written of various avant-garde authors, principally Mallarmé, Autrbamont, Artaud, and Joyce, in this vein. Also like Arendt, she signals her faith in the possibility for a more authentic modernity with the argument that a truly autonomous public sphere would itself be a work of art. Yet unlike Arendt, Kristeva is more attuned to emotional dilemmas and contradictions. Wearing her psychoanalytic hat, she argues that the telling of narratives fractures as much as unifies identity; she asserts that language is only ever an emotional holding operation against the disruptive emotional impact of lost loves, repressed pasts, displaced selves.

In her more recent work, especially *Black Sun* (1989), *New Maladies of the Soul* (1993), and *Crisis of the European Subject* (2000), Kristeva analyzes the psychic turmoil produced by contemporary culture with reference to the themes of depression, mourning, and melancholia. In depression, says Kristeva, there is an emotional disinvestment from the symbolic power of language and intersubjectivity. The depressed person, overwhelmed by sadness (often as a result of lost love), suffers from a paralysis of symbolic activity. In effect, language fails to fill in or substitute for what has been lost at the level of the psyche. The loss of loved ones, the loss of identity, the loss of pasts: as the depressed person loses all interest in the surrounding world, in language itself, psychic energy shifts to a more primitive mode of functioning, to a maternal, drive-related form of experience. In short, depression produces a trauma of symbolic identification, a trauma that unleashes the power of semiotic energy. In the force field of the semiotic—silences, rhythms, changes in intonation, semantic shifts—Kristeva finds a means to connect the unspoken experience of the depressed person to established meaning, thereby permitting for a psychic reorganization of the self.

How might such psychoanalytic sensibilities be relevant to debates over globalization, and especially the moral and political challenges facing the European Union? Here Kristeva's recent work is instructive. *Crisis of the European Subject,* for example, is a sustained meditation on the globalization of culture, which amounts in effect to a history of the drastically shrinking world of transnational capitalism. Culture is in the broad sense for Kristeva the very stuff of politics, and one of her central claims is that a sense of cultural belonging or identity has begun to stall in the face of globalizing social forces. Her political critique focuses on how worldwide social transformations—and particularly European cultural shifts—are becoming more and more suited to the successes of the far Right and a general climate of hostility to immigration, and less and less open to voices speaking up for cultural difference, moderation, or reason. While it may not be exactly clear which globalizing forces Kristeva has in mind, it is evident that she writes, among other things, as an intellectual exile, anxious over the consequences of NATO high culture, particularly attempts by transnational corporations to legislate the winners from the losers of globalization. Kristeva's primary purpose is to return to European national identities a sense of what is missing or absent from much of the excited talk on global culture. She is out to probe the unwitting ways in which globalization, and particularly the insidious influence of cultural Americanization, inaugurates new levels of psychic repression and emotional denial. To this end, her work is full of sinuous reflection on the transformative power of grief, mourning, and melancholia in political life, coupled with a detailed examination of cultural memory and the power of imagination. In Kristeva's culturalist version of psychoanalysis, nations, just like individuals, must work through grief and trauma. In the same manner that depressed individuals lose interest in the surrounding world, so, too, nations become traumatically disconnected from their historical past.

From this angle, Kristeva argues that the emergence of the European citizen in our new world of globalization will surely not amount to much unless nations undertake the difficult task of working through specific cultural pathologies, from virulent nationalism to the cult of militarism. This, one might consider, is something of a tall order. But Kristeva makes an urgent plea for citizens to try to "think the horror" of their specific cultural pasts and national histories. Drawing from her own past, Kristeva reflects on the Bulgarian Orthodox Christian tradition, speculating whether Eastern conceptions of identity and culture offer an emotional corrective or political supplement to the rationalistic excesses of West European life.

What her argument comes down to, in effect, is that any concept of culture, civil society or publicness as an *identity* (think, once again, of Habermas's claim to "a European-wide public sphere") is constituted and sustained only through an abjection of nonidentity, difference, and otherness. What is at stake for Kristeva is not only that globalization processes flatten out or threaten other, non-Western forms of life (though this is certainly of central political concern to her), but rather that the current regeneration of the European subject involves psychic damage—in particular, the short-circuiting of mourning, melancholia and depression. A powerful blend of poststructuralist motifs (nonidentity, difference) and psychoanalytic themes (affect, the psyche) is thus evident in Kristeva's social theory.

As Kristeva forcefully argues, the link between national identity and national citizenship is clearly more than a matter of economics, of transformed patterns in employment and prosperity. For the structural impact of economically driven migrations inevitably carries high consequences for personal life, intimacy, and self-identity, and it is against this backdrop that Kristeva raises the question of the regeneration of European identity in progressively multicultural societies. While acknowledging that the debate over multicultural models of identity and citizenship has been forced on the political agenda as a consequence of globalization and the regionalization of migration, Kristeva sharply questions the coarseness and reductionism of various "hyperglobalists"—those who evoke globalism as an image of proliferating interrelationships, of better communication between cultures and polities of standardized political democratization where old class, gender, ethnic, and racial forces of cultural conflict dissipate. She maintains that the implications of globalization for the autonomy of modern states, and for the practices of democracy, are multidimensional and ambivalent. And against those dismissive of arguments that globalization equals the bland Americanization of global consumer markets, she warns of the dangers that globalizing processes pose to the specificity and uniqueness of regional and national identities.

The remembering, repeating and working through of "unnameable urges," "semiotic ruptures" and "uncanny strangeness" that Kristeva has proposed for the West's ailing democracies may seem irredeemably subjectivist or psychically reductionist. Yet the political force of her argument surely stems from the curious and wonderful mixture of various forms of otherness—sexual, racial, ethnic, cultural, religious—that are called upon to probe the dynamic of "globalized culture." All such facets of the social unconscious, or of institutionalized otherness, are analyzed with reference to those that benefit from, as well as those that suffer at the hands of, globalization, and as we have become accustomed to in Kristeva the emphasis is on the two-way traffic between cultural forms and psychic states. "I don't think," she writes, "that there is a global 'popular psychology,' because I believe in the singularity of individuals" (Kristeva 2000: 177).

If this sounds like the kind of individualist rhetoric routinely advanced by psychoanalysts, Kristeva's exit from the simple Freudian conscious/unconscious dualism is doubly disarming—she is at a firm distance from the repression-expression binary that posits that distorted communications can be incorporated into consciousness; she is similarly doubtful of the presuppositions for deliberative democracy, again for reasons of excluding the singularities of human subjects as well as the strangeness or otherness of the Other. Certainly from this angle, Habermas's "talking cure"—from distorted or deformed public spheres to free and transparent political channels of communication—begins to look faintly absurd. As Kristeva notes, "a 'completed' mourning would be a detachment, a scar, indeed a forgetting" (Kristeva 2000: 166).

Kristeva speaks then not only of individual singularities but also the singularities of cultures, organizations, religions, sexualities. She designates this as the *grammar of mentalities*. Mentalities, at once personal and social, provide the bass rhythm of psychic transformations that underlie all other social and political changes. What Kristeva's account in particular underscores, *pace* Habermas, is the ongoing force of *specific cultural imaginaries:* of the unconscious, symbolic texture of particular lives unfolding daily, routinely, in relation to the rhythms of the individual psyche and imagination, of the internal world, and historically, in relation to the shifting socioeconomic and political forces of advanced modernity. She emphasizes that cultural demands and human needs cannot be translated into the political process without a remainder; the political trials and historical traumas of, say, Ireland or Denmark, or indeed the peripheries of Europe of which she evocatively writes, cannot be made fully transparent within public political dialogue, but instead register as forms of enigmatic signification, semiotic rupture, undecoded trauma.

Kristeva's argument that grieving for past identities, as well as the loss of imagined communities, is politically progressive is certainly interesting—partly because this argument offers a striking counterpoint to dominant Western notions, which tend to down grade the psychological benefits arising for citizens able to express grief in respect of destructive actions undertaken by the nation-state. In an age of the trivialization of cultural memory all the way from self-help manuals to theme-parks, however, one might well wonder whether mourning or grieving for the past is, in fact, necessarily politically progressive. Certainly Kristeva sometimes gives the impression that an affective engagement with loss or grief on an individual level is itself tantamount to social and political transformation. In her essay "Bulgaria, My Suffering" in *The Crisis of the European Subject*, for example, her valorization of psychotherapeutic and religious forms of transformational experience takes on a decidedly isolationist tone:

> We can also devote ourselves to ourselves, take care of our autonomy, its desires, its dignity; undergo a psychoanalysis or psychotherapy, try some religious experiences: the asceticism of the Protestants, the joy of the Catholics, and why not others as well? Return to Orthodoxy, rattle its cage, make its communitarian demands more concrete and more effective. Rediscover the meaning of value, speak them, transform them, leave them open, keep on renewing them. . . . This will take a long time, a very long time, Bulgaria, my suffering. (2000: 182)

The constructive side of Kristeva's argument is that there are a good many political issues as well as social movements that are by no means adequately attentive to the emotional literacy of human subjects—and from this angle, her call to "devote ourselves to ourselves" is interesting and politically relevant. Yet by extending the imperial sway of the individual over and above the social and political matrixes of identity, Kristeva is surely in danger of advocating a monadic political practice, one potentially disconnected from common culture.

At this point, we can return to Habermas's reworking of the normative dimension of the public sphere and explore further some of the vulnerable assumptions on which this approach rests. Many commentators have cast doubt on the universalizability of Habermas's theory of communicative action within the framework of the public sphere. It is a conceptual and political proposal, according to these critics, that ultimately violates not only the heterogeneity of language games and discourses of modern societies but also the politics of difference. Some commentators, in particular, argue that Habermas's notion of rational consensus seems excessively rationalistic, indeed much too proceduralist. Now Kristeva's reflections on the public political sphere are interesting in this context, precisely because her account of the relationship between maladies of the soul, language, and politics offers significant illumination regarding the advent of cosmopolitan, global culture in a fashion that Habermas is unable to confront. Her stress on the plurality of mentalities characteristic of the contemporary epoch is compelling, and it directs our attention to the murky, ambivalent waters of affect, human suffering, and emotional trauma as embedded in, and contained by, the political process. Yet this, in turn, raises the thorny conceptual issue of how to theorize about the influence of psychic mentalities and emotional life upon public political life.

SUBJECTIVE SUBVERSIONS,
DISCURSIVE DELIBERATIONS

Kristeva's initial reformulation of the relationship between language, meaning, and subjectivity is set out in *Revolution in Poetic Language* (1984). To map the intersubjective structuring of identity through language, Kristeva draws extensively from the writings of Lacan. Following Lacan, Kristeva claims that the formation of selfhood in the mirror stage, as well as the latter trajectories of the small infant in negotiating the Oedipal drama, results in the intersubjective structuring of human identity within a set of temporal and spatial sociohistorical meanings. In acquiring language, Kristeva concurs with Lacan: The individual subject is inserted into a Symbolic Order that organizes unconscious desire within the systemic pressures of that structure. This argument, dating from Lacan's seminars in the 1950s, directly connects the endless return of "lack" at the heart of psychical life on the one hand, and the order of language and symbolization on the other. For Kristeva, as for Lacan, the subject attempts to signify itself through a symbolic system that he or she does not command and that rather commands identity. Yet while desire may become fully prey to the signifier through entry to language, it is only through the intersubjectivity of speech that the distorted and partially repressed autobiography of the subject can be reconstructed or restored at the level of *meaning* for the individual.

How might Kristeva's approach to language, meaning, and subjectivity relate to that proposed by Habermas? At first sight, there appear to be few similarities, especially given the structuralist and poststructuralist tendencies of Kristeva's work. The looming presence of Lacanian theory would also seem to sharply distinguish Kristeva's social theory from that of Habermas. Intriguingly, however, Peter Dews (1999: 92) has argued that Lacan's conception of intersubjectivity is "arguably far closer to that of Habermas than to the French contemporaries with whom he is habitually associated." If Dews's argument is correct, this then necessarily carries implications for any comparison of Kristeva, indebted as she is to Lacan, and Habermas.

But, first, let us follow Dews. His argument is that there are striking convergences between the interpretations of Freud offered by Habermas and Lacan. According to him, both Habermas and Lacan argue that Freudian psychoanalysis must not be viewed naturalistically, as a theory of the dynamics of quasi-biological drives, but rather as an account of linguistic distortions of symbolic structures at the level of self-formation and the process of intersubjectivity. According to Habermas, for example, unconscious repression arises from distortions of language in general, and from communication in particular. In *Knowledge and Human Interests,* Habermas (1971: 285) states emphatically: "The conception of the instincts as the prime mover of history and of civilization as the result of their struggle forgets that we have only derived the concept of impulse privately from language defamation and behavioral pathology. At the human level we never encounter any needs that are not already interpreted linguistically and symbolically affixed to potential actions." In tying repressed desire and language deformation ineluctably together, Habermas reconstructs the conscious–unconscious dualism as a prime example of "systematically distorted communication." In this communications reading of Freud, consciousness contains discourses derived from the public sphere, while the unconscious contains those needs and desires prevented or denied access to communicative action. Repressed desire is formed through a process that Habermas, following Lorenzer, calls "desymbolization." This involves a splitting off of desires, needs, and representations from daily interactive communication.

Dews finds a remarkably similar underscoring of the power of intersubjective dialogue in Lacan's "return to Freud." He notes the emphasis Lacan put on speech throughout his seminars and papers. As Lacan argues: "It is through the intersubjectivity of the 'we' which it assumes that the value of a language as speech is measured" (Lacan cited in Dews 1999: 93). Moreover, it is just this emphasis on the intersubjective structuring of identity and culture that Kristeva takes, and further develops, from Lacan, primarily with her notion of the "thetic" (see, e.g., Elliott 1999: 200–11).

Notwithstanding coming to psychoanalysis from linguistics, however, Kristeva (1995: 18) argues that contemporary psychoanalytic theory must attend to the heterogeneity and polyvalence of psychic representatives—in particular to attend to the eroticization of lost loves that dislocates the individual subject's capacity to use words:

> The development of semiology has led to the conception of different signifying systems (iconic code, musical code, etc.) that are irreducible to language (the latter being envisaged as a structure or a grammar, a language or a discourse, a statement or an utterance. This has shaken "linguistic imperialism." Concurrently, a return to Freud, and in particular to the Freudian concept of representation, takes into account a plurality of psychic representatives: thing-representation, word-representation, representation of drive, representation of affect. The ensuing result is a "laminated" model of the psychic signifying process with heterogeneous *traces* and *signs*.

What, exactly, are these psychical traces and signs—radically heterogeneous—of which Kristeva speaks? Kristeva's own response to this has been to displace the Lacanian emphasis on language and intersubjectivity with the notion of a "semiotic" signifying process, a realm of prodiscursive experience (including the tone and rhythm of utterances, gestures and bodily sensations) that is necessarily prior to symbolic representation and entry into the cultural network. The semiotic is construed here as the most direct appearance in consciousness of the drives. Kristeva suggests there is a connecting track between semiotic displacement, or the unconscious rupture of language, and the folding back of repression into a symbolic signifying process through which the eroticization of language perpetuates and normalizes itself.

This emphasis on the primacy of semiotic or prelinguistic desires differentiates Kristeva's conception of intersubjectivity from Habermas's conception, whether of language, communication, or interpersonal relationships. In particular, Kristeva connects her analysis of the semiotic with maternity. According to Kristeva, a semiotic longing for the pre-Oedipal maternal is part and parcel of selfhood, making itself felt through tonal rhythms, slips, and silences in everyday speech. These semiotic forces, she insists, are potentially subversive of Symbolic Order, primarily since they are rooted in a prepatriarchal connection with the mother's body. Hence, the subversive or disruptive potential of the semiotic is closely interwoven with femininity. However, it would be a mistake to say that the semiotic belongs exclusively to women. On the contrary, the semiotic is a pre-Oedipal realm of experience. The semiotic comes into being prior to sexual difference. If the semiotic is "feminine," this is a femininity always potentially available to both women and men in their efforts to transform identity and gender power.

What, then, of these different conceptual understandings of desire, language and political discourse? In the end, the gulf between Habermas and Kristeva runs deeper than language. Habermas stresses the necessity of deliberative democracy for the production of open and flexible channels of communication between the public sphere and the political realm. The autonomy of the subject or citizen, he argues, can develop "only on undeformed public spheres." A Habermasian is thus one who views the public sphere as a space in which nondistorted communication leads to the intersubjective discovery of truth and justice. Kristeva, by contrast, sees the public sphere as an agonistic space, constituted and reproduced through narrativization of ongoing psychic conflicts and political crises. It is no wonder then that language, for Kristeva, both establishes *and* erases meaning. It is in this sense that Kristeva speaks of the public sphere less as a "system" or "process" for the founding of truth than as a domain that reflects the painful reality of psychic and political life. For Kristeva, the public sphere is an index of "endless mourning" (2000: 169).

To speak of mourning, depression, and other unnameable desires in relation to the public political sphere, as Kristeva does, is once again to advance an altogether more emotionally literate conception of freedom and autonomy than that developed in Habermas's communications theory. There is, one might speculate, an almost academicist fear of directly reckoning with the darker, more tragic dimensions of personal subjectivity and the psyche in Habermas's sociological writings, and this may be why it is difficult to imagine a Habermasian social theorist affirming the importance of Kristeva's stress on the polymorphic plasticity of both language and mentality. By contrast, Kristeva has given us a sense of autonomy that is not dependent on Reason or transcendence or escape.

EXCURSUS: HABERMASIAN SOCIAL THEORY

It is common for advocates of contemporary critical theory to insist on the conceptual superiority of Habermas's work to that of the early Frankfurt School. From the communication-theoretic standpoint, the defects of the philosophy of history outlined by Horkheimer and Adorno are all too evident. The thesis of social domination sketched in *Dialectic of Enlightenment* is both politically one-sided and conceptually unconvincing. Horkheimer and Adorno's thesis leads to a totalized model of the domination of nature, of others and ourselves. The negativism of critical theory thus represents that point at which the reflective task of a search for social critique succumbs. By contrast, Habermas's concept of communicative action offers an alternative framework for analyzing structures of social conflict, a framework that suggestively underscores the human capacities needed to reverse social domination in the interest of human freedom. Or so some have argued.

There is, undeniably, some truth to this version of the history of German critical theory. Recent critiques of the philosophy of human subjectivity show the inadequacy of the early Frankfurt School's rather solitary, monadic conception of selfhood (see Dews 1999; Whitebook 1995; Elliott 1999). For this view relied on the pretheoretic assumption that a devastating repression of inner nature is the price paid for individuation. However, the transition from the philosophy of consciousness to intersubjectivity—as formulated by Habermas and others—shows that subjectivity is not established in one fell swoop through a uniform, repressive introjection of the law; it is, as Habermas argues, formed through structures of communication which involve both autonomy and heteronomy.

Having sorted out these conceptual difficulties, the reconstruction of critical theory is today generally thought secure. Like the great bulk of social-theoretical traditions, critical theory is not partial to reviewing what it has "disproven." (This task has generally been left to "outside" commentators—many of whom argue that, although the shift to intersubjectivity may be a conceptual advance, contemporary critical theory has lost sight of the inner repression and psychic fragmentation of the subject, a fundamental theme of the early Frankfurt School.) Instead, Habermas and his disciples have been more concerned to "test" the theory of communicative action by recourse to series of moral learning processes and empirical studies of intersubjective mechanisms, processes, and procedures. That being said, a number of distinguished writers within the critical theory campus have recently raised concerns about the adequacy of the theory of communicative action—thus calling into questions the current stock market fortunes of Habermas's social theory. In what follows, I want to look briefly at the work of Honneth (1991), McCarthy (1991) and Braaten (1991) in order to raise questions about the modifications of critical theory attempted by Habermas and of future paths for social theory.

Honneth, McCarthy, and Braaten are united in their commitment to the key tenets of Habermas's theory of communicative action. All stress that the critique of reason should be founded in the pragmatic presuppositions of communicative language; that complex modern societies require a high degree of systems differentiation and administrative coordination; and that, in regard to politics, the project of emancipation depends on building networks that foster free and open communication. At the level of critique, however, each of these authors specifies a different impasse in contemporary critical theory.

Honneth's *The Critique of Power* attempts to trace the issue of social conflict as it is conceptualized in the first generation of critical theory (examining the work of Horkheimer and Adorno), in poststructuralist thought (specifically Foucault's theory of power), and in communication-theoretic terms, initiated by Habermas. The guiding thread is the elucidation of a critical social theory that can comprehend both grids of social domination and the social resources for its practical overcoming. In this connection, Honneth argues, the dynamic of "social struggle" has consistently eluded critical social thought. This is evident in the early Frankfurt School, he believes, since society is reduced to the dimension of social labor. This leaves Horkheimer and Adorno to see technological rationality as applying in all spheres of society and thus prevents an analysis of social conflict within everyday cultural life. In the poststructuralist writings of Foucault,

Honneth finds a new disclosure of the sphere of social interaction. Power infuses the strategic exchanges between human subjects in this perspective. Yet Foucault's critique of power, he argues, can be made intelligible only if we assume a normative standard of evaluation that this standpoint actually lacks. That is, Honneth believes Foucault's critical claims about social control cannot be reflexively grounded since they are situated outside normative understanding—and hence reasons why oppositional attitudes or political dissent should be directed against specific forms of power cannot be given or justified. In the end, a diagnosis of the times is presented in which social domination becomes self-autonomous—in Horkheimer and Adorno, through a prescientific critique of the mutilation of reason; in Foucault, through a purely systems-theoretic explanation. "A central problem," writes Honneth (1991: xiv), "of a critical social theory today is thus the question of how the conceptual framework of an analysis has to be laid out so that it is able to comprehend both the structures of social domination *and* the social resources for its practical overcoming."

The unique feature of Habermas's work, Honneth argues, is that he allows us to see that this unquestioned coercive model of social rationalization remains dependent on processes of communicative action. That is, what Horkheimer and Adorno as well as Foucault misperceived as society operating in a totalitarian manner is actually the restructuring of domains of action according to rules of purposive rationality. In this connection, Honneth agrees with Habermas that "systems reproduction" (administrative and bureaucratic institutions) has become progressively uncoupled from the communicative spheres of the "lifeworld." The central disturbance to social development is that the organizational domains of the economy and the state have been severed from internal communicational demands and now function through a perverse, instrumentalizing logic of their own. This is, in short, Habermas's thesis of the colonization of the lifeworld by systems reproduction—which is also seen by Honneth as *the* social pathology of modernity:

> In the end it seems that, through the stages of the development of his social theory, Habermas has worked his way up to a diagnosis of the times that, like Adorno's and Foucault's analysis of the present, concentrates on the social consequences of power complexes that have become autonomous. Habermas locates the developmental tendencies of the present within the dualism of system and life-world, as Adorno had within the dualism of organisation and individual and Foucault had within the dualism of power apparatus and human body. The penetration of systemic forms of steering into the previously intact region of a communicative everyday practice represents for Habermas the pathology of our society. (1991: 302)

Can the extremely unbalanced relationship between power complexes and their increasing penetration into the communicative foundations of the life-world, however, be reversed? In a nutshell, Honneth believes the answer is yes. However, he contends that Habermas's own work fails to give due recognition to the spheres of social conflict which are vital to any reconquest of the life-world through communicative action. The conceptual difficulties here concern principally Habermas's attachment to systems theory. As Honneth argues:

> Habermas views communicative action as the fundamental mechanism of reproduction of all societies. His critique of positivism and his critique of one-sided concepts of rationality are the unique witnesses of a communicative theory of society aspired to along the path of a theoretical argument with competing tendencies. Only this approach puts him in the position to interpret the phenomena of a dialectic of enlightenment, observed by Adorno and Foucault, in such a way that they can be criticised as one-sided, purposive-rationality directed forms of social rationalisation. He is no longer deprived of the standards in connection with which a critique of the capitalist model of socialisation could be indicated. However, Habermas is so wedded to the basic convictions of the technocracy thesis that he attempts to conceive the domain of material reproduction as a norm-free, purely technically organised sphere of action. Hence, he excludes it from the definitions of his own theory of communication. This ultimately pretheoretic decision lets him take hold of the means of systems theory in order to be able to analyse evolutionary processes within the historically differentiated spheres of the economy and politics as systemically steered processes of purposive-rational action. Thus, the action spheres in which material reproduction is today organised finally appear as domains of norm-free sociality that, as a closed universe, stand over against the sphere of communicative everyday praxis. (1991: 302–3)

For Honneth, the concept of systems—as the "norm-free" organization of material reproduction through purposive-rational action—leads Habermas to break with his earlier recognition that there are no spheres of social life in which processes of intersubjective understanding are not operative. By viewing politics and the economy as purely technical, systematically steered processes of purposive-rational action, Habermas disconnects these forms of social rationalization from this own theory of communicative action.

To overcome these limitations, Honneth argues that we should interpret "the process of rationalization as a process in which social groups struggle over the type and manner of the development and formation of social institutions." This is a point of considerable importance, I think, to contemporary critical theory. Against Habermas's tendency to see systems integration as at the core of regulating the moral and action orientation of individuals, Honneth wants to recover the notions of *praxis* for rethinking constituted systems of action. That is, the communicative processing of social action takes place against the backdrop of social struggle. Struggle and conflict, he insists, are rooted in both the life-world and systems reproduction. The potential for social transformation, Honneth concludes, depends on an institutionally mediated communicative restructuring of asymmetrically distributed power.

So too, McCarthy foregrounds the dynamics of communicative interaction. His analysis of social reproduction in *Ideals and Illusions* highlights an important distinction within systems domains: formal and informal organizations. Like Habermas, McCarthy argues that the formal aspects of organizational processes—rules and regulations, systems of norms and roles, and so forth—can result in damage to mechanisms of mutual understanding. However, McCarthy rejects the viewpoint that systems integration has become wholly autonomous, operating outside of communicative processes. To say that organized domains of action are not primarily structured through communicative interaction, he argues, is *not* to say that these processes are not coordinated by consensual requirements at all. The informal aspects of systems—the sentiments, needs, and desires that underpin interpersonal relations within organizations—are of key importance to the analysis of social rationalization. For McCarthy, interaction mediated by power is at once institutionally and socially integrated.

The recognition of a fragility between social processes and communication leads McCarthy—billed as "the foremost interpreter of Habermas in the English-speaking world"—to argue for a *less* formalized conception of communicative reason than Habermas has proposed. To do this, McCarthy suggests the need for a careful integration of poststructuralist techniques and deconstructive motifs into a critical social theory of communication. Drawing from Rorty, Foucault, Heidegger, and Derrida, McCarthy contends that poststructuralist social theory illuminates the decentering effects of cultural processes in the late modern age on identity and rationality. However, McCarthy's "integration" of these social-theoretical traditions is of a typically cautious brand. He feels that poststructuralist critique is itself unintelligible without the presupposition that the viewpoint criticized can be rationally justified. In this connection, he notes that deconstruction relies on modernist assumptions about reason that this tradition of thought actually seeks to undercut. But exactly why McCarthy should want to incorporate poststructuralist social and political thought into critical theory is not entirely self-evident. In any event, he contends that the deconstruction of reason, when integrated into a pragmatic approach to communication, should permit "the socially necessary construction of concepts, theory, techniques, laws, institutions, identities, and so on with greater sensitivity to what doesn't fit neatly into our schemes." Disappointment might be in store, I suspect, for followers of McCarthy's social-theoretical project. It is unlikely that critical theorists, whose primary concern is the formal structures of communicative language, will want to bother with such notions as *difference* and the Other. Similarly, many poststructuralists and postmodernists are bound to see this proposal as another academicist fantasy, an attempt to corner the Other only to outflank it.

From a different angle, Braaten has sought to develop Habermas's ideas with specific reference to empirical social research. In particular, she seeks to apply Habermas's account of the increasing complexity of modern society to everyday cultural life in the United States. Against this backdrop, she reviews the American reception of Habermas's work in social research. She analyzes Nancy Fraser's feminist critique of Habermas's distinction between systems and the life-world. She points out that many specific phenomena cross-cut the boundaries of this scheme—for example, family life is not just a network of life-world reproduction but is also constituted by exploitative exchanges of labor, power, sex, and money. The conceptual separation of the public and private in Habermas's scheme, she argues, goes hand in hand with traditional male values and thus poses acute problems for a feminist critical theory. Like Fraser, Braaten argues that the life-world and systems reproduction should be seen not as "un-coupled" but rather as interactive. It is only if we see communicative processes as deeply embedded in both personal and institutional settings that the material conditions of human suffering can be brought to light and thus transfigured.

The Habermasian mind-set might be a communication-making champion, denouncing the philosophical limits of monadic subjectivity and the political dangers of relativism, but this is not, in itself, a cause for celebration. Dialogue may be our preferred political pathway and democratic method, but something has to be done to communication to make it personally meaningful and emotionally significant in the lives of individuals. The act of communicating, in other words, is not sufficient; something has to be added on an internal plane for the emotional processing, unconscious digestion, and symbolic registration of dialogical messages. In Freud's view, words must be made available to internal transformation. Too many rules and regulations, too much process (and here one cannot but be reminded of Habermas's more recent obsessive worrying away over propositional truth, validity claims and the normative consensus underpinning a discourse ethic) and dialogue can soon jam—as an antitransformational object, neither nourishing nor interesting. The view that Freud offers, and that is so evocatively elaborated by Kristeva, is that our ways of experiencing creative and novel social engagements depend on the twinning of dialogue and affect, politics, and the passions. Only then can we creatively transform what we are discursively given by others into thoughts for thinking and questions, in the service of imaginative recombinations.

II

CENTRAL ISSUES IN CONTEMPORARY
SOCIAL THEORY

6

Sexualities: Social Theory and the Crisis of Identity

"Sex," writes Charles Lemert (2002: 203), "touches human beings at the quick, at the root, at the core, at the heart of the most intimate feelings. This is why analytic cultures want so to organise it. It is too dangerous to be left to its own." If the prevailing analytic categories of modern culture at once denigrate and despise the sexual realm, this is so, according to Lemert, because sex suggests a dangerous underside to social convention, stock notions, the family; the sexual imagination, working within us as both a transindividual and hyperindividual force, represents a kind of radical unconscious, that which continually gives the slip to societal order building, or rights, duties, obligations, conventions, and customs. There is in any case something intriguingly enigmatic or transgressive about the sexual domain, such that objects of analysis and contestation (sexualities, bodies, desires, and pleasures) are called into question—brought undone, as it were—through an unending erotic compulsion to invert, displace, condense. This may be why various sociological conceptions of knowledge have long sought to protect scientific discourse from becoming too deeply entangled with the erotic, the unconscious, sexualities—or so the practitioners of mainstream sociology have imagined. As Lemert (2002: 205) notes, "sex is the last relation social thought wishes to think because it so powerfully reminds us of the animal within that is free of the analytic rules and barriers of Society."

There is a sense, then, in which the modernist redeployment of sex constitutes a self-identical subject of Culture that all but cancels the erotic energies of Nature. This, presumably, is what Freud was getting at when he spoke of glimpsing the "return of the repressed" in the erotic free associations of his analysands. And it is just this notion of an unconstrained, spontaneous sexuality very deep within the self that knowledges and discourses of sexual liberation during the postwar, post-Freudian era have sought to promote.

In an age in which sexuality is increasingly uncoupled from modernist anchorings such as prescribed interpersonal obligations, heteronormative marital bonds and traditional family structures, the imponderabilities of the erotic necessarily involve a reflective engagement with personal interiority. The postmodern redeployment of sexuality, we might say, is about this problematic, often painful, search for expressing inner desires in a world where there are no longer definite guidelines on how to express yourself. What is sometimes painful is the search for a personal balance in sexual expressions of the self that are neither too definite (the frustrations stemming from the decline of modernist certitude) nor indefinite (the perversity of "anything goes" in postmodern enactments of eroticism).

In the last few decades, sexuality has become a topic that is increasingly discussed and debated among social theorists. Indeed, sex and desire have become the focus of intense social-theoretical, philosophical, and feminist fascination, and it is against this backcloth that social theorists have sought to rethink the constitution and reproduction of sexualities, bodies, pleasures, desires, impulses, sensations, and affects. How to think sexuality beyond the constraints of culture is a question that is increasingly crucial to the possibilities of political radicalism today.

The cultural prompting for this turn toward sexuality in social theory is not too difficult to discern. In the aftermath of the sexual revolution of the 1960s, and particularly because of the rise of feminism, sexuality has come to be treated as infusing broad-ranging changes taking place in personal and social life. The politics of identity, sexual diversity, postmodern feminism or postfeminism, gay and lesbian identities, the crisis of personal relationships and family life, AIDS, sexual ethics, and the responsibilities of care, respect, and love: These are core aspects of our contemporary sexual dilemmas.

This turn to sexuality in social theory, as I have said, is relatively recent. Social theorists, for many years, largely ignored sex. This neglect is perhaps less odd than it first appears, since the pleasures of the flesh were not considered a substantive or proper scientific matter for the social sciences—especially at a time when positivistic or naturalistic philosophies of natural science dominated the methods of the social sciences and humanities. There were, it is true, scattered texts—Wilhelm Reich's *The Function of the Orgasm* (1968) or Norman O. Brown's *Love's Body* (1990). Yet it was only in the wake of social protests and movements in the 1960s and 1970s that sociologists and social theorists turned their attention to the analysis of sexuality in any detailed fashion.

In this chapter, I shall explore the central discourses of sexuality that dominate contemporary social theory and the social sciences. These approaches can be grouped under five broad headings: psychoanalytic, Foucaultian, feminist, sociological, and queer theory. I make no claim in this analysis to discuss all the significant themes raised by these discourses or theories. Rather, I seek to portray the contributions of particular theorists in general terms, to suggest some central questions that the analysis of sexuality raises for social theory today.

FREUD AND PSYCHOANALYSIS

The founder of psychoanalysis, Sigmund Freud, initiated a trend in twentieth-century thought that attributed primary place to human sexuality in the organization of culture and society. The theory Freud developed views the mind as racked with conflicting desires and painful repressions; it is a model in which the self, or ego, wrestles with the sexual drives of the unconscious, on the one hand, and the demands for restraint and denial arising from the superego, on the other. Freud's account of the complex ways in which the individual is tormented by hidden sources of mental conflict provided a source of inspiration for the undoing of sexual repression in both personal and social life. In our therapeutic culture, constraints on, and denials of, sexuality have been (and, for many, still are) regarded as emotionally and socially harmful. The Freudian insight that personal identity is forged out of the psyche's encounter with particular experiences, especially those forgotten experiences of childhood, has in turn led to an increasing interest in the secret history of the self (see Elliott 1998).

Many psychoanalytic critics working in the humanities and social sciences have sought to preserve the radical and critical edge of Freud's doctrines for analyzing the discourse of subjectivity and desire (see Elliott 1994, 1999). For these theorists, psychoanalysis enjoys a highly privileged position in respect to social critique because of its focus on fantasy and desire, on the "inner nature" or representational aspects of human subjectivity—aspects not reducible to social, political and economic forces. Indeed, social theorists have been drawn to psychoanalytic theory to address a very broad range of issues, ranging from destructiveness (Erich Fromm) to desire (Jean-François Lyotard), communication distortions (Jürgen Habermas) to the rise of narcissistic culture (Christopher Lasch).

It is perhaps in terms of sexuality, however, that Freud and psychoanalysis have most obviously contributed to (and some would also say hampered) social and cultural theory. Psychoanalysis has certainly been important as a theoretical resource for comprehending the centrality of specific configurations of desire and power at the level of "identity politics," ranging from feminist and postfeminist identities to gay and lesbian politics. It is possible to identify three key approaches through which psychoanalytic thought has been connected to the study of sexuality in social theory: (1) as a form of social critique, providing the conceptual terms (repression, unconscious desire, the Oedipus complex, etc.) by which society and politics are evaluated; (2) as a form of thought to be challenged, deconstructed, and analyzed, primarily in terms of its suspect gender, social, and cultural assumptions; and (3) as a form of thought that contains both insight and blindness, so that the tensions and paradoxes of psychoanalysis are brought to the fore. While I cannot do justice here to the full range of psychoanalytic-inspired social theories of sexuality, I shall in what follows concentrate on the seminal contributions of Herbert Marcuse and Jacques Lacan.

Herbert Marcuse

A member of the Frankfurt School, Herbert Marcuse developed a radical political interpretation of Freud that had a significant impact upon those working in the social sciences and humanities, as well as student activists and sexual liberationists. Marcuse added a novel twist to Freud's theory of sexual repression, primarily because he insisted that the so-called sexual revolution of the 1960s did not seriously threaten the established social order but rather was another form of power and domination. Instead of offering true liberation, the sexual revolution was defused by the advanced capitalist order, through its rechanneling of released desires and passions into alternative, more commercial outlets. The demand for individual and collective freedom was seduced and transfigured by the lure of advertising and glossy commodities, the upshot of which was a defensive and narcissistic adaptation to the wider world. This narcissistic veneer characterizing contemporary social relations, Marcuse argued, was in fact evident in the conservative rendering of Freudian psychoanalysis as ego psychology in the United States—a brand of therapy in which self-mastery and self-control were elevated over and above the unconscious and repressed sexuality.

A range of psychoanalytic concepts—including repression, the division between the pleasure principle and the reality principle, the Oedipus complex, and the like—have proven to be a thorn in the side of political radicals seeking to develop a critical interpretation of Freud. Freud's theories, many have argued, are politically conservative. Marcuse disagrees. He argues that political and social terms do not have to be grafted onto psychoanalysis, since they are already present in Freud's work. Rather, social and political categories need to be teased out from the core assumptions of Freudian theory. The core of Marcuse's radical recasting of Freud's account of sexuality lies in his division of repression into basic and surplus repression, as well as the connecting of the performance principle to the reality principle. Basic repression refers to that minimum level of psychological renunciation demanded by collective social life, in order for the reproduction of order, security and structure. Repression that is surplus, by contrast, refers to the intensification of self-restraint demanded by asymmetrical relations of power. Marcuse describes the "monogamic-patriarchal" family, for example, as one cultural form in which surplus repression operates. Such a repressive surplus, he says, functions according to the "performance principle," defined essentially as the culture of capitalism. According to Marcuse, the capitalist performance principle transforms individuals into "things" or "objects"; it replaces eroticism with masculinist genital sexuality; and it demands a disciplining of the human body (what Marcuse terms "repressive desublimiation") so as to prevent desire from disrupting the established social order.

What chances personal and social emancipation? Marcuse is surprisingly optimistic about sociosexual change. He argues that the performance principle, ironically, opens a path for the undoing of sexual repression. The material affluence of the advanced capitalist societies, says Marcuse, is the basis on which a reconciliation between culture and nature can be undertaken—the ushering in of a stage of social development he calls "libidinal rationality." Although maddeningly vague about this undoing of sexual repression, Marcuse sees the emergence of emotional communication and mature intimacy issuing from a reconciliation of happiness with reason. "Imagination," writes Marcuse (1956: 258), "envisions the reconciliation of the individual with the whole, of desire with realization, of happiness with reason."

Jacques Lacan

Perhaps the most influential author who has influenced recent debates about sexuality is Lacan, whose pioneering departures in French psychoanalysis were critically examined in chapter 3 as concerns their potential import for critical social theory. Like Marcuse, Lacan criticizes the conformist tendencies of much psychoanalytic therapy; he was particularly scathing of ego psychology, a school of psychoanalysis that he thought denied the powerful and disturbing dimensions of human sexuality. Also like Marcuse, Lacan privileges the place of the unconscious in human subjectivity and social relations. Unlike Marcuse, however, Lacan was pessimistic about the possibilities for transforming the sexual structure of modern culture and the dynamics of gender relationships.

In an infamous "return to Freud," Lacan reads psychoanalytic concepts in the light of structuralist and poststructuralist linguistics—especially such core Saussurian concepts as system, difference and the arbitrary relation between signifier and signified. One of the most important features of Lacan's psychoanalysis is the idea that the unconscious, just like language, is an endless process of difference, lack and absence. For Lacan, as for Saussure, the "I" is a *linguistic shifter* that marks difference and division in interpersonal communication; there is always in speech a split between the self which utters 'I' and the word 'I' that is spoken. The individual subject, Lacan says, is structured by and denies this splitting, shifting from one signifier to another in a potentially endless play of desires. Language and the unconscious thus thrive on difference: signs fill in for the absence of actual objects at the level of the mind and in social exchange. "The unconscious," Lacan argues, "is structured like a language." And the language that dominates the psyche is that of sexuality—of fantasies, dreams, desires, pleasures, and anxieties.

This interweaving of language and the unconscious is given formal expression in Lacan's notion of the Symbolic Order. The Symbolic Order, says Lacan, institutes meaning, logic and differentiation; it is a realm in which signs fill in for lost loves, such as one's mother or father. Whereas the small child fantasizes that it is at one with the maternal body in its earliest years, the Symbolic Order permits the developing individual to symbolize and express desires and passions in relation to the self, to others, and within the wider culture. The key term in Lacan's theory, which accounts for this division between imaginary unity and symbolic differentiation is the phallus, a term used by Freud in theorizing the Oedipus complex. For Lacan, as for Freud, the phallus is the prime marker of sexual difference. The phallus functions in the Symbolic Order, according to Lacan, through the enforcement of the name-of-the-father (*nom-du-père*). This does not mean, absurdly, that each individual father actually forbids the infant–mother union, which Freud said the small child fantasizes. Rather, it means that a "paternal metaphor" intrudes into the child's narcissistically structured ego to refer her or him to what is outside, to what has the force of law—namely, language. The phallus, says Lacan, is fictitious, illusory, and imaginary. Yet it has powerful effects, especially at the level of gender. The phallus functions less in the sense of biology than as fantasy, a fantasy which merges desire with power, omnipotence, and mastery.

But how, exactly, is the phallus situated in relation to psychic individuation and sexual difference? According to Lacan, the desire of the child—of either sex—is to *be* the exclusive desire of the mother. The child is, in effect, psychically held in thrall to the Imaginary lures of maternal containment. Yet the child, somewhat painfully, learns that the mother herself is lacking. That is, the child becomes aware that the mother's desire is invested elsewhere: in the father and his phallus. Significantly, the child's discovery that the mother is lacking occurs at the same time that she is discovering herself in language and culture, as a separate individual identity. This arises, says Lacan, with the entry of a third person (the father) or term (language). It is the symbolic function of the father, as possessor of the phallus, to prohibit oedipal desire—a prohibition that at one stroke constitutes the repressed unconscious. Lacan argues that the sexes enter the symbolic order of language as castrated. The moment of separation from imaginary plenitude is experienced as a devastating loss, the loss of connection with the imaginary, archaic mother. The pain of this loss *is* castration. The child imagines the phallus as the source of the mother's desire, and from this perspective both males and females experience loss, depression, and a profound sense of emptiness.

It is against this complex psychoanalytic backdrop that Lacan sketches a global portrait of the relation between the sexes. Males are able to gain phallic prestige, he says, since the image of the penis comes to be symbolically equated with the phallus at the level of sexual difference. "It can be said that the phallic signifier," comments Lacan (1977: 287), "is chosen because it is the most tangible element in the role of sexual copulation . . . it is the image of the vital flow as it is transmitted in generation." Masculinity is thus forged through appropriation of the sign of the phallus, a sign that confers power, mastery, and domination. Femininity, by contrast, is constructed around exclusion from phallic power. Femininity holds a precarious, even fragile, relation to language, rationality and power. "There is no woman," says Lacan (1975: 221), "but excluded from the value of words."

This viewpoint, as the reader might have already gathered, is hardly likely to win much support from feminists; and, in fact, Lacan has been taken to task by many feminist authors for his perpetuation of patriarchal assumptions within the discourse of psychoanalysis. However, it is perhaps also worth holding in mind that more fluid possibilities for gender transformation are contained within Lacan's formulation of sexual difference and its cultural consequences. Beyond the bleak Oedipal power of the phallus, Lacan deconstructs sexuality identity as fiction or fraud. Desire, he maintains, lurks beneath the signifiers on which identity and sex are fabricated. Gender fixity is always open to displacement.

Lacan's "return to Freud" has exercised an enormous influence on debates over sexuality in social theory, especially in the area of feminist studies—of which more shortly. However, his work has also been criticized for its structuralist leanings, its failure to attend to the inner complexities of emotion and affect, and its pessimistic account of the possibilities for personal and social change (see Elliott 1994, 1999; Frosh 1987).

FOUCAULT ON THE DISCURSIVE PRODUCTION OF SEXUALITY

For the French philosopher and historian, Michel Foucault, sexuality is intricately bound up with advanced systems of power and domination within our broader culture. Foucault's major studies in the 1960s and 1970s, such as *Madness and Civilization* (1965), *The Archaeology of Knowledge* (1972), and *Discipline and Punish* (1977a), examine the deeper social implications of configurations of knowledge and power in the human sciences—for example, psychiatry, sexology, criminology, penology, and demography. Giving a novel twist to Bacon's dictum that "knowledge is power," Foucault argues that scientific discourses, while aiming to uncover the truth about "the criminal" or "madness" or "sex," are in fact used to control individuals. In his genealogies of power/knowledge networks, he argues that scientific disciplines and discourses shape the social structures in which culture defines what is acceptable and unacceptable: what can be said from a position of authority, and by whom and in what social conditions. In a society such as ours, writes Foucault (1980b: 93):

> There are manifold relations of power which permeate, characterize and constitute the social body, and these relations of power cannot themselves be established, consolidated nor implemented without the production, accumulation, circulation and functioning of a discourse. There can be no possible exercise of power without a certain economy of discourses of truth which operates through and on the basis of this association. We are subjected to the production of truth through power and we cannot exercise power except through the production of truth.

The production of discourses, texts, and knowledges is deeply interwoven with the operation of power in society. The individual subject is viewed by Foucault, in this early phase of his career, as an upshot or product of discursive positioning and fixation; the individual is increasingly subjected to new forms of power and control in what Foucault terms our "disciplinary society"; in Weberian terms, the Foucaultian subject is caught up in the iron cage of modernity (see O'Neill 1986; Turner 1993b).

In the later part of this career, Foucault problematized global conceptions of sexuality (e.g., those portrayed in psychoanalytic, social-constructivist and feminist theories), and developed powerful genealogies of the self and subjectivity. He explained his shift of analytical focus from power and domination to sexuality and the self in the following terms:

> If one wants to analyze the genealogy of the subject in Western civilization, one has to take into account not only techniques of domination, but also techniques of the self. One has to show the interaction between these two types of the self. When I was studying asylums, prisons and so on, I perhaps insisted too much on the techniques of domination. What we call discipline is something really important in this kind of institution. But it is only one aspect of the art of governing people in our societies. Having studied the field of power relations taking domination techniques as a point of departure, I should like, in the years to come, to study power relations, especially in the field of sexuality, starting from the techniques of the self. (Foucault 1985: 367)

Foucault's concerns about the culture of sexuality were prompted, in part, by his own homosexuality; in particular, he was troubled by what he saw as the intolerant and repressive heterosexual regime governing sex in French society. He became increasingly fascinated with the sexual liberation movements of the 1970s and 1980s, especially the politicization of gay and lesbian identities. He regarded political demands for sexual liberation, as defined by theorists like Marcuse, to be of crucial importance in redefining configurations of normal and pathological desires, acts, and identities. However, he was suspicious of the claims of various sexual liberationists that desire was repressed in Western societies; he was even more troubled by the notion that, if sexuality were released from existing personal and social constraints, society might achieve greater levels of autonomy. Rejecting what he described as "the Californian cult of the self"—the notion that the scrutinizing of sexuality would reveal the essence of the "true self"—Foucault sought to develop a radically different approach to analyzing the culture of sexuality, desire, and sexual identity.

At the core of Foucault's approach was a rejection of the modernist assumption that sex should be understood as a natural or biological foundation, upon which an imprinting of "sexuality" and "gender" is added. Turning such conventional wisdom on its head, Foucault argues that the idea of sex as origin, as base, or as given to identity and social relations is itself the outcome of a discursive regime of sexuality. As Foucault (1980a: 155) explains:

> We must not make the mistake of thinking that sex is an autonomous agency which secondarily produces manifold effects over the entire length of its surface of contact with power. On the contrary, sex is the most speculative, most ideal, and most internal element in a deployment of sexuality organized by power in its grip on bodies and their materiality, their forces, energies, sensations and pleasures.

Preexisting types of sensual pleasure, says Foucault, become "sex" as the creation of discourses about it—such as medical texts, therapeutic books, self-help manuals, and the like—bring about an ordering of "normal" and "pathological" sexual practices. The human subject, according to Foucault, is not "sexed" in any meaningful sense prior to its constitution within a discourse through which it becomes a carrier of a natural or essential sex.

In *The History of Sexuality,* Foucault (1980a) sets out to overturn what he calls "the repressive hypothesis." According to this hypothesis, the healthy expression of sexuality has been censured, negated, forbidden; at any rate, this is held to be the case in the West. Sexuality as repressed: this theorem has been crucial not only to Freudian and post-Freudian theory but also to various sexual liberationists. Foucault, however, rejects the thesis of sexual repression. Sex, he says, has not been driven underground in contemporary culture. On the contrary, there has been a widening discussion of sex and sexuality. Sexuality, says Foucault, has flourished. Sexuality for Foucault is an end effect, a product, of our endless monitoring, discussion, classification, ordering, recording and regulation of sex.

As an example, Foucault considers attitudes toward sexuality in the Victorian age of the late nineteenth century. Victorianism, he writes, is usually associated with the emergence of prudishness, the silencing of sexuality, and the rationalization of sex within the domestic sphere, the home, the family. Against such conventional wisdom, though, he argues that the production of sexuality during the Victorian era as a secret, as something forbidden or taboo, created a culture in which sex then had to be administered, regulated and policed. For example, doctors, psychiatrists, and others catalogued and classified numerous perversions, from which issues about sex became endlessly tracked and monitored with the growth of social medicine, education, criminology, and sexology.

According to Foucault, this fostering of a science of sexuality arose from the connection of confession to the growth of knowledge about sex. The Roman Catholic confessional, Foucault contends, was the principal means of regulating the individual sexuality of believers; the Church was the site in which subjects came to tell the truth about themselves, especially in relation to sexuality, to their priests. The confessional can be regarded as the source of the West's preoccupation with sex, particularly in terms of the sanctioned inducement to talk of it. Confession became disconnected from its broad religious framework, however, somewhere in the late eighteenth century and was transformed into a type of investigation or interrogation through the scientific study of sex and the creation of medical discourses about it. Sexes became increasingly bound up with networks of knowledge and power, and in time a matter for increasing self-policing, self-regulation, and self-interrogation. In other words, instead of sex being regulated by external forces, it is much more a matter of attitudinal discipline, which is in turn connected to issues of, say, knowledge and education. Psychotherapy and psychoanalysis, says Foucault, are key instances of such self-policing in the contemporary era. In therapy, the individual does not so much feel coerced into confessing about sexual practices and erotic fantasies; rather, the information divulged by the patient is treated as the means to freedom, the realization of a liberation from repression.

Foucault's writings have been sharply criticized on the grounds of sociological determinism—that is, that his definition of power primarily in terms of its disciplinary consequences on passive bodies denies the active place of human agency (Giddens 1981b; Habermas 1987a, 1987b). His writings on sexuality and the self have also been criticized for their neglect of gender dynamics (see McNay 1992). Notwithstanding these criticisms, however, many social theorists, ranging from sociologists to literary critics, have drawn from Foucault's critique of sexuality to debunk traditional notions of rationality, the unified subject, and sexuality as the foundation of identity.

FEMINISM AND SEXUALITY

Feminists have adopted many different approaches in exploring the theme of sexuality and gender. Some feminists have offered perspectives on the social role of women from the viewpoint of our patriarchal society, in which women are the targets of sexual oppression, abuse, harassment, and denigration. Others have concentrated on, say, the regimes of beautification or modes of self-presentation to which women submit in adopting "masks of femininity," to function as objects of men's sexual desire. Still other feminists have examined the broader influences of economics and public policy in the reduction of women's sexuality to the tasks of child rearing and household duties. In these contrasting approaches, the issues of sexual difference, gender hierarchy, social marginalization, and the politics of identity achieve different levels of prominence. For the purposes of this brief discussion here, I will explore the crucial links between sexual subjectivity and gender practices as elaborated in contemporary feminist thought, cultural analysis, and psychoanalysis.

The interlocking relations of subjectivity, gender, and society were powerfully theorized in the late 1970s by the American feminist sociologist Nancy Chodorow. In *The Reproduction of Mothering* (1978), which is now considered a classic feminist statement on sexuality and gender, Chodorow combines sociological and psychoanalytic approaches to study the reproduction of gender asymmetries in modern societies. Her idea was to focus on the emotional, social, and political ramifications of exclusive female mothering, giving special attention to the construction of masculinity and femininity. Against the tide of various socialization theories, Chodorow contends that gender is not so much a matter of "role" as a consequence of the ways in which mothers emotionally relate to their children.

In explaining the sex roles to which women and men are expected to conform, Chodorow argues that the developing infant acquires a core gender identity that functions as a psychological force in the perpetuation of patriarchy. The core of her argument concerns gender difference. Mothers, she says, experience their daughters as doubles of themselves, through a narcissistic projection of sameness. The mother emotionally relates to her daughter as an extension of herself, not as an independent person; the daughter, as a consequence, finds it extremely difficult to disengage emotionally from her mother and to create a sense of independence and individuality.

Chodorow sees gains and losses here. Empathy, sensitivity, and intimacy are the gains that flow from this narcissistic merging of mother and daughter. Daughters, she argues, are likely to grow up with a core sense of emotional continuity with their mother, a continuity that provides for strong relational connections in adult life. In this account, girls become mothers since their mothers' feminine selves are deeply inscribed within their psyche. However, the losses are that, because daughters are not perceived as separate others, women consequently lack a strong sense of self and agency. Feelings of inadequacy, lack of self-control, and a fear of merging with others arise as core emotional problems for women.

By contrast, Chodorow sees masculine sexual identity as based on a firm repression of maternal love. Boys, she says, must deny their primary bond to maternal love—thus repressing femininity permanently into the unconscious. This is not a psychic task that boys complete by themselves, however. Mothers, according to Chodorow, assist boys in this painful process of psychic repression through their own tacit understanding of gender difference. That is, because mothers experience sons as other, mothers in turn propel their sons toward individuation, differentiation, and autonomy. Mothers thus lead their sons to emotionally disengage from intimacy. The mother, in effect, prepares her son for an instrumental, abstract relation to the self, to other people, and to the wider society; this, of course, is a relation that males will be expected to maintain in the public world of work, social relations, and politics.

Chodorow's work is an important contribution to feminist scholarship; her psychoanalytically oriented sociology has influenced many feminists researching gender identity in the wider frame of families and communities. Her general claim that women mother in order to recapture an intensity of feeling originally experienced in the mother–daughter relation has been especially fruitful. For such a claim connects in Chodorow's work to a wider social explanation of gender alienation and oppression. Women's emotional lives are drained and empty since men are cut off from interpersonal communication and sexual intimacy. From this angle, the desire to have a child is, in part, rooted in the repression and distortion of the current gender system. Against this backdrop, Chodorow argues for shared parenting as a means of transforming the current gender regime.

A similar focus on the mother–daughter relationship is to be found in the writings of the French philosopher Luce Irigaray. Like Chodorow, Irigaray is out to analyze the deeper symbolic forces that limit or constrain women's autonomy and power. Unlike Chodorow, however, Irigaray proposes a more formalistic or structuralist thesis. Taking her cue from Lacan, Irigaray contends that woman is, by definition, excluded from the Symbolic Order. On this view, the feminine cannot be adequately symbolized under patriarchal conditions. As Irigaray (1985: 143) argues: "there is no possibility whatsoever, within the current logic of sociocultural operations, for a daughter to situate herself with respect to her mother: because, strictly speaking, they make neither one nor two, neither has a name, meaning, sex of her own, neither can be 'identified' with respect to the other."

Similarly, Kristeva (1984) argues against the patriarchal bent of the Lacanian Symbolic Order, to which she contrasts the "semiotic"—a realm of pre-Oedipal prolinguistic experience, consisting of drives, affects, rhythms, tonalities. According to Kristeva, as discussed in chapter 5, semiotic drives circle around the loss of the pre-Oedipal mother, and make themselves felt in the breakup of language—in slips, silences, tonal rhythms. These semiotic drives, she suggests, are subversive of the symbolic Law of the Father since they are rooted in a pre-Oedipal connection with the maternal body. The subversive potential of the semiotic is thus closely tied to femininity, and Kristeva devotes much of her psychoanalytic work to the analysis of motherhood and its psychical consequences.

Most recently, the development of a social theory of sexuality has been transformed by the writings of the American feminist poststructuralist Judith Butler. Butler seeks to debunk the work of theorists, such as Chodorow, who appeal to women as a foundation or basis for feminist theory and politics. She argues that notions of "identity" or "core gender identity" serve to reinforce a binary gender order that maintains women's oppression. Like Kristeva and Irigaray, Butler sees sexual identity as shot through with desire, fantasy, emotion, symbol, conflict, and ambivalence. Unlike Kristeva and Irigaray, however, Butler argues that desire is not so much some inner psychic force as a result of the internalization of gender images upon the surface of our bodies. Drawing on the work of Foucault, Butler contends that the link between sex and gender power is produced, not through nature, biology or reason, but through the deployment of knowledge, discourses, and forms of power, actualized through acting bodies and sexual practices.

In *Gender Trouble: Feminism and the Subversion of Identity* (1990) and *Bodies That Matter* (1993), Butler argues that sex and sexuality are constituted and reproduced through the body that performs—the production of masculine and feminine bodies, lesbian and gay bodies, the sexy body, the fit and healthy body, the anorexic body, the body beautiful. Gender, says Butler, is not the outcome of the "true self" or "core sex identity" but rather a matter of performance, the performance of a corporeal style. Individuals for Butler model their gender performances after fantasies, imitations and idealizations of what we think it means to be a "man" or "woman" within the range of cultural representations of sex in the current gender regime. Butler's notion of performance, of the body that performs, encompasses the copying, imitation and repetition of cultural stereotypes, linguistic conventions, and symbolic forms governing the production of masculinity and femininity.

THE SOCIOLOGY OF SEX

Among changes now pervading our culture, sociologists argue that few are more profound than those transforming the texture of family life. In many advanced societies, we are moving to a situation in which nearly half of first marriages end in divorce, and the statistics are even worse for second and subsequent marriages. Among conservatives, this decline is often cast as a sign of society's moral decay; the lament is attributed to several sources. From sexual permissiveness to feminism, from new parenting arrangements to the spread of overt homosexuality: our new era, so many conservatives argue, is one that spells the end of family ties that bind.

A key reference point here is a recent study of American families, *A Generation at Risk: Growing Up in an Era of Family Upheaval*. Paul Amato and Alan Booth (2000), the authors of the study, argue that the costs of our separating and divorcing society are simply too high. Divorce might suit adults, but not children. For it is children who suffer the painful and destructive long-term impact of divorce in their own sense of self, sexuality, and intimate relationships. Based on an analysis of married couples of over fifteen years, the authors of *A Generation at Risk* suggest that unhappy parents should try to stay together for the sake of their children. It is acknowledged that children can suffer if remaining with parents in what is termed a "high-conflict marriage," but the authors argue that in most "low-conflict marriages," couples ought to make certain sacrifices in order to fulfill their parental and societal responsibilities.

Some rather obvious criticisms might be made of this argument. For one thing, it pays little or no attention to the emotional damage sustained by children living in family contexts of disrespect, to say nothing about lack of love. For another, it seems excessively prescriptive and moralistic. Who, exactly, is to say whether conflicts experienced in marriage are to count as "low-level" or "high-level"? Emotions, after all, are not exactly skilled workers. On a deeper sociological level, there is something awry with arguments about "the breakdown of the family." Certainly the rise of one-parent families, as well as the dramatic increase of births outside marriage, indicates that broad-ranging changes are sweeping through society. And divorce undeniably looms as a feature of family and domestic arrangements. Yet liberal and conservative critics do not readily acknowledge the fact that people very often remarry. The implications of this are far-reaching, and some sociologists are now suggesting that, rather than family breakdown, the family is undergoing a constructive renewal.

Sexual relationships today, conducted inside and outside marriage, embrace what has been called the movement toward "individualization." Individualization refers principally to self-construction and self-design, in which the forging of identity and sexuality becomes less dependent on social traditions and customs and is organized instead around personal decision-making and choice. The self-staging of individualization is inevitably undertaken through a host of traditional social, economic, political, and cultural constraints. However, individualization, as Ulrich Beck argues, is a paradoxical compulsion that takes the individual into a posttraditional social setting, a setting where the person must live as an individual agent and designer of her or his biography. There is a new contingency at the level of the self, identity, and sexuality, says Beck. What this means as far as families and domestic arrangements are concerned is that the stress today on choice and individual autonomy provides a radicalizing dynamic that, in turn, alters the interpersonal realm in which relationships are rooted.

Beck claims that many patterns of family development suggest that traditional expectations ("till-death-us-do-part") are being put aside, and instead domestic relationships are increasingly based on the growth of the individual as well as the care for others. The individualized individual, says Beck, engages in relationships in which trust is the key anchor. If trust evaporates, so, too, does the relationship; traditional ties no longer bind in the way they once did. Beck connects this redesign of family living to the changing ways in which individuals experience sex, sexuality, relationships, and intimacy. "The traditions of marriage and the family," writes Beck (1997: 96), "are becoming dependent on decision-making, and with all their contradictions must be experienced as personal risks."

Beck's social theory permits the illumination of very broad transformations at the level of personal and social relationships. Many parents are now stepparents as well as biological parents, and the clear trend is toward new commitments to others across family boundaries. This can be viewed positively for children, in so far as it involves an "opening out" of childhood to relationships in the deepest sense of the term. As Beck notes, there are many social forces at work here, including more flexible employment options, recent gains in autonomy for women, newly emerging definitions of masculinity, as well as rising experimentation across diverse heterosexual and homosexual lifestyles. Add to this the variety of options in the area of reproductive technologies—such as in vitro fertilization and embryo freezing—and changes in human attitudes to sexual reproduction become increasingly transparent. These developments usher in a world of new possibilities and risks for people.

Anthony Giddens also sees the modern social world as unleashing positive and negative developments at the level of the self, sexuality and intimacy—as discussed in chapter 2. Like Beck, Giddens argues that the self is increasingly individualized today—the self becomes something that is reflected upon, reworked, altered, even reshaped. "The self," writes Giddens (1991: 32), "becomes a reflexive project." By reflexivity, Giddens means to underscore a disposition of continuous self-monitoring, in which social practices are constantly examined and reformed in the light of new information and fresh developments about those very practices.

Again, marriage is a key example. According to Giddens, statistics about marriage and divorce do not exist in a separate realm from the flesh-and-blood human agents that comprise those statistics. On the contrary, Giddens's sociology emphasizes the knowledgeability of social agents, and in particular the manner in which social transformations affect the reflexive organization of the self. The coming of a divorcing society, says Giddens, penetrates to the core of our personal lives, such that it is virtually impossible to equate romantic love with the "forever" or permanence of the marriage contract. When people marry today, they do so against a backdrop of high divorce statistics—knowledge that, in turn, alters their conception and understanding of the permanence of relationships. "In struggling with intimate problems," writes Giddens (1991: 12), "individuals help actively to reconstruct the universe of social activity around them."

In *The Transformation of Intimacy: Sexuality, Love and Eroticism in Modern Societies* (1992b), Giddens speaks of "the pure relationship," a relationship created and maintained through the mutual trust of partners. As Giddens explains:

A pure relationship has nothing to do with sexual purity, and is a limiting concept rather than only a descriptive one. It refers to a situation where a social relation is entered into for its own sake, for what can be derived by each person from a sustained association with another; and which is continued only in so far as it is thought by both parties to deliver enough satisfactions for each individual to stay within it. (5)

At the heart of this account of contemporary, postmodern intimacy and lifestyle lies a radicalization of gender and sex. For if relationships are indeed designed and maintained through personal commitment, trust, and emotional satisfaction, then it follows that contemporary men and women are demanding equality to provide ongoing consent to the posttraditional world of intimacy in which they find themselves. Feminism and the women's movement, says Giddens, are crucial to this process of democratization in the sphere of gender, sexuality and intimacy.

A related emphasis on reflexivity in the construction and deconstruction of sexuality is to be found in the work of the British social theorist and cultural historian Jeffrey Weeks. In a series of publications, Weeks developed a social constructivist approach to the study of sexuality, in which sex is less a matter of inner desires and personal behavior than a site where ideologies, cultural norms, and institutions interweave. Weeks contends that the notion that homosexual practices reveal a distinct identity—"the homosexual"—did not arise in the West until the late nineteenth century. Prior to this, the policing of homosexuality was undertaken not through the monitoring of deviant persons, but through the punishing of particular acts, organized under the general category of sodomy. By drawing attention to the ways in which homosexuality was socially fashioned in relation to specific identity traits, psychological dispositions, and cultural markers, Weeks attempts to underscore the patterns of social fabrication underpinning modernity's regimes of sexuality.

QUEER THEORY

The history of the label "queer theory" is set against a backdrop of the radical sexual politics of the 1970s, in particular the assumption that homosexuality is a foundation or identity of minority sexual experience in the sociocultural order. The development of this theoretical approach to sexuality arose not only from emerging social divisions around the meaning of homosexuality throughout the 1980s but also from new attempts to avoid exclusionist and separatist strategies of political opposition to the masculinist, heterosexual dynamic of Western culture. If the first generation of gay, lesbian, and feminist activists and theorists sought to analyze homosexuality as a minority experience, then the focus of queer theorists has been to contest the binary divide between majority and minority experience, as well as the social dynamics of heterosexuality and homosexuality.

The theoretical grounding of queer theory lies in poststructuralism and literary deconstructionism, and the influence of social theorists such as Foucault, Lacan and Derrida looms large. Less a unitary coherent body of thought than an assemblage of conceptual tools and political strategies, queer theory attempts to subvert the cultural stereotypes used to understand gay, lesbian, or bisexual people—to bring into focus the "queer knowledges" that modernity has unleashed in its framing of sexual identities and differences. As Teresa de Lauretis (1991: v) explains this transgressive edge of queer theory:

> Today we have, on the one hand, the terms "lesbian" and "gay" to designate distinct kinds of lifestyles, sexualities, sexual practices, communities, issues, publications, and discourses; on the other hand, the phrase "gay and lesbian," or more and more frequently, "lesbian and gay" (ladies first), has become standard currency. . . . In a sense, the term "Queer Theory" was arrived at in an effort to avoid all of these fine distinctions in our discursive protocols, not to adhere to any one of the given terms, not to assume their ideological liabilities, but instead to both transgress and transcend them—or at the very least problematize them.

So queer theory embraces not only lesbian, gay, and bisexual people but also sadists, fetishists, voyeurs, drag queens, transsexuals, transvestites, butches, gender benders, and all other practices that attract the label "deviant sexualities" within the asymmetrical power relations of patriarchy.

In *Essentially Speaking* (1989), Diana Fuss develops a poststructuralist critique of the homosexual/heterosexual binarism. Questioning identity categories, Fuss asks:

> Is politics based on identity, or is identity based on politics? Is identity a natural, political, historical, psychical, or linguistic construct? What implications does the deconstruction of "identity" have for those who espouse an identity politics? Can feminists, gay, or lesbian subjects afford to dispense with the notion of unified, stable identities or must we begin to base our politics on something other than identity? What, in other words, is the politics of "identity politics"? (100)

Fuss questions here what it might be like to live our lives outside or beyond the anxious grip exerted by identity categories. Here she develops a queer critique of feminist theorizing. Heterosexuality, says Fuss, derives meaning in relation to its opposite, homosexuality; the sexual foundation of the former is framed on an exclusion and repression of the latter; the production of hetero-/homosexual divisions and differences is crucial to the workings of sexual oppression. This carries radical implications for understanding sexual identity, and especially the construction of gay and lesbian identities. Fuss argues that the hetero-/homosexual opposition constitutes a fixed normativity for sexual identities, a rigid cultural order in which sexual differences are forever displaced and denied. Thus, the assertion of identity-based gay and lesbian communities has the paradoxical effect of reinforcing heterosexuality and homophobia as the key dynamics of sociosexual organization. In contrast to the politics of identity, Fuss urges sexual radicals to contest, and hence destabilize, the hetero-/homosexual hierarchy. She urges, in short, a politics of relational identities.

Eve Kosofsky Sedgwick, sometimes dubbed "the mother of queer theory," goes one step further. In *The Epistemology of the Closet* (1990), she argues that the hetero-/homosexual binarism not only shapes and structures sexual identities and differences, but informs key categories of Western thought and culture. For Sedgwick, the hetero-/homosexual binarism organizes people's experience and knowledge of the world, particularly forms of self-knowledge, self-disclosure, and self-revelation. "Coming out" and the "closet" are key terms for understanding the experiences of gay and lesbian people; but these broad categories of self-definition also deeply affect heterosexuals, who situate their own identities and practices in relation to homosexuality, especially the power of homosexuality to disturb and displace. The contemporary crisis of homo-/heterosexual definition is at root a desire for certainty at the level of sexual knowledge. Following Foucault, Sedgwick argues that the secrecy surrounding knowledge of the closet is both maintained and frustrated because of the risk of the secret's disclosure. Somewhat akin to Lacan's description of the phallus as a "master signifier," Sedgwick describes the hetero-/homosexual division as pivotal to the cultural logic of the advanced societies. Knowledge of the closet and its secrets, Sedgwick says, is invested with much energy and anxiety, a set of fears and fantasies, which underwrites spacings between appearance and reality, norm and pathology, power and powerlessness. Due to the intense anxieties and fears in our culture associated with the closet and coming out, we can never know the truth about self, sexuality, or gender. The closet, Sedgwick argues, is the disturbing underside of "normal sexuality," always threatening to open or be opened.

Sedgwick's work has been very influential in queer theory, primarily since she has moved debate beyond narrow definitions of the politics of identity, as well as the basic oppositions of oppression and resistance. Refusing to accept that the world can be easily divided between homosexuals and heterosexuals, Sedgwick seeks to underline (1) that knowledge is the consequence of bodies; (2) that sex is not the center or foundation of the human subject; (3) that sexual identities are fundamentally provisional, mobile, and fractured; and (4) that the instability of the hetero-/homosexual binary opposition holds out possibilities for the reinvention of identities, desires, practices, communities, knowledges, and social structures.

7

The Reinvention of Citizenship

"In the twentieth century," wrote T. H. Marshall (1973: 84), "citizenship and the class system have been at war." The advancement of the democratic potential of modernity, according to Marshall's classic analysis, has occurred as a complex, negotiated trade-off between the evolution of capitalism (and the oppressive effects of class inequalities), on the one hand, and the integrative effects of an extension of citizenship to social rights and social equality, on the other. "The expansion of social rights," Marshall says, "is no longer merely an attempt to abate the obvious nuisance of destitution in the lowest ranks of society. . . . It is no longer content to raise the floor-level in the basement of the social edifice, leaving the superstructure as it was. It has begun to remodel the whole building" (1973: 96–97). On this view, the development of citizenship as a cluster of social and political rights has provided sources of social solidarity for processes of democratization. Civil society, underpinned by an appreciation of civil or legal rights, is based on the widening and deepening of rationality and solidarity.

Marshall's work on citizenship provided a powerful alternative interpretation of modernization and modernity to that offered by radicals on the left. As Anthony Giddens develops this point:

Marshall's views were strongly shaped by a critical reaction to Marx and Marxism. Marshall wanted to defend the claims of reformist socialism as contrasted to its bolder and violent cousin, revolutionary communism. He wanted to show also that class conflict was neither the main motor of social transformation nor a vehicle for political betterment. With Max Weber, Marshall accepted class inequality as an inherent element of a capitalistic industrial society. Class division, however, in Marshall's view is only one dimension of such a society. The other, integrative, dimension is that of universal involvement in the national community, given concrete form in the welfare state. (1996: 208)

Marshall's account of the formation of citizenship rights, as Giddens emphasizes, is intricately interwoven with the nation-state and welfare institutions. In Marshall's conception, citizenship rights, and the political and cultural struggles associated with them, have a certain parallel with the principles of the national community as understood in the liberal tradition.

The foundations of citizenship, then, belong to the nourishing sphere of the nation-state and its welfare systems. Yet identifying the institutional locus of Marshall's analysis allows us to see that such an approach can no longer grasp the core prospects and risks for civil society at the turn of the twenty-first century. For ours is the era of globalization, reflexive metamodernism, and postmodernization. The nation-state today has to react to the twin forces of globalism and localism, and its associated transformation of the world economy. One comprehensive result of these transnational events or structures is that the nation-state is no longer the main regulator of sociosystemic order and thus no longer politically accountable for finding solutions to major and traumatic crises. "The Welfare State is dead," or so argue the neoliberals. Such critics have attacked welfare systems for promoting dependency and apathy—and, by implication, socioeconomic stagnation. While many question and critique the glaring inadequacies of the neoliberal interpretation of the world of the late twentieth century, one would surely have to conclude that a model of citizenship contextualized in the frame of the national state no longer holds good, if it ever did.

Some social theorists argue that the deep impact of globalization and new media technologies on mass culture signifies that citizenship is best approached as an ideology, a kind of hangover from the Enlightenment's privileging of rationality and individuality. Hence, reports are spreading about the "death of the citizen" (see Turner 1993a: 10–12). However, the poststructuralist or semiotic critique of the end of citizenship is based on mistaken, and somewhat simplistic, assumptions about the eclipse of modernity and modernism in the light of postmodernist theory.

In this chapter, I propose to analyze some very general trends affecting the cultural conditions of citizenship in the context of a mixed model of modernity and postmodernization. As Bauman (1991, 1995, 1997) has argued, postmodernization does not spell the end of the project of modernity; postmodernity is rather "modernity without illusions"—as social practice is increasingly geared to reflect back upon itself, to examine its guiding assumptions and aspirations. Accordingly, I want to examine the concept of citizenship in the frame of both modern and postmodern life strategies, set within the broader institutional possibilities and risks inaugurated in an age of globalization. My suggestion is that citizenship need not be theorized pessimistically (despite the hazards and dangers confronting cultural communities and the global social order), but can instead be located as a new departure point for the chronic tension and struggle of civil (or intersubjective) interchange.

STRATEGIES OF IDENTITY, MODERN
AND POSTMODERN

Much talk these days is about identity: identity and its problems, the transformation of identity, and, perhaps most fashionably, the end or death of the subject. Nowadays notions of identity seem inevitably to capsize into either modern or postmodern forms of theorizing. In modern theorizing, the catchword for identity is that of 'project'; in postmodern theorizing, it's that of 'fragmentation'.

The 'project' of modern identity is that of identity building. By identity building, I mean the building up of conceptions of oneself, of one's personal and social location, of one's position in an order of things. It is such restless self-activity that replaces the ascriptions of tradition and custom. Freed from the rigidities of inherited identity, human beings are set afloat in the troubled waters of modernity—in its unpredictability and flux, its global transformations, cultural migrations, and communication flows. Modernity, we might say, is much preoccupied with identity as an end in itself: people are free to choose the kind of life they wish to live, but the imperative is to "get on" with the task and achieve. To put it in another way, the order-building, state-constructing, nation-enframing ambitions of modernity require human subjects capable of picking themselves up by their own bootstraps and making something of life, with no rationale beyond the market driven imperatives of constructing, shaping, defining, transforming.

Perhaps the most comprehensive analysis to date that we have of this modern conception of identity building has been provided by the British sociologist Anthony Giddens (1991, 1992a), who lists 'life-planning', 'internal referentiality', and 'colonization of the future' as defining features. But the paradox of self-construction, if we read Giddens against himself, is that modern craving of identity maintenance or identity preservation results in a drastic limiting of life stories, the denigration of meaning in the present and its projection into the future. What Giddens calls the future colonized is a spurious form of self-mastery, if only because the predictable, the routine, and the determined always involve destructive forms of unconscious repetition.

Indeed, the psychic costs of life lived as project are grave. For the founder of psychoanalysis, Sigmund Freud, the crux of the problem is that of delayed gratification. In *Beyond the Pleasure Principle* (1921), Freud argues that psychic violence erupts in that gap between demand for pleasure and pleasure actually attained. "What we call happiness," writes Freud, "comes from the (preferably sudden) satisfaction of needs which have been dammed up to a high degree, and it is from its nature only possible as an episodic phenomenon." The more culture presents itself as future colonizing and project oriented, the more life becomes repressive: the very contingencies of human experience are imagined to be insured against by the promise of future certainty, a certainty always tantalizingly out of reach.

Elsewhere, in his magisterial cultural analysis *Civilization and Its Discontents*

(1930), Freud speaks of the modern adventure as a drive for order, a drive that he links to the compulsion to repeat. The trimming of pleasure into that of order, says Freud, spares us the painful ambivalence of indecision and hesitation.

So, too, the French psychoanalyst Jacques Lacan sees the human subject as marked by the impossibility of fulfillment, an empty subject constituted through a primordial lack or gap of the Other. Indeed, such a decentering of the subject is at the heart of 'Lacan's Freud'. Lacan (1977: 171) states, "If we ignore the self's radical eccentricity to itself with which man is confronted, in other words, the truth discovered by Freud, we shall falsify both the order and methods of psychoanalytic mediation; we shall make of it nothing more than the compromise operation that it has, in effect, become, namely, just what the letter as well as the spirit of Freud's work most repudiates."

In broader social terms, Lacanian theory has often been unproblematically inserted into the whole discourse of postmodernism, as if the critique of the withering of imaginative cultural production could be generated up from unconscious desire itself. But it might be just as plausible to see Lacanian psychoanalysis as symptomatic of the modern adventure in identity building. For the Lacanian Mafia, without knowing it, offers up a superb portrait of the limits and dead-ends of *life lived as project*. A subject marked by lack and gap is, one might say, an accurate portrayal of that brand of modern identity that is always on the move, hungering for new (and better) destinations, but never actually arriving. From the National Socialism of Hitler's Germany to the present-day resurgence of nationalism in Europe, identity building is framed on an exclusivist, violent negation of the Other. Life lived as an identity project, then, is defined by *pleasure in discontent*. This is a discontent that leads modern women and men to the view that "things can always be better," to the denigration of the here and now, and to the desire for smooth-functioning, regulated identities (always in the future, or around the next corner).

By contrast, in what are increasingly called "postmodern" times, the status of identity-projects diminishes. Postmodern sentiments recognize that the sociopolitical consequences of modernity clash strongly with its programmatic promises (see Bauman 1991, 1995, 1997). Instead of the search for the ideal identity (complete, finished, self-identical), we find instead a celebration of cultural heterogeneity and difference. Ours is the age of what Jean-François Lyotard (1988: 31–36) describes as 'open space-time', by which he means that identities are liquidated into episodes, a flow of drifting moments, eternal presents, transitory encounters. The postmodern condition—with its globalization of the market, its proliferation of media simulations, its cult of technologism, its self-reflexive pluralism—unleashes a multiplicity of local identities without any 'central' or 'authoritative' coordination.

The American cultural critic Christopher Lasch (1981) some years ago made a crablike move toward the idea of a postmodern life strategy, which he summarized as a "minimal self." This new self is one drained of ego strength and autonomy, a narcissistic self focused only on the experience of living "one day at a time," the comprehension of reality as a "succession of minor emergencies." Daily life, in the postmodern, becomes a matter of shifting anxieties and drifting concerns, always changing, always episodic. It is as if we live in a constant state of information overload. Crisis, in short, has become the norm. Living in a world of constant crisis means, necessarily, adjusting one's emotional response level. There is no citizen who can adequately monitor all that is going on; and any attempt to do so can only lead to psychic burn-out. So, players in the postmodern game of life develop an air of indifference and aloofness, sure only in the knowledge that all new improvements, social and technological, will create further problems down the track.

Postmodern life is episodic, a fractured and fracturing world, with little in the way for continuity or the making of meaningful connections. Yet one can also view the personal consequences of the postmodern in a somewhat more positive light. Imagination, it appears, has been given a considerable boost as a result of new technologies and electronic advances. Computers, word processors, faxes, the Internet, DAT: we now have technology that ushers in the possibility of different kinds of pleasures, different thoughts and feelings, different imaginings. In psychical terms, one may say that the trademark of postmodernity is a radical 'decentering' of the human subject: the limiting of omnipotence, not in Lacan's sense of a separation of subject and Other, but rather in terms of a *reflexive scanning of imagination* (see Elliott 1996). By reflexive scanning, I mean to draw attention to the complexity of fantasy itself, as a medium of self-construction and other-directedness. This fantasized dimension of our traffic with meaning is underscored powerfully by contemporary theorists such as Julia Kristeva (1995), who speaks of 'open psychic systems', Cornelius Castoriadis (1997), who speaks of 'radical imagination', Christopher Bollas (1995), who speaks of 'personal idiom', and Jessica Benjamin (1995), who speaks of 'the shadow of the other subject'.

Viewed from this perspective, the postmodern can promote a heightened self-understanding of imagination and desire in the fabrication of meaning in daily life. Against this backdrop there are risks and opportunities. The risks are that there is no guarantee that the reflexive scanning of imagination will prove solid enough to sustain interpersonal relationships; the gains are the capacity to proceed in personal and cultural life without absolute guidelines—in short, an increased toleration of ambivalence and contingency.

Perhaps the most important feature to note, however, concerns the durability of human imagination. New technologies and postmodern aesthetics can extend the richness of the sense-making process, furthering the questioning of preexisting categories by which we make sense of personal and social life. In people's changing attitudes to technology and globalization, identity has become problematic all over again. From the most intimate, personal relationships through to global processes of political governance (e.g., the UN), social life has become more and more structured around ambivalence and contingency. The dynamics of mind and world are increasingly treated as puzzling, and simple descriptions and explanations of social processes are discarded.

These identities of which I've spoken, the modern and postmodern, represent different ways of responding to the globalization, bureaucratization, and commodification of contemporary culture—of which I'll say more about in a moment. But let me stress now that we should not see these identity strategies as simple alternatives: the postmodern as something that eclipses the modern. Modern and postmodern identities are better seen, as Zygmunt Bauman (1991, 1997) has powerfully analyzed, as simultaneous strategies deployed by contemporary societies. Constructing a self today is about managing some blending of these different modalities of identity: a kind of constant interweaving, and dislocation, of modern and postmodern states of mind. If, for example, the signifier 'America' can today be used to fashion identities framed on a sense of global interconnectedness, democratic cosmopolitanism, and a postnational way of belonging, it can also easily be deployed in a more defensive manner, the production of identities held in thrall to the fetus and the flag.

INDIVIDUALIZATION: OR, STRUCTURALLY NECESSITATED IDENTITY CREATION

What are the broader social transformations underpinning such modern/postmodern identity strategies? What are the institutional reference points marking out the dimensions within which identities are fabricated today? And how might these modernist and postmodernist identity strategies affect citizenship?

There has recently emerged a massive level of interest in the notions of globalization, globalism, and global culture. Indeed, theory in the space between globalization and culture has been on the boil for some time now, having reached a level of pressure that is at once a deepening and a displacement. On the one hand, the discourse on globalization opens up new political, social, and economic flows that classical notions of nation, state, and society seem ill equipped to comprehend. On the other hand, the attention theory has lavished on globalism has often been at the cost of denying the significance of the regional, local, and contextual, the long-running poststructuralist emphasis on difference and otherness notwithstanding.

What has fueled such interest has been the emergence of a range of socially produced, institutional transformations: these include transnational communication systems, new information technologies, global warming, holes in the ozone layer, acid rain, the industrialization of war, the collapse of Soviet-style socialism, and universal consumerism. The globalization of financial markets, the increasing importance of international trade, and the advent of new technologies, in particular, define the contours of an advanced capitalist order, in which general deregulation and the marketization of culture reign supreme. The political ambivalence of globalism is nowhere more obvious than in the split it introduces between macro and micro levels of social life. In terms of macro considerations, it can be said that, if globalism has bulked so large in contemporary theory, it is because the deregulation of society and economy is fundamental to late capitalism. But deregulation is only one aspect. The other side of a labor market that demands complete flexibility and mobility is that of an increasingly regularized and standardized micro world. In this respect, social integration is portrayed as a blending of normalization (as described by Foucault) and the seductions of the market, the thrills of simulated pleasure seeking (as described by Baudrillard).

The division between a deregulated public sphere and hyperregularized private sphere is, however, surely unconvincing. For me, this is really but a variant of the idea of big institutions dominating individual lives, such as we find in the Frankfurt School's concept of the 'totally administered society' or Habermas's thesis of an 'inner colonization of the life-world' by technical systems. Perhaps the most interesting development in social theory in this context has been around the idea of individualization, an idea elaborated by the German sociologist Ulrich Beck in his recent books *Risk Society* (1992), *Ecological Politics in an Age of Risk* (1994), *The Normal Chaos of Love* (1995), and *The Reinvention of Politics* (1997). Beck's argument, bluntly stated, is that contemporary society is marked by reflexive individual decision making in a context of growing uncertainty, risk, and hazard. At once stripped of its traditions and scarred by all kinds of menacing global risks, contemporary culture radicalizes individual decision making and individual initiative. "Certainties," says Beck (1997), "have fragmented into questions which are now spinning around in people's heads." By this I take Beck to mean that the very definitions of social co-ordinates, ranging from love and sex through marriage and family to politics and democracy, are up for grabs, with new modes of life being worked out, arranged, and justified. Quite spectacular individual opportunities arise in this respect, as decisions (sometimes undecidable or painfully ambiguous ones) lead to further questions, dilemmas, problems.

Before anyone concludes that all this is little more than some manic upgrading of the narcissistic illusions of the ego at the level of theory, let me point out that Beck is not suggesting that individualization processes produce unfettered autonomy. On the contrary, individualization presupposes the internalization of social regulations, laws and precepts. Thus, the very social conditions that encourage individualization (e.g., detraditionalization and internationally mobile capital) produce new, unintended consequences (e.g., psychic fragmentation and the privatization of public, moral issues).

But the other side of opportunity is more than simply danger in posttraditional society. It is *risk,* says Beck, and risk on an astonishing global scale. In an age of commodified multiple choice, instrumental rationality, and genetic, chemical and nuclear technoscience, there is a diminishing protection of social life: We live to today in an 'uninsured society'. Whereas expert knowledge was once imagined to offer a sense of security from external risks, today science, technology, and industry are seen as deeply intertwined with the very origins of global risk. Global awareness of menacing risks is routinely discussed, interrogated, criticized, made use of, and agonized over. How can anyone know, for example, what possible effects the nuclear meltdown at Chernobyl might have on human bodies fifty years from now? And what, precisely, might be the long-term effects of global warming, psychologically, ecologically, and politically?

These are important questions, and experts disagree about the answers. Politically speaking, however, it is nearly impossible to predict the likely scenarios, energizing and catastrophic, arising from global interconnectedness. The critical point that Beck makes is that risk management and risk avoidance are constitutive of personal and cultural life today, if only for the reason that we are confronted by hazards and risks that previous generations didn't have to face: we live with risk on a global scale. After all, no one can "opt out," says Beck, from the consequences of ecological catastrophe or nuclear disaster.

But there are important political limits to the sort of reflexive risk calculation that Beck claims late modernity has ushered into existence. Perhaps most important, what gets displaced here are some of the more pernicious effects of deregulation on social reflexivity. In a deregulated, market-driven society, significant constraints impinge on our capacities for risk monitoring and risk calculation. Of key importance here is the *privatization of risk*. Today, risk is increasingly "dumped" into the individualized world of acting subjects; risk is presented as a series of technical problems to be individually coped with and reacted to through individual effort. More and more, our cultural know-how is shaped by scientifically preselected and predefined risks. But rather than acknowledge the hiatus between global processes of risk production that are largely beyond the control of their victims and the denial of risk in the public sphere, we are returned to the dumping of risk at an individual level, a dumping that can be connected with the individualization and subpoliticization of civic concerns, of which more shortly.

NEW PATHS OF CITIZENSHIP

Let me, at this point, extend the preceding discussion by focusing on the new paths—at once personal and political—of citizenship created by the institutional influences of globalization, mass media and new communication technologies, modernity and postmodernization. A systematic account of citizenship in an age of reflexive risk and postmodernization might be elaborated as follows:

Context	*Modes*	*Sites*
Subjectivity	Subject/self relation, as mediated by conscious/ unconscious dualism	Psyche, body, identity, differentiation

Intersubjectivity	Self/other relation, as mediated by boundary maintenance of identity/difference	Association, relationship, emotional literacy
Subpolitics	Communal points of opening/ closure	Civic discourse, disruption, reproduction
Globality	Global/local nexus	Mass media, United Nations, social movements, transdisciplinarity

In the realm of modes and sites, there are many points of overlap—such that it makes little sense to attempt to define any axiomatic neatness here. Nonetheless, we can identify these categories in summary form.

1. The self-construction, self-elaboration, self-staging and self-revision of the *subject as citizen* is a new mode of arranging life strategies. What is at issue here is not the traditional connection of welfare policies and national solidarity as a means of confronting the social inequalities of late capitalism, but rather the reflexive scanning of the subject at those nodal points in which identity, biography, citizenship, social networks, and administrative systems are looped. This may, of course, and it often does, take the form of the individual as citizen in the frame of welfare systems (i.e., unemployment and health benefits). The important point today, however, is that involvement in welfare systems constitutes individuals as at once *subject to subsystems of administration and regulation, and also bearers of individual rights.*

"Most social welfare rights," says Beck (1997: 97),

are *individual* rights. Families cannot lay claim to them, only individuals, more exactly, working individuals (or those who are unemployed but willing to work). Participation in the material protections and benefits of the welfare state presupposes labour participation in the greatest majority of cases. . . . All these requirements . . . do not command anything, but call upon the individual kindly to constitute himself or herself *as an individual,* to plan, understand, design and act—or to suffer the consequences which will be considered self-inflicted in case of failure.

Individualization in this context might be taken to mean "do-it-yourself citizenship," as various governmental and collective agencies—including the education system, welfare networks, and the labor market—compel people to devise new ways of life and interaction. In these circumstances, the personal or subjective dimensions of citizenship are raised to the second power. Questions and issues surrounding self-identity, sexuality, gender, the body, as well as the relationship between human beings and nature, become political in a new sense: Today's world is becoming increasingly reflexive in terms of the problematization of human subjectivity, and crucially this raises matters concerning both economic and cultural resources for the development and expansion of citizenship.

Indeed, much recent social theory has concentrated on the suffering and frailty of the human body as a basis for human rights and civic concern (Turner 1993a, 1993b, 1997; Morris 1996; Clarke 1996). Such attempts to place citizenship studies in the wider context of a sociology of self and body reflect an individualization of culture to the degree that there is a questioning of the traditional division between private and public, and in particular a questioning of the personal/political vicissitudes in which civics is experienced and embodied. This type of *individualization of citizenship* demands a thorough-going revision of the groundwork of what counts as community and solidarity, and thus it presumes high levels of autonomy and self-reflection—capacities that, due to the insidious influence of commodification and technoscience, are more and more under threat.

2. The language of citizenship is framed, reproduced, and redefined through intersubjective involvement in the sociopolitical field, those spaces in which self and other embrace and define boundaries of identity and difference. Citizenship, in this sense, liberates us from the prison house of self-referentiality and becomes a primary social-historical site for explorations in both solidarity and subordination.

The prime theorist of intersubjectivity in social theory is Habermas. Against the backdrop of the Frankfurt School's Weberian antimodernism, Habermas's innovation was his introduction of the distinction between "life-world" and "systems reproduction" in the context of an intersubjective theory of communication. Instrumentalization—the colonization of the life-world by systems logic—is Habermas's version of Horkheimer and Adorno's "dialectic of enlightenment"; but, crucially, he is also able to unpack the more progressive, democratic advances of modernity. Habermas sees political conflict and ambivalence as central to the world of late modernity, and it is here that issues about citizenship and civic intervention arise.

However, partly for reasons associated with his interpretation of Freud and psychoanalysis, and partly for reasons associated with his privileging of methodological concerns over more substantive issues, Habermas's theory of intersubjectivity is a highly idealized one—concerned as it is with the justification of certain universal norms. Many commentators have criticized his intersubjective realm for its purely cognitive, linguistic and formalistic bent, while others have pointed out that it reinstates rationalistic oppositions between reason and unreason, subject and object, knower and known, active and passive, and so forth (Benhabib 1992; Elliott 1999; Whitebook 1995).

The complexities of these debates are not my central concern here. Rather than trace these out, what I want to note is both the Habermasian theory of intersubjectivity, as well as attempts to develop a post-Habermasian account of intersubjective contexts (see Benjamin 1998), are important for analyzing the shifting, differentiated components of citizenship, culture, and society. For intersubjectivity, in both its Habermasian and post-Habermasian varieties, signifies the subject-to-subject context in which individuals and groups live with, work through, and manage the uncertainties and anxieties of contemporary civics.

The intersubjective underpinnings of citizenship, with its constant cognitive and affective interchanges among individuals and groups, is at the heart of processes of individualization. In the Habermasian frame of intersubjective solidarity, strategies tend to be project oriented, with clearly defined forms of policy regulation, political territoriality, collective goals, as well as a strict normalization of the behaviors and boundaries considered appropriate to civil society. In this frame, the language of citizenship functions through forms of inclusion and exclusion, usually through the institutional domain of the nation-state. In particular, various minority groups—such as aboriginal groups in the white-settler societies of Australia, New Zealand, Canada, and the United States—are excluded and subordinated in modernist patterns of citizenship; and there is no doubt that the idea of assimilation has been one of the most brutal ways of destroying aboriginal cultures. Such repressive types of citizenship definition, however, are increasingly subject to postmodern critique. In the post-Habermasian frame of intersubjective solidarity, strategies tend to be more fluid, revisable and self-questioning. In the case of excluded aboriginal groups and cultural minorities, the postmodern critique of modernist citizenship focuses squarely on the pernicious influence of ethnocentrism, evolutionism, sexism, and colonialism in collective decision making or community activities.

The civil condition so deeply socialized and disciplined in modernist and postmodernist cultural politics can be defined as *attitudes of mind with varying degrees of openness and reflectiveness.* Oakeshott's (1991) discussion of what he calls "intelligent relationship" has certain parallels with modernist encodings of civic expression; civil association, Oakeshott says, "is not organic, evolutionary, teleological, functional or syndromic relationship but an understood relationship of intelligent agents." In other words, modernist prescriptions of civic engagement emerge from purposive, procedural, instrumental rationalities, with tight and strictly circumscribed limits for defining the common political interest.

By contrast, postmodernity reconstitutes and recontextualizes the community spirit, at once enlarging the very definition of the political (via deconstructing binary divisions of private/public, center/periphery, real/imagined) and narrowing genuine interest in politics (through privatization, deregulation and sociocultural fragmentation). What Susie Orbach (1994) has termed "emotional literacy" is perhaps a key intersubjective resource in the postmodern framing of regional, local, national, and supranational civic communications. "Emotional literacy," writes Orbach,

> is about hearing another's distress without being impelled to smother their feelings; about allowing the complexity of emotional responses to coexist with commandeering them to simplified categories of good and bad; about finding a way to accept the differences between us without resorting to prejudice or emotional fundamentalism.

Emotional literacy is the call for a new agenda in which we restructure our institutions to accommodate and enhance our emotional, social and civic selves.

In other words, emotional literacy is both condition and outcome of postmodern responses to citizenship.

3. Entry to and exit from communities are regulated in many different ways, and these are based not just on gender, race, and class but also age, nation, region, empire and colony. All in all, the new spirit of community is one based on *strategic flexibility* in negotiating multiple forms of oppression, and such utopian civics implicitly rejects modernist modes of thinking in favor of postmodernist cultural politics. That is, politics breaks open beyond the formal institutional domain (witness the breakdown of solidarity forging through local government, trade unions, etc.) into zones of *subpolitics* and *subpolicy* (Beck), the politicization of social relations and institutional structures previously treated as *un*political. "Subpolitics," writes Beck (1997: 103), "is distinguished from politics in that (a) agents outside the political or corporatist system are also allowed on the stage of social design . . . and (b) not only social and collective agents, but individuals as well compete with the latter and each other for the emerging power to shape politics." This ranges from "single issue" actions involving local initiatives or health precautions to "planetary issue" actions involving global warming or the depletion of the ozone layer.

What matter from the vantage point of citizenship, in particular, are the communal points of opening and closure in the fabrication of relations of power that the realm of subpolitics now constitutes. As Bauman (1995) writes of the more fleeting, transitory citizenship practices of the postmodern:

> Like other events, such collective causes burst into attention for a brief moment only to fade out to make room for other preoccupations. . . . Very seldom do such "single issues" manifest or enhance the sentiment of moral responsibility for common welfare. Much more often they mobilize sentiments against, not for; against closing down a school or a mine here rather than elsewhere, against a bypass or a rail link, against a Romany camp or travelers' convoy, against a dumping ground for toxic waste. What they would wish to achieve is not so much making the shared world nicer and more habitable, but redistributing its less prepossessing aspects: dumping the awkward and unpleasant parts of it in the neighbors' back-yard. They divide more than they unite.

Bauman's citizenry of subpolitics appears as almost apolitical—no sooner constituted as collective project than divided, no sooner focused than fragmented. Yet the disruption and disordering of institutionalized political space are perhaps more energizing and associative than Bauman's account recognizes; after all, the civic inhabiting of "other spaces"—the margins and crevices of the social system—can be seen, as many postcolonial, postfeminist, and postmodern critics have argued, as vital to alternative critical imaginaries. But what Bauman does bring to our attention is an underlining of the fragmentation of the civic imagination; he highlights the immense difficulties in exploring thought, and also passion (which is distinct from excitement), in the "shared world."

There are also other reasons why a decline in shared public commitments and solidarity forging occurs in these conditions. Much has recently been written about various global flows, principally economic and financial in character, but the importance of immigration and tourist flows is also increasingly important to grasping the changing dimensions of citizenship. One of the most crucial implications arising from the massive global flows of tourists, according to John Urry, lies in its restructuring of people's conceptions of home, and with that the relationship between the home society and other societies. "Citizenship rights," says Urry (1995: 165) "increasingly involve claims to consume other cultures and places throughout the world. A modern person is one who is able to exercise those rights and who conceives of him or herself as a consumer of other cultures and places." If, as Urry contends, citizenship in the postmodern world is more a matter of consumption than of rights and duties, then this might be said to shatter once and for all the reciprocity of rights against, and duties toward, the political community that the liberal-democratic conception of citizenship is based on.

Yet it is unlikely that things are so cut and dried. For if people in some robustly entrepreneurial nations have been able to consolidate some travel and tourist gains *as rights,* it is also the case that such people are themselves transformed as citizens in the process. That is, how people define themselves as citizens is increasingly bound up with, and constructed with reference to, the changing world of space and place into which an increasing number of societies are being thrust. This is a point not lost on governments either, as the shift from taxation of income to consumption begins to take hold everywhere.

This is why consumerist notions of citizenship demand more critical attention than they have otherwise attracted. The critique of the consumerist citizen as the *negative index* of modernist citizenship is surely lacking in critical depth, since it allows one to reject the development of postmodernity as intrinsically repressive or oppressive. This is not to say that the privatization and deregulation of governmental and state agencies have not carried devastating consequences for the boundedness of communities and community spirit. Clearly, they have (see Elliott, forthcoming). Politics is today less and less defined in relation to notions such as "the public interest" or "common interests" than ever before; but the reasons for this have a good deal more to do with far-reaching upheavals in the social, economic, and political organization of world society than current rhetoric about civic apathy.

4. Behind these interlockings of subjectivity, intersubjectivity, and subpolitics lies the assumption that citizenship needs to be comprehended from the vantage point of a global perspective, or global paradigm, in the social sciences and humanities. And behind this, in turn, lies the current upsurge of interest in social theory about the collusion between globalization and regionalization, or proc-

esses of global-systemic power and rupture. While these issues are of core importance to grasping the reinvention of citizenship at the current social-historical
juncture, there can be little doubt that students of civil society have too easily
imagined a simplistic binary opposition between globalization and its others (difference, particularity, region, specificity). Yet what is clear is that there is an
increasing interdependence between these domains in contemporary social life,
such that neat conceptual distinctions between globality and locality become
increasingly forced and implausible.

As Roland Robertson (1992: 52–53) explains the need to overcome such simple opposites: "The distinction between the global and the local is becoming very
complex and problematic, to the extent that we should now perhaps speak in such
terms as the global institutionalization of the life-world and the localization of
globality." As concerns citizenry, we might well say that globalization is always
experienced (and constructed) from highly local situations, just as we might also
speak of the global production of the local concerns of citizens. Nobody, of
course, has ever witnessed a globality, in the sense of having directly seen global
warming or the depletion of the ozone layer. Rather, people are likely to find
themselves in situations where, to make sense of the risks surrounding the pollution of the Earth's atmosphere or of a limited nuclear exchange, the scientific-
technical knowledge of experts is drawn on and deployed to set about confronting
and transforming the local/global environment. This, after all, is how radicals
came to urge the imperative to think globally and act locally.

The point, anyway, is that globalization implies a radicalization of citizenship,
primarily because it brings into focus problems, risks, and hazards that are operating at a great distance from the individual; this is the global compression of risks
and responsibilities to which the *transdisciplinarity of globality* (Robertson) is a
response, at the level of the academy certainly, but also from time to time in
public debate.

Understanding the globalization of citizenship opens up interesting avenues for
examining why, in conditions of postmodernization, civil, cultural and political
dilemmas are at once rendered omnipresent and ordinary, overwhelmingly catastrophic, and genuinely common. Much has been written on how a sense of social
or cultural crisis today is being rapidly replaced by the more postmodern blend
of cynicism and distance, local spaces in which global risk environments are con-
jured into their opposite, or at least stripped of their power to shock and disturb.
Giddens (1991: 184) argues that today "crisis becomes normalized." Crisis
becomes "normal" in the sense that high-consequence environmental, economic,
and military risks pervade the fabric of everyday life, either experienced directly
or via the mass media.

More deeply, the postmodern thrust of civics and citizenship today is altered
because it is increasingly evident that the meaning of "political community"
involves a complex, contradictory blending of regional, national and global
domains. Gender politics, ecology, homosexual rights, the rights of children

against parents or the state, AIDS: civic rights today may arise from various inter-lockings of regional and global struggles, but the final court of appeal is increas-ingly centered on the world stage (e.g., United Nations' legislative enactments of civil and human rights). As Held (1995: 281) explains: "The political space for a cosmopolitan model of democracy . . . is being made by numerous transnational movements, agencies and institutional initiatives pursuing greater coordination and accountability of those forces which determine the use of the globe's resources, and which set the rules governing transnational public life." To this it might be added, transnational civic life is being *invented,* which itself is a *rein-vention* of the politics of citizenship.

CONCLUSION

In this chapter, I have sought to examine, mostly in broad stokes, some current dilemmas facing the social theory of citizenship. I have primarily concentrated on the complicated relationship between modernity, postmodernization, and the reinvention of citizenship, and I have examined in particular the altered global conditions of citizenship formation. In noting the institutional settings that under-pin the constitution and reproduction of modern and postmodern citizenship, namely the nation-state and globalization, I have attempted to show how some of these sociological concerns might be more satisfactorily analyzed in the frame of both personal and political life strategies. I then set out, in a strictly tentative and provisional manner, a range of issues concerning contemporary civic politics. These new paths of citizenship were divided in four key areas: (1) the individual-ization of citizenship; (2) the intersubjective framing of regional, local, national, and supranational civic communications; (3) the reinvention of citizenship within altered contexts of subpolitics; and (4) the radicalization of citizenship in terms of the interlacing of globalization and regionalization. My argument throughout has been that the foregoing issues are of the utmost importance to the analysis of citizenship in contemporary social theory.

8

Politics and Social Theory

Political science, it would seem, is a discipline currently in crisis. Today, at the dawn of the twenty-first century, those who like to regard themselves as political scientists are struggling to come to grips with quite profound changes in contemporary political life. These very considerable changes—such as the impact of processes of globalization, transnational communication systems, the industrialization of war, the collapse of Soviet-style socialism, and the increasing privatization of public issues—have dramatically altered the very "object" of analysis of political science: the contemporary political world. However, these institutional developments are highly complex in character, and it is by no means clear that political science is currently able to meet the challenges posed by these concrete political changes. In a period when political research is less well funded than it was, the discipline of political science, it would seem, remains unable to break from the hold of traditionalist conceptions of power, reason, subjectivity, and knowledge; the foundational assumptions of political science as a discipline and its dominant configurations of knowledge render it unable to engage with, or account for, the transforming political practices and discourses of the twenty-first century. Indeed the American political scientist and feminist scholar Jane Flax (1995: 3), delivering the keynote address to the 1995 Australasian Political Science Association Conference, has contended that "the gap between contemporary political life and the issues that preoccupy the discipline is growing."

How accurate is such a view of the current intellectual stock market fortunes of political science? Certainly many leading political thinkers would reject the suggestion that the discipline is in any kind of crisis. There is undoubtedly a conventional view that the key terms of political science—power, the nation-state, democracy, and the like—are adequate to the task of analyzing a range of institutional issues which are the proper province of the discipline; and, from this angle, the relation between theoretical and institutional concerns in political science is

166

one of complementarity. This conventional standpoint is not one that I wish to discard altogether. But I do want to argue, like Flax, that there is a growing gap or lag between contemporary political life and the key intellectual concerns of political science. My suggestion is that this disjuncture has its roots in the current insulation of political science from a series of transitions in critical social theory particularly and the social sciences more generally. These transitions relate to both substantive and epistemological matters, and they include radical reconceptions of the nature of power and domination, new theories of human subjectivity and human agency, and the problematizing of knowledge, truth, and justice. While these transitions derive from a wide range of intellectual sources, they have come to be predominantly associated with the intellectual traditions of critical theory, psychoanalysis, and postmodernism.

In this chapter, I want to discuss the problematic of power in relation to both political science and current problems in social theory. In discussing ways in which power is reacted to, and dealt with, in political science, I shall argue that there are two different *political modes* of conceptualizing power: one modern, the other postmodern. I shall argue that the drafting and perpetuation of modernist power have been central to political science as an intellectual tradition, and I shall endeavor to trace displacements of postmodernist power in contemporary political science as rooted in anxiety, an anxiety over the present uncertainty of contemporary political life. Throughout the chapter, I shall explore both the way that political science enables a comprehension of power relations and the way social theory opens questions about the intellectual adequacy of political science, especially with regard to the question of power. My general argument is that contemporary transformations in social-theoretical thinking as a whole are not only relevant to the core concerns of political science, but, if treated with full seriousness, they radically restructure the connections between political science and politics more broadly conceived.

Some provisos are in order here, however. First, I make no claim in this chapter to cover all of the significant issues raised by the ambiguities of power in the discourse of contemporary political science. Many core issues in political science touch on the question of power, such as democratization and the nation-state, that I mostly gloss over. What I am instead attempting to consider are some of the key contributions of social theory to the analysis of power and further to examine ways in which the complex structuration of power relations in the late modern age is constituted and sustained in the discourse of political science. Accordingly, I have necessarily sketched the contours of political science in broad strokes, in order to suggest ways in which the discipline might draw with profit from contemporary social theory.

Second, it must be stressed at the outset that the framework I develop in this chapter for the analysis of modernist and postmodernist power relations has little to do with the understanding of contemporary political life promoted in poststructuralist circles. While certainly drawing on some core ideas associated with poststructuralism, I think it must be recognized that there are significant limitations to the understanding of modernity and postmodernity as advanced by poststructuralist thinkers. This is especially the case as regards the view that postmodernity is a political epoch beyond modernity. Current controversies about postmodernity should perhaps rather be seen as the mapping of a world in which advanced modernity has run up against its limits as a social and political order. From this angle, postmodernity is not conceived as a stage of development beyond modernity. Instead, postmodernity—as Zygmunt Bauman (1991, 1997) has brilliantly analyzed—is modernity coming to terms with its paradoxes; it is modernity becoming reconciled to its own impossibility—and deciding, for better or for worse, to live with it.

MODERNITY, OR ENFRAMING POWER

Politics today produces fundamental shocks and challenges. Against the backdrop of the fall of the Soviet Union and political transformations in Eastern Europe, universal consumerism is now the order of the day in the world capitalist economy. Suddenly democracy is embraced by all, even throughout those nation-states in which the dark forces of nationalist and racist ideologies have violently resurfaced. The explanation for this state of affairs, according to the celebrated view of Francis Fukuyama (1992), is that history has come to an end. With the internal decomposition of communism, says Fukuyama, the spread of liberal democracy prevails and is prized for its capacity to generate social solidarity and autonomy. The end of history, for Fukuyama, spells a twilight for the time-binding and time-bound exercise of power politics as a force in world construction.

Yet such a view of current institutional transformations is at best one-sided. Characteristic of our lives today are also troubles that thoroughly penetrate, and indeed constrain, global politics. The pollution of the Earth's ecosystems, overpopulation, the awesome destructive power of nuclear weapons, the instability of global economic mechanisms, and the persistence of sexual violence: These are some of the most difficult problems facing contemporary culture and politics. But what chances for an exercising of political imagination in the face of multinational, geopolitical networks of contemporary power arrangements? If history has not come to an end but is rather reflexively pushed to its limits in social and cultural life today, how are we to think of the political products of power in the crisis management of world affairs?

Power is, perhaps, the one constant principle of all political strategies. The effects of power involve, among other things, a shifting of attention from the realm of the possible to the realm of necessity; a transmutation from the socially fashioned and culturally constructed to that of immutable laws, rules, and regulations; a transmutation that invisibly strips the frantic political interactions that shape deployments of power of their own constitution, magically transforming the exercise of power into an ideological, naturalized realm of the 'forever'. But if to think of power—and especially to think it otherwise—is itself to engage in politics, what frames the conceptualization of power in political scientific models? What is the politically constructed status of power in political science?

I propose that there are two core *political modes* that inform our understandings of power in the contemporary critical climate, one modernist and the other postmodernist. I further propose that political science remains predominantly wedded to a modernist view of power relations, a view of power that it in some part helped to construct, and for which reason the discipline has been reluctant to embrace an alternative, postmodernist conceptualization of power (a conceptualization either drained of substance or cast as "outside" the discipline by many political scientists).

Certainty, order, control, and mastery inform the very assumptions of mainstream, modernist political science. Political science can be narrated as a story of the self-mastery of the political field, a field heterogeneous and plural but that under the intellectual supremacy of political scientists is rendered knowable, open to rational calculation, and, above all, subject to the administrative and bureaucratic refashioning of the state (see, e.g., Easton, Gunnell, and Graziano 1991; Dryzek and Leonard 1998). Power—political, coercive, economic—is in this sense constructed as a narrative of the dominating group and the dominated; this is a narrative that is, it might be added, especially to the liking of the power shapers and power holders of modernity. Yet this one constant principle of all political strategies—that is, power—refuses containment, classification, ordering. "Unfortunately," Talcott Parsons (quoted in Lukes 1974) writes, "the concept of power is not a settled one in the social sciences." Or at least it is not settled to the liking of an intellectual strategy bent on certitude.

Modernity emerged against the backdrop of the disintegration of the *ancien régime*—the guiding ethos to substitute rationalistic, calculated, purposeful activity for the dead weight of tradition. The political form of what Jürgen Habermas (1987b) has termed the 'project of modernity', although assuming various guises, was one of progressivism: the conception of a single direction to history, the grounding of all human experience and representation in reason, and the endeavor to develop a rationalistic program of collective emancipation. Like modernity, political modernism set itself against tradition and in this sense contrived to bring the anticipated and unanticipated products of power under the scrutiny of Enlightenment rationality. Political intervention into the social world, and especially the conscious direction of power, was seen as essential to the remaking of the world according to rational design. In liberal political theory and political economy of the nineteenth century, juridical power—in its hierarchical, administering, prohibitive form—was very closely intertwined with the production and organization of state control. The regulation of state and economy according to rationalistic procedures could produce nothing but social good and moral advancement, thus guaranteeing freedom because of the assumption that conformity to an abstract neutrality and universality lent to politics an a priori certainty. In the case of political legislation, this meant the shaping of human beings according to the rules of Enlightenment rationality, the transmutation from that prepolitical state of nature theorized by Locke and Rousseau to the political legitimacy of the rights-bearing citizen.

Liberal political theory offers a specific interpretation of the constitution of modernity and also presents a specific view *of* modernist politics. In this modernist frame, power is a resource, to be administered according to universally applicable procedures of reason and that accordingly supplies legitimate claims to political order and control. Such a view of power is surely very limited, and it is no doubt for this reason that political theory in the late nineteenth and early twentieth centuries comes to concentrate increasingly on latent conflicts of power. The framing and intensifying of the bureaucratic power of the state, in particular, are perhaps the most important characteristics of social and political thought in this context. For bureaucratic and administrative power, beginning with Max Weber, is not only essential to the modern codification of rules (described by Weber as *procedural rationality*), but is in part constitutive of the regimentation of day-to-day social life. To the impact of capitalism and industrialism Weber adds the influence of bureaucratic regimentation in order to comprehend the complex, contradictory dynamic of power in modernity. With the regimentation of bureaucratic life—the strict definition of organizational roles, impersonal rule-guided activity, and the like—power becomes increasingly covert; indeed, it is this specific, veiled aspect of power relations that is brilliantly analyzed in the early writings of the French historian and social theorist, Michel Foucault. As Foucault (1977: 220–21) sees the transformation of power relations in the modern epoch:

> If the economic take-off of the West began with the technique that made possible the accumulation of capital, it might perhaps be said that the methods for administering the accumulation of men made possible a political take-off in relation to the traditional ritual, costly, violent forms of power, which soon fell into disuse and were superseded by a subtle, calculated technology of subjection.

Modern social and political organization for Foucault involves a transformation from overt violence to covert 'disciplinary power', characteristic of the prison and the asylum but also of organizations as functionally diverse as hospitals, schools, psychiatric clinics, industrial plants, and business firms.

Broadly speaking, in the evolution of the field of political science, until roughly the early 1970s, there was something like a "general consensus" concerning the nature of political power. This consensus was inextricably entwined with a positivist philosophy of science and the long-standing dominance of behavioralism. By no means all political scientists and theorists affiliated themselves with this agreement—one might instance, for example, Hannah Arendt, Herbert Marcuse, or Michael Oakeshott—but it did command the support of the majority of professional political scientists. The hegemonic position of this positivistic, behavioral construction of political science had several core features (of which more no doubt could be found): It sought to construct the science of politics as derived from the logical foundations of natural science, it designated quantitative methods of analysis as the preeminent method of research, it sought to displace political theory in favor of the development of empirical theory, and it dissolved the concerns of political theory and political science as interwoven.

Mapping discourses of power in political science and international relations, Albert Paolini has argued that—although such discourse has been fiercely contested within the social sciences and humanities—it has been remarkably free of dispute within politics, particularly in the dominant realist school. "'Power,'" writes Paolini (1993: 103),

> as understood in international relations is unaffected by the debates in contemporary social theory which have shaken the concept loose from its behaviouralist and positivist foundations. Power is simply not a contested concept in international relations. Its significance as an explanatory concept of the international system may be perennially challenged by the various critics of realism. It may be denied by the idealists. It may even be refined and made more intellectually appealing by rationalists and neo-realists. But the understanding of how power works, how it is manifested, is shared and constant. The operation of power, the "form" of power is viewed in similar terms by these theoretical positions.

A number of leading practitioners might be mentioned here in support of Paolini's thesis. Famously, Robert Dahl (1957: 202–3) defined power in strictly behavioralist terms: "A has power over B to the extent that A can get B to do something that B would not otherwise do." In time, this behavioralist view was supplanted with a more complex analysis that recognized distinctions between subjective and objective power interests. Lukes's supposedly "radical" view defined power as "A exercises power over B when A affects B in a manner contrary to B's interests" (1974: 34). Nonetheless, power was to remain a fairly one-dimensional concept. For example, Morgenthau (1978: 31), though recognizing both overt and covert manifestations, sees power principally in terms of domination and control—as an "expectation of benefits," a "fear of disadvantages." Kenneth Waltz (1979: 191) views power as the ability to apply "one's capabilities in an attempt to change someone else's behaviour in certain ways."

The background to this positivistic, behavioral institutionalization and professionalization of political science, as John G. Gunnell's (1993) recent genealogy of the discipline uncovers, is perhaps best understood as a kind of disembedding of concrete political power from the abstract rhetoric constitutive of modernist, academic authority. Scientific political analysis, says Gunnell, required the displacement of political engagement and critical interpretation in favor of the collection of data and the application of scientific techniques in order to render the complex, contradictory political field subject to imagined conceptual control and prediction. This indeed is evident enough in the construction of political science as "the study of *who gets what, when, and how"*—as emphasized in the writings of Harold Lasswell—but it is also implicit in the pseudotheoretical empiricism of political scientists such as Seymour Martin Lipset, David Easton, V. O. Key, David Apter, and others (see Merriam 1934; Laswell 1936; Wright Mills 1956). Significantly, Gunnell (1993: 263) summarizes the state of the discipline in the late 1960s in the following manner:

> At the very historical moment that events such as the civil rights movement, the urban crisis, the Vietnam War, and upheavals on university campuses such as Berkeley and Columbia were taking place, political science research seemed to ignore these matters in favour of the study of such things as voting. It had, paradoxically given the historical context, tended to endorse Daniel Bell's argument about "the end of ideology" as a conscious affirmation of the values that marked the unreflective complacency, conformity, and chauvinism of the previous decade. Social and political scientists such as Seymour Martin Lipset defended Western liberal democracy and pluralist politics not as the "way" toward the good society but as "the good society in operation," and political scientists studying comparative politics adopted this as both a description of and prescription for politics in other countries.

Politics, says Gunnell, has been disconnected from the discourse of political science. Moreover, this aversion to politics has continued to influence political science in Gunnell's view; a wedge has been driven, so to speak, between concrete political life and academic political discourse. It should perhaps be noted that Gunnell argues that the recent history of the discipline is one that contributes to a reversal of this trend—although in a limited and partial fashion. For example, he argues that critical theory, especially the work of Marcuse and Habermas, has helped to reinvigorate a critical academically based political theory and science. But to this countertrend he rightly points out that critical theory, while influential, does not command the support of mainstream political science.

There is much of interest, I believe, in Gunnell's genealogy of political science, but it needs to be substantially recast, especially if we are to adequately comprehend the dialectical interplay of modernist and postmodernist versions of power, domination, and subordination in the contemporary epoch. Let me briefly sketch out a somewhat different interpretation of political science and its theorization of power (and specifically modernist power) here.

Contemporary political science, while internally complex and divided, continues to find itself caught within this ruthless division between power and knowledge, public and academic discourse—or so I want to propose. Two recent examples are rational choice theory and the theory of deliberative democracy. Rational choice theory is among other things an attempt to think rationally on a normative basis and to locate social decision making as structurally similar to individual choice. As Jon Elster (1991: 117) details this:

The central *explananda* of rational choice theory are *actions*. To explain an action, we must first verify that it stands in an optimizing relationship to the desires and beliefs of the agent. The action should be the best way of satisfying the agent's desires, given his beliefs. Moreover, we must demand that these desires and beliefs themselves be rational. At the very least, they must be internally consistent. With respect to beliefs we must also impose a more substantive requirement of rationality: they should be optimally related to the evidence available to the agent.

This analysis of the rational, with its strong emphasis on action, agency, consistency and evidence, is grounded in a modernist dualism of subject/object, representation/action, knowing/doing, discourse/practice. Significantly, it contains highly problematic assumptions about psychical life and the mental processing of experience. For even the most cursory reading of psychoanalysis highlights that human desires and beliefs are always eccentric to themselves, shot through with the desire of the Other, located within the instabilities and discontinuities of language and symbolic signification. The search for internal consistency in rational choice is a search for subjectivity on the solid ground of reason, a ground that displaces and represses the specificity of the body, sexuality, pleasure, desire—as revealed in psychoanalytic, feminist, Foucaultian, and queer theory. But rational choice theory also functions as a double-encoding of modernist power, in Foucault's sense of the specific power relation between discourse and knowledge. To say this is to say that rational choice theory not only treats the political field as the effect of the rational/irrational calculation of action, but that in so doing it also fixes this dulled and degraded, instrumental relation to knowledge as central to social practice; the scientific discourse of rational choice enters into, and reconstitutes, the political field that it purports to describe.

So, too, the theory of deliberative democracy, as developed in the writings James Fishkin, Joshua Cohen, and David Miller, might be regarded as a good instance of Foucault's theorem of the interrelations of power and knowledge. Deliberative democracy, as represented by these authors, is a conception of democracy that treats human subjects as autonomous agents capable of self-reflection and of forming reasoned decisions; it accepts that politics is a contested arena, an arena that raises many questions which have no clear-cut answers; and proposes therefore that it is necessary to attempt to institutionalize mechanisms that facilitate open discussion in the process of collective decision making. "The emphasis in the deliberative conception," writes Miller (1993: 57), "is on the way in which a process of open discussion in which all points of view can be heard may legitimate the outcome when this is seen to reflect the discussion that has preceded it, not on deliberation as a discovery procedure in search of a correct answer."

The deliberative ideal, like rational choice theory, is essentially a modernist enframing of power politics however. It encodes modernist assumptions in so far as it treats individual subjects as autonomous and self-identical (and thus represses the critical insights of psychoanalysis in relation to the condition of human subjectivity as internally split and divided by the operations of desire itself). Furthermore, despite the emphasis on the open-endedness of collective decision making, it fails to explore and interrogate contemporary political specificities of difference and otherness (most notably, in the fields of sexuality, gender, and race) and of how in particular deliberation is itself regulated by the imperatives of patriarchal power, the lures of cultural conformity, the fantasized and sociosymbolic structuration of race/gender relations, and the like.

The political science discourses of rational choice and deliberative democracy not only are dominated by modernist notions of subjectivity, reason, power, politics, and the state but also (re)inscribe a modernist mixture of a properly secure knowledge and scientism at the heart of political authority, of authority as the central organizing category that marks the turbulent relationship between intellectual life and mass culture. That is, these discourses, in some more properly structural sense, are bids for power: an invoking of authority and power in the designation of a scientific relation between rationality and politics or of democracy and politics; a bid for articulating the discursive location of the political within Enlightenment metanarratives of science; a commitment to the modernist split between the intellectual classes, the political classes, and the masses. As power bids, these discourses reflect and reproduce a core dimension of our collective thinking and our collective fantasies about politics and reality. To such a dimension correspond not only those conceptual bids for power (the authority of sure knowledge) inscribed in the tracking down of the sphere of the rational and of the democratic but also the specific domain of specialized training and practice that helps to secure the elevated social position of academic discourse and of which the sociologist Pierre Bourdieu (1984) designates as part and parcel of the twentieth-century self-mastering dialect of 'distinction'. By contrast, the conception of postmodernist knowledge, as we will see, is an attempt to cut through this particular dilemma of self-mastery through a turning of politics and the political back against itself.

To summarize all this, there is a broad modernist approach to the conceptualization of power in political science as a discipline (see also table 8.1). Such a modernist conception of power is varied in its conceptual, institutional, and political effects, permitting the exercise of professional and political authority through the production of truth regimes and fixing the time–space designation of the political sphere through the intertangling of scientific production and institutional reorganization. There are several core attributes to this modernist construction of power in political science:

1. The production of structures of power, domination, and oppression are analyzed against a conceptual backdrop of the distinction between scientific knowledge and political reality, with the former firmly separated from the latter and imagined immune to the interlockings and transformations of

power itself. This modernist construction of power expresses itself as a search for objectivity, sure knowledge, certitude, mastery (encoded as the professional authority of academic discourse).

2. Modern politics is grounded in a series of binary oppositions, such as subject/object, individual/history, psychological/social, masculine/feminine, nature/culture, truth/falsehood, knowing/doing, representation/action, and discourse/practice. Such oppositions underpin the disciplinary assessment of relations of power and modes of political legitimation.

3. Structures of political power involve the elevation of a privileged group at the expense of other, subordinated groups. Such political positions are constructed as generally fixed and stable; the juridical conception of power is one of hierarchy and prohibition. The effects of power are thus determined and determinable, subject to a natural science logic of cause and effect.

4. Relations of power, domination, and oppression are the result of very different structural levels of human activity—generally divided between the political, the coercive, and the economic. While in reality these different forms of human activity overlap in complex ways, modernist constructions of knowledge create a functional link between such categorizations and the determination of power.

POSTMODERNITY, OR THE PLURALIZATION OF POLITICAL POWER

All this, let me repeat, takes place as political science *making itself* (a making of itself in which the political unconscious has been central): the training and/or drilling of political scientists; the refashioning of complex, contradictory fields of social interaction into orderly and systematic rules governing the operations of power; the conceptual construction of authority and domination as differentiated in the name of universalization. But if certitude and order are crucial to the thinking of power in modernity, knowledge of the contingency of power relations becomes increasingly prevalent during the postmodernist stage of modernity. For the postmodern mind, power is inherently fragmented, discontinuous, multifaceted, drifting, and unstable. Indeed, most attributes of the postmodern conception of power, listed persuasively by Gilles Deleuze, disrupt a continuous, linear con-

Table 8.1. Modernist forms of political power

Form	Resources	Institutions
Political power	Domination	The nation-state
Coercive power	Violence	The military, police, prisons, etc.
Economic power	Class	Commercial enterprises

struction of political domination and serve to problematize and transform existing intellectual and pragmatic frameworks of the topic in politics. Where
modernist and postmodernist conceptualizations of power differ, and differ fundamentally, concerns the containability, or rather uncontainability, of the political activity of producing, perpetuating and transforming symbolic forms; and, as
poststructuralists have gone a long way in showing, the issue of containment is
not something from which the academy is itself protected.

On this uncontainability, Deleuze's Nietzchean discourse discloses a world of
power that is multidimensional, shifting, fractured. Deleuze recasts power as
"nomadological" and "rhizomatic"—the site of unexpected libidinal intensities,
new productivities with other objects and persons, multiple forces of difference
(Deleuze 1988, 1990, 1994; Deleuze and Guattari 1987). His analysis points to
the constitutive dynamics of space, spatialization, and movement in power relations, dynamics that imply the unexpected and the eruption of the heteronomous.

Postmodern power, one may say with the Foucault of *The History of Sexuality*,
is a political force in the production of significations, representations, values, sentiments, desires. Power appears here not as simply a constraining force but as a
mobilizing phenomenon; it is this that prompted Foucault to describe the generative capabilities of power as "biopower" or the "anatamo-politics of the human
body," capturing the political points of tension of technologies of bodily management. Power, says Foucault, is "capillary"; it penetrates to the core of the human
body; it is this that establishes the generative link between flows of biopower and
expert systems of political domination. Today, for example, human beings are at
once empowered and constrained by political programs aimed at the regulation
and standardization of bodily existence as well as the reproduction of normative
discourses of sexuality, especially dominant heterosexual discourses. A range of
expert systems, from public health and family planning to social work and psychotherapy, are relevant here. However, those that are subject to biopower are not
necessarily submissive in their reactions to it; on the contrary, human subjects
are implicated in a mobile assemblage of force relations, an assemblage in which
individual and collective strategies and counterstrategies realign and transform
relations between power, domination, and subordination.

This specifically postmodern phenomenon of the pluralization of power is
more diffuse and heterogeneous than Foucault's work recognizes, however. (This
is the case because, as Peter Dews has cogently argued, Foucault's work examines only the installation of power in social practices and institutions and not the
modes of psychical/subjective elaboration in which power is reacted to, made use
of, and coped with. See Dews 1987. For a more detailed discussion of Foucault's
neglect of the turbulent constitution of the subject in power relations see Elliott
1996: chapter 2.) Paradoxically, deployments of power are brittle and short-lived
for the reason that a dismantling or deconstruction is built into its very operations
in postmodern times. For the relations of domination and subordination constituting oppression go hand in hand with that decomposition of politics today into a

flow of episodes. From this angle, power is the product of episodic contestation, and it renders visible, according to Jean-François Lyotard, the fundamental significance of *transformations* in the postmodernization of politics. The postmodern, writes Lyotard (1988: 31–32), is a perpetual present of transformations "in which the universe presented by a phrase is exposed and which explodes at the moment the phrase occurs and then disappears with it."

This is more, however, than just an underwriting of that linguistic uncertainty that poststructuralism maps; it is rather an uncertainty that haunts power politics itself. Politics in an age of uncertainty, like everything else, is discontinuous: politics, and here I include the politics of government, is about responding to problems as they happen; deployments of power increasingly take the form of problem solving in the short term (trading on the knowledge that public attention will have moved elsewhere by tomorrow); political forces appear today as a multitude of happenings, with little in the way for linking academic and public discourse, or indeed of personal and communal concerns (precisely for the reason that governments everywhere are deregulating and privatizing the activity of political living).

But this is also, and above all, the reconstruction of political pathways by which power now asserts itself. For the rise of inconsequential and forgettable episodes in the postmodernist stage of modernity springs from a reemergence of the passions in politics today. This is not just a matter of passion unleashed from the iron cage of a degrading, instrumental rationality; it is rather an affective reenchantment of the *political mode* itself. Postmodern politics, and the modes of power it spawns, is a world in which the constitutive role of human imagination is pushed to its limits (and here the extraordinary one-man effort of Cornelius Castoriadis in highlighting the creative dynamics of 'radical imagination' in European philosophy is of signal importance). This self-grasping of political imagination, which Anthony Giddens calls 'reflexivity' and Ulrich Beck 'reflexive modernization', might be thought of as a personal and cultural setting afloat on the troubled waters of contemporary society: tolerating uncertainty and confusion; living with otherness and difference valuing an orientation of 'not-knowing' as a fundamental precondition for reflective, critical thinking; and attempting to think the unthinkable within the turbulence of collective political identities.

What makes this self-grasping of political imagination radical, as Michel Maffesoli has argued, is that it forces a confrontation with the fragility of political association and action. Maffesoli (1988) speaks of *neotribalism* to describe a world of heightened contingency and indeterminacy. Neotribal power, which contrasts with the tightly structured boundary maintenance of ancient tribes, is a kind of power that is continually on the brink of complete self-destruction; membership is far from being determined once and for all but is rather a matter of self-identification, imaginary solidarities, and symbolic attachments—all of which can dissipate as fast as they surface. For the power of neotribes, says Maffesoli (1988), is a power that disqualifies its own self-perpetuation: generated as a defensive reaction to the flux of postmodern times, neotribes react to the inevitable frustration and indeterminancy of politics through their own deconstructing, dismantling, and replacement. The resurgence of nationalism throughout Europe, as well as in other political sectors of the world today, has been substantially based on such an unleashing of primordial sentiments and attachments at the local, regional, national, or continental levels, exposing the fractured and dispersed structure of the imaginary basis of intolerance (to the 'outsider' or 'other' of 'our community') as well as the defensive rejection of ambivalence and uncertainty in the context of globalization.

It is this fragmentation and dislocation infusing *spacings of power*, of its never complete construction as well as the deconstruction, dismantling, and reconstruction of its very forms, that frame postmodern attitudes and orientations to the integration and the discord between authority and knowledge, law, and judgment. In the postmodern framing of power detailed in table 8.2, the phenomenon is recast as part of an intersubjective dialectic in which relations between self and society are uncertain and unpredictable. Here the ebbs and flows of power relations are spread out between four interconnected points: identity, difference, society, and politics. The matrix through which power is constituted and reproduced encompasses the idea of identity (as a complex, contradictory 'wrapping' of desires, wishes, fantasies, pleasures, bodies, and practices) as refracted through difference, otherness and alterity; and it is this traffic between identity and difference, or sameness and otherness, that is inextricably interwoven with sociosymbolic discourses, knowledges, and forms of politics. The fractured, dispersed force of power relations is at once coming from nowhere (in the sense of there being no originating cause) and embedded in the vast structuration of activities and contexts in and through which we live, and give meaning to, politics. Power as a never-ending zigzagging of meaning and force confronts postmodern men and women as a ubiquitous feature of daily life, and indeed it against this shifting, discontinuous experience of power in the late modern age that the fragilities of subjectivity and knowledge, as well as the hopes and dreads of cultural life, are mapped and charted.

POLITICAL MODERNIZATION, OR THE POSTMODERNIZATION OF POLITICS?

It is perhaps surprising that, among the numerous works of political scientists who have concerned themselves with the epistemological implications of postmodernism in a critical manner, so few have analyzed the postmodernization of politics as a substantive transformation of political agency and political structures in a geoeconomic frame of globalization. Because of this, postmodernism is accorded some relevance to problems of knowledge in current disciplinary concerns; but it remains the case that postmodernity as an institutional problematic

Table 8.2. Postmodernist forms of political power

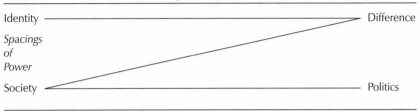

is politically and intellectually neglected in political science. A recent example is an edited volume by the political theorist David Held, *Political Theory Today* (a volume that contains contributions from such eminent political scientists as Claus Offe, Jon Elster, John Dunn, Susan Moller Okin, and Agnes Heller). In the introduction, Held (1991) raises the question of postmodernism for political theory and political science as primarily an epistemological one, characterizing modernist and postmodernist political analysis in oppositional terms:

> With their critique of all 'grand narratives' and their emphasis on the necessary plurality of heterogeneous claims to knowledge, theorists of postmodernism insist that philosophy and science have no privileged cognitive status. Most, if not all, of the contributors to this volume would seek to break with the objectivistic illusions once common in philosophy and science. Indeed, none believes that political theory can rest on any simple doctrine of an objective social good or pre-given reality. But all seemingly equally accept—contra postmodernism—that a coherent political theory is possible, and that systematic political knowledge, embodying generalizations about patterns of political life, can be achieved. (19)

Note the pitting of postmodernism against 'coherent political theory' here—a move that is as conceptually questionable, I would suggest, as it is politically loaded. In the book itself, however, there is no discussion of postmodernity as a political issue, nor is there any discussion of postmodern theorizing as concerns power, reason, subjectivity, sexuality, gender, truth, knowledge, or justice. The substantive issues usually associated with postmodernity are certainly raised as urgent matters for political reflection (issues such as the impact of globalization and transnational communication networks), but the question of the postmodern as such is eliminated.

Such a restrictive view of the implications of postmodernity is of crucial significance for political science and its potential futures. Indeed, if the implications of the postmodern for selfhood, culture and politics are as far-reaching as contemporary commentators imply—and here I invoke Fredric Jameson's classic headings ("The Waning of Affect," "Euphoria and Self-Annihilation," "Historicism Effaces History," "The Breakdown of the Signifying Chain," "The Hysterical Sublime" and "The Abolition of Critical Distance")—then political science is clearly called on to undertake a major rethinking of its key categories of analysis or risk sliding into conceptual, as well as practical, irrelevance. The coordination of the political with the fragmented, dispersed, and disconnected world of the postmodern would seem to have a conceptual urgency that is linked to very significant political and strategic consequences. Yet somehow it is this very call for a transmutation in the conceptual underpinnings of political science itself that generates anxiety across the discipline, leading often to a further intensification of theoretical denial and withdrawal, and sometimes to the more violent accusation that all this talk about the postmodern, the posttraditional, or the postcontemporary is nothing less than an ideological ruse that masks the legitimation crises affecting present-day politics. I have a good deal of sympathy with those who seek to reject the call of poststructuralists and postmodernists for the conceptual downgrading of key terms in modernist politics: *power, democracy, nation-state, hegemony, totalitarianism,* and the like. And I would further argue that the call for a 'transmutation' or 'delegitimizing' of the discourse of political science is itself vacuous since the advent of a postmodern political condition—or at least that condition analyzed by poststructuralist thinkers—renders the very idea of any such transformation pointless. More modestly, however, I think it can be maintained that something like a 'politics of postmodernity', as well as a 'politics of modernity', is required in political science. And significantly—contrary to poststructuralist theory—such a development does not imply that we give up the systematic study of politics. On the contrary, provided the poststructuralist account of postmodernity is rejected, there is little reason why the study of the 'politics of postmodernity' cannot generate a theory that is coherent, accurate, systematic, and, hopefully, critically reflexive.

This latter task, I suggest, is one that might best be achieved by treating modernity and postmodernity as distinct but interlocking modes of political activity, reasoning, orientation, practice, strategy. Politically speaking, we have not transcended modernity (even though modernist political forms are being pushed to their limits), nor have we entered a postmodern political condition writ large. Instead, it can be argued—following the pathbreaking work of Bauman—that the contemporary political world is one that deploys modern and postmodern forms of power simultaneously, although certainly not without significant tensions, ambiguities, and ambivalences. "Postmodernity," writes Bauman, "is modernity without illusions"; to which we might add that postmodern political power is a reflective deployment of authority which reckons into account the shortcomings of modernist strategies bent on certitude, order, and mastery.

Is it true that the rise of the postmodern uniformly drives out politics? Answers vary widely. Some view the postmodernization of the political as a lifting of the aesthetic to the *n*th degree, involving a vast shrinking of the formal political system and a concomitant explosion of interest in the individualizing identity politics of sexuality, gender, self-identity, ethnicity, race, and the like. The spread of such individualized or do-it-yourself politics is, according to critics, intrinsically *antipolitical,* a retreat toward privatism, egoism, narcissism, and hence tantamount to taking our eyes off the established democratic and economic rules of the game. This is obviously a critique that could only emanate from those entirely at one with the professionalization of politics and the bureaucratization of political parties. Other political commentators have taken much more seriously the growing levels of cynicism and disillusionment of citizens the world over with established political institutions. Various political experiments, sometimes labeled hypermodern or postmodern, are seen as resulting from this institutional crisis, and the predominant reaction has been to develop serious challenges to the institutional political sphere at the level of subinstitutional processes or mechanisms. As Beck (1999: 91–92) explains:

> [As] the formal political system shrinks, politicians and political scientists continue to look for the political in the formal political system and only in that system. . . . But why can or should the political be at home or take place only in the political system? Who says that politics is possible only in the forms and terms of governmental, parliamentary and party politics? Perhaps the truly political disappears in and from the political system and reappears, changed and generalized, in a form that remains to be comprehended and developed, as sub(system)politics in all the other fields of society. My thesis is that opportunities for alternative action are opening up in all fields of activity—technology, medicine, law, the organization of work—under the pressure of changed challenges and fundamental convictions. The old industrial consensus built into the social system is encountering new and different fundamental convictions: ecological, feminist, and many others. Technocracy ends when alternatives erupt in the techno-economic process and polarize it.

The spread of subpolitics, from the politics of cultural difference to the rise of ecological protest, is bringing a general sharpening of methods of organizing steering across all fields of political life. Each subpolitical demand might be said to draw from, and scan, the possibilities opened by scientific and technological advances only to outflank "objective knowledge," thus keeping politics local, self-reflexive, practical, and, above all, dependent on the needs and desires of citizens. For Beck, this signals a shift from modernist politics (systems over subjects) to late modern politics (subjects reflexively engaged with political systems).

Political theory, writes John Dunn (1985: 1), is primarily an institutionalized attempt from within the discipline of political science to grasp "what is really going on in the world," and what is going on in the world is itself structured by what is happing in society. It follows for Dunn that modern political theory stands in need of dramatic rethinking, or overhauling, "because it is philosophically so feeble and politically so maladroit." To which one is tempted to add, in the context of the present discussion, if political science in general and political theory in particular are "maladroit" in interpreting individual and collective political action, then this is surely a consequence of the failure of the discipline to keep pace with dramatic changes in political, economic, and social organization in recent decades. Although any such rethinking is not easy, the obvious point is that it is unlikely to become easier to engage with the given practical world unless a sustained, critical, and reflective engagement with the postmodern condition of politics is undertaken.

I cannot pretend that the discussion of modernist and postmodernist conceptualizations of power undertaken here has made a substantive contribution to such a rethinking of political theory and political science. But the discussion has at least attempted to address some of the issues surrounding the postmodernization of politics and in particular to suggest that modern forms of the political continue to survive alongside the advent of new fractured, episodic, self-reflexive, individualized, and subpolitical instantiations of individual and collective activity—in short, postmodern politics. The nub of the problem, as I see it, is whether the discipline can get around the methodological and sociological narrowness of its theoretical operations in the recent period and instead tackle head-on the vital and indispensable forms of political association and subpolitical activity that are transforming the postmodern political habitat.

9

Social Theory, Morality, and Ethics

"**M**odern technology," writes Hans Jonas (1984: 7–8), "has introduced actions of such novel scale, objects, and consequences that the framework of former ethics can no longer contain them." Living in a globalizing hi-tech world means living in a world where daily, routine, local actions may potentially affect thousands or even millions of individuals throughout the world, and not just in the here and now. Actions contributing to, say, global warming or the proliferation of nuclear weapons may have the most lethal repercussions for future generations—for our children's children. For Jonas, this is where the moral problem of our globalizing world lies—in that ever-widening gap between individual imagination and moral capacity, on the one hand, and the conditions of rampant technology and globalization, on the other. Indeed, it would seem that our individual imaginations are increasingly blunted in terms of ethical choices and moral responsibilities by the far-away consequences of our actions—thanks to the forces of capitalist commodification, the development of technologies, and globalization.

To understand the sociological and philosophical weaknesses of our ways of thinking about our moral responsibility to each other requires a rethinking of traditional conceptions of ethics. Matters of ethical significance, as Jonas has rightly drawn our attention, have for too long been narrowly circumscribed in terms of their temporal and spatial human consequences. But the problem runs even deeper. Moral responsibility, according to the modernist conception, was essentially rule governed in character; ethics had to do with laws, prescriptions, regulations, principles, duties. Today moral duty increasingly gives way to ethical dilemmas, and political philosophers endeavor to find new ways of framing moral-practical issues. But it is important to situate ethics in social context. This means looking at ethics and moral responsibility without losing sight of politics and culture.

Many postmodern sociological theories privilege a conception of ethics as open-ended, multiple, fragile, and self-reflexive, which is in turn further linked to the implosion of identity and fragmentation of the subject (see Smart 2000). However, there have been few detailed sociological studies of ethics as discourse or ideology. With the notable exception of the recent work of Bauman (1993, 1995, 1996, 1997), few of the major sociological theorists have in recent years carried out sustained and systematic examination of either the grand texts on ethics in modernist/postmodernist philosophy and sociology or the everyday practices that draw from, and help reconstitute, the moral and ethical domain. In this chapter, I shall examine both modernist and postmodernist texts and discourses on morality and ethics with the purpose of reflecting on what they tell us about identity and culture in contemporary societies.

ETHICS AS SOCIALITY, OR ORGANIZED MORALITY

The development of a moral world, as organized and organizing, is of major significance in connecting what at first sight look to be quite opposed outcomes: the legislating of an ethical code founded on Law, and the eradication of moral sentiments and moral responsibilities. What distinguishes the regulation and enforcement of "coded ethics" across modern, Western nation-state cultures is the sheer colonization of world space, established and reproduced through global capitalism and liberal political administration, in and through which individuals come to define and redefine the conditions of their subjecthood and its moral contours. The modernist drive for order, control, and predictability has generated a coded ethics of prescriptions and prohibitions, which in part has permitted the building of successful economic lives free from the strain of ethical turmoil, or without struggle in the daily linking of private and public, personal, and moral ideals; yet in the very act of so regulating identities, moral predispositions, impulses, inclinations, and emotions, the ethical sphere itself has, in fact, become liquidated of autonomous moral self-understanding. In this frame of organizing experience—what I shall call "ethics as sociality"—morality is at one with social rights and responsibilities, and more often than not moral principles are conceived in the image of Law and Order. There are, as we will see, different versions of ethics as sociality, and such orientations routinely advance rhetoric of an ethics free of conflict, disturbance, and anguish. Society, or the political state, or community, is viewed in this frame of reference as a supracollective foundation, exercising legislative authority and making juridical pronouncements in the name of ethical rationalities. At its best, ethics as sociality is realist in orientation, focused on policy questions, anchored in social context and security, and concerned above all with economic and political prosperity. At its worst, ethics as sociality is conformist, utilitarian, shallow, superficial, and passionless.

Since the dawn of what has come to be termed the modern era, the political state incarnates ethics, through a relentless modernist drive for order, control, regularity, and predictability—in a celebrated tradition from Thomas Hobbes to Jeremy Bentham. If modernism (the culture of the modern age) dreamed a single, unified dream of how ethics should be, modernity (daily life as lived in the modern age) took up this dream as challenge—legislating practices, codes, laws, and ideas in and through which it was thought society could move progressively toward a better world. A properly moral world, as derived from classical liberal political theory, sought to specify something more than just socially sanctioned rights and responsibilities; that something was the founding of morality in Law, ranked according to principles, prescriptions, rules, procedures, and laws. In civil society, the state drills citizens with the proper ethical sensibilities, inculcates moral qualities, and cultivates enlightenment and virtue as a way of life. From Hobbes onward, political thinkers have stressed that, only under the threat of coercion, will people act in a moral (read: systematic) manner.

"Certain principles of justice," insists John Rawls (1971: 21), "are justified because they would be agreed to in an initial situation of equality." Rawls's own theory of justice, which has raised methodological concerns in contemporary political philosophy to the second power, seeks to delineate procedural principles to which literally everyone would agree in a modern society by assuming "ignorance" of one's own particular material and social interests, or what Rawls calls "the original position." People in the original position are placed behind a "veil of ignorance" that makes them unaware of, say, their social status, their race or their gender. By delimiting the power and influence of personal and social interests in this way, Rawls attempts not only to define certain circumstances to which all people would come to agreement but specifically to ensure *impartial principles* to guide human action. Hence, the cool-eyed, sober, and judicious (though one suspects relentlessly manic, for as Freud noted the elevation of rational calculation is always and everywhere at the expense of repression of desire) search for principles—"the Liberty Principle," "the Difference Principle," "the Fair Opportunity Principle"—in *A Theory of Justice*.

Critics of Rawls have not been slow to note that his theory incorporates elements into the original position that are not fair and that his whole conception of justice is one biased in favor of individualist, commercial culture (see, e.g., Wolff 1996). What may immediately strike the sociologically informed reader here, though, is the uptightness of this entire discourse—that is, of both Rawls and his critics. This is an uptightness that prevents ethics from getting too deep or going too far. The important thing, after all, is the delineation of principles, the activity of formulating, detailing and monitoring "principled actions," and thereby keeping a firm distance from that "lesser" realm of moral calculating known as personal disposition, emotional response, or subjective feeling. Of course, the idealism is almost attractive, until one reflects on how hard followers of Rawls have had to work to reconnect the theory to any practical outcome. Here is one such commentator, picked almost at random:

It is important to try to keep clear that Rawls is *not* saying that this is what people in the world are really like. People are often envious, or irrational, and we certainly often do care very much about how other people's lives go. Rather, he is creating a hypothetical-fictional model of a person who will take part in the original position. . . . we end up with a view of people in the original position who are very unlike real people. But this is not a criticism of the theory. The conditions of the original position, behind the veil of ignorance, are not meant to describe the nature of a person, but to act as a methodological device; a device which helps us come to a view about the correct principles of justice. (Wolff 1996: 173)

Rawls's methodological device, it transpires, assists in a desubjectivization through which an allegedly impartial process about principles of justice can be derived.

The proceduralism inherent in such a conception of justice, morality, and ethics is particularly shocking when it persuades people that human desires, passions, needs, and intuitions are a shelter from principled ethical engagement—in effect a diversion from the prescriptions of moral life. In Wolfe's (1989: 125) rendition, "in a world where people raise children, live in communities, and value friendships, a moral theory that demands rational cognition to the degree that Rawls's does is little help and may well be a burden. It teaches people to distrust what will help them most—their personal attachment to those they know." We could add to this insight that, in the proceduralist reworking of justice, the ethical sphere is often reduced to proving and protecting yourself as an individual while laying claim to an approved moral position in society. Such sought-after principles create an ethics individualistic and conformist at the same time.

It is this codification of morality (laws, rules, principles) that modern men and women have inherited, and in which desires, beliefs, and interests are transformed via the purely instrumental space of rule-guided reason in the constitution of the social agent as a "moral person." The lived experience of identity in this mode of organizing morality is one of discipline; individuals committed to social morality are always mindful of rights, responsibilities, goals, and projects; such individuals have a strong emotional investment in appearing normal, decent, uncomplicated, and, above all, reasonable. In effect, these are people who can always be relied on "to do the right thing"—provided the "right thing" is fairly clear and obvious, does not require too much critical introspection, and above all will discharge the burden of social responsibility. This then is ethics as practiced by the Moral Majority, where rule following is culturally valued because it confers order, and order is thought to bring safety. Proliferation of rules and regulations is of course needed because morality left to itself would simply be too ambivalent, too unpredictable, and too risky.

Rule-bound morality is, by definition, intimately interwoven with the guidelines presented by moral preachers, ethical educators, and legislators of normative principles. Today, such guidelines come in the form of do-it-yourself manuals, in which ethics is modeled on technical know-how and organizational ability in the realm of social doings. Today's experts preach, lecture, advise, prod, push, admonish, cure. Critical theorists see in such social practice the arresting of self-reflection and human autonomy: The insidious effect of an expert discourse on ethics is the prevention of moral people from thinking their own thoughts, reflecting on the ethical impulse, or establishing internal communication with their own moral sentiments.

My preliminary remarks on "ethics as sociality" take their cue primarily from classical and contemporary liberal theory, along with modernist attempts to anchor morality in secure foundations, rationality, and legal conduct. Too much intellectual history, not enough sociology! Or at least this is arguably so for my analysis to be relevant to today's world of globalization, information revolution, and permanent cultural uncertainty. Yet the organizing of morality, or what I am terming "ethics as sociality," lies at the heart of the political paradoxes of contemporary social life; it would certainly be naïve to imagine that this classic mode of organizing moral conduct has dissipated. However, current social transformations have altered the internal composition of "ethics as sociality," and it is in present-day communitarianism, I think, that similar stories can be told about the nexus of ethical certitude, on the one hand, and the eradication of morality, on the other.

To pluralize the concept of culture, and to underline the political, critical, and emancipatory value of diverse communal memberships, is the stated intention of communitarians. In both its more academic guise and its more popularly elaborated versions, communitarianism—whose leading lights include Charles Taylor, Michael Walzer, and Amitai Etzioni—laments the decline of community in contemporary political life. If it is difficult to see quite how this critique applies to such deeply entrenched communities and forms of political culture as we find in Northern Ireland or the Middle East, it is perhaps easier to argue that the twin forces of globalization and the market produce a range of *closed communities*— defensive cultural enclaves, in which the rights-bearing citizen is regarded as central to the "superior" ethics of Western life. And it is precisely the rise of such closed communities that communitarians see as threatening the ethical fabric of politics altogether; to counter this state of affairs the argument is developed that solid, diverse, and pluralistic communal membership is crucial to advanced civics, ethics, and a mature sense of self-identity.

Communitarianism is only too familiar with the mutability and flux of contemporary social life, especially as this relates to the elevation of privatized existence over and above different manifestations of communities of tradition and history. But here the relation between society and the individual, between public and private, is apprehended, first, as a "problem" of a new philosophy of individualism, and second, as transformable through prescriptive legislation promoting the furtherance of public involvement. As befits a doctrine influenced so powerfully by American political culture over recent decades, the communitarian ideology is one that views society as disintegrating under the weight of the *primacy of privacy:* Too many rights, too few responsibilities is the key slogan emanating from the communitarian critique of morality.

Liberal political theory holds that no image of the good life is to be promoted by the State; liberals tend to the view that the principle of equality or nondiscrimination would be transgressed if society advanced a particular conception of the good life at the expense of another conception of what is good. Liberalism has thus long been unable to adequately cope with the issue of cultural rights. However, an unusual liberal version of the case for protecting and supporting differential cultural rights is advanced in Will Kymlicka's (1995) *Multicultural Citizenship: A Liberal Theory of Minority Rights.* Rather than place cultural specificity in opposition to universal rights, Kymlicka argues that cultural rights can be viewed as promotional of each individual and his or her ethical and moral development. "The primary good," Kymlicka writes in odiously utilitarian style, "is the cultural community as a context of choice, not the character of the community or its traditional ways of life". What this boils down to is that public policy may legitimately promote culturally specific rights, but the political aims or objectives of such legislative action remain firmly fixed on an individual plane. For liberals like Kymlicka, forms of life are valued not out of any particular ethical concern with the integrity or survival of a specific cultural form but rather because diverse cultural communities breed a multitude of choices, which the individual can then celebrate in true liberal vein as promotional of human self-development. Just how this argument works in the case of the political activities of the National Front or the Ku Klux Klan may not be immediately obvious. But what is clear is that Kymlicka's liberal rendering of cultural rights theory has been embraced with considerable enthusiasm by many seeking to come to grips with the postmodern recasting of citizenship and multiculturalism.

Communitarians such as Taylor and Walzer strongly criticize the hyperindividualist, utilitarian bent of liberalism. For Taylor in particular, any adequate political theory of the self, of morality and of ethics must recognize the foundational importance of interpersonal, moral frameworks, which in turn are strongly anchored in communal forms. The rise of subcultural demands made by communities in postmodern times testifies, according to Taylor and Walzer, to the diversity of claims for recognition and justice. The challenge communitarians set for society is then the protection of individual rights and the safeguarding of minority communities struggling to maintain themselves. Like any delicate balancing act, choosing between individual right and cultural cohesion is extremely difficult and complex. Taylor's own version of communitarianism proposes a model of deep diversity, composed of a unity of cultural identities without this translating into tyrannical uniformity—the measures taken by Quebec governments to promote the survival of French language and culture being the case that Taylor, a Canadian, worries over endlessly.

The communitarian critique of morality has been sharply criticized by many commentators, and it is worth briefly restating the more prominent of these. First, it is sometimes argued that communitarians, in calling for a renegotiation of private rights and public responsibilities, fail to acknowledge the importance of power and economic resources to the redrawing of communal boundaries. The communitarian diagnosis, as one critic (Smart 1999: 176) aptly argues, "steers clear of any critical consideration of the socio-cultural and economic forces which arguably are responsible for the undermining and fragmentation of social cohesion, and diminution of a related collective sense of belonging which has to be regarded as constitutive of community."

Second, and perhaps more damning, it has been argued that communitarianism is inherently oppressive and authoritarian, and ultimately dismissive of individual autonomy. Taylor's argumentation for the "goal of survivance," as one critic (Bauman 1996: 83) deconstructs it,

> calls for the right of the community to limit or pre-empt the choices of younger or not-yet-born generations, to decide for them what their choices should be like. In other words, what is demanded here is the power of enforcement; to make sure that people would act in a certain way rather than in other ways, to taper the range of their options, to manipulate the probabilities; to make *them do what they otherwise would not do,* to make them less free than they otherwise would be.

Notwithstanding their talk of "dialogue," "authenticity," and "cultural pluralism," communitarians, such as Taylor, construct identity as an impotent reflex of its social conditions; individuals can only construct "meaningful identities" from within the protected cultural traditions of their society, but this in turn means streamlining human autonomy. Communitarianism is thus at the same time individualistic and conformist. The trouble with communitarians, we might say, is that the discourse delivers one up to the (preestablished) culture, but not to know anything or change anything at the level of contemplating societal viewpoints or idioms, and certainly not to interrogate or question the self.

There is something resolutely defensive in all of this. In ethics as sociality—in which I have woven together conservatism, liberalism, and communitarianism as morally reductionist—the complex interplay between ethics and culture does not arise as a question, since ethics is regarded as a priori cultural. While reductionist, this is not necessarily a drawback, or at least not so for those whose habits of mind incline toward the ordered predictabilities of structured social life. Indeed, it is perhaps interesting to view political ideologies such as Reaganism or Thatcherism as the stunningly successful culmination of modernist powers of ethical enforcement, of moral security and tranquil ethics—however wholeheartedly economic libertarianism (with its intrinsic threat to moral certainty) was in fact preached in the doctrines of such political parties. This is the "realism" of ethics as sociality: Moral choices and moral acts are anchored firmly in concrete social processes and cultural conventions, and ethics is what happens within the limits set by society for interpersonal relationships and political association.

But there is also another sense in which ethics as sociality can be described as realist, and this concerns limitation and limits. The key message conveyed in various versions of ethics as sociality is that no amount of idealism or utopianism will bring us together as self-identical moral individuals and communities. There are just different versions of individualism, each of which fits more or less readily with prescriptive cultural forms, and the problem is how best to balance competing demands of self and society in a practical and rational fashion.

At this point, however, the drawbacks of ethics as sociality become plain. Inevitably, ethics in this frame of reference can only appear as stabilized, partly by cultural shaping and partly by self-control. Stabilized ethics is an ethics of discipline, of rule following, of knowing not only the right thing to do, but when and how to do it. Ethics here is, by and large, conceived as a structure of rules and regulations; such rules provide a means of escape from our moral capacity, not a means of exploring ourselves and our relation to others and the wider world. Yet subjective distance from our moral capacities is not the only drawback, since in some versions of ethics as sociality the autonomy of the self is displaced altogether. The most immediate consequence of ethics as sociality is to cast morality in antisubjectivist terms, and in particular to configure human subjects as mere ciphers of culture and social practice.

INDIVIDUALIZED ETHICS, OR POSTMODERN MORALITY

Let me now turn to individualized ethics, or postmodern morality. For many, the idea that postmodernity might be thought to spawn new ethical connections and obligations is faintly absurd. For these commentators, the postmodernist construction and consequence of ethics represents a wholesale individualization of the entire culture of contemporary social life; in our individualized world, moral problems are dispersed within a political culture defined by consumerist hedonism, reified technologism, the aestheticization of the social, and the pervasiveness of global risk. Against this societal backdrop, and perhaps not surprisingly, some theorists of the postmodern condition argue that we are witnessing the "death of ethics." Morality, from this viewpoint, has been replaced by a mix of consumerism and aesthetics—the attitude of "anything goes."

Thankfully, this is only part of the postmodern narrative. In a venerable tradition from Jean-François Lyotard, postmodern ethics signifies a version of social theory highly attuned to particularistic claims, minority opinion, local diversity, and cultural difference. If postmodernism lends itself to the development of an ethical program, it is one that privileges the debunking of universalism and totality, prizes appeals to instinctual intuition and passion in the formation of judgment, values irony and cynicism as a means for keeping a firm distance from intellectualism and elitism, while all the time remaining committed to self-reflexive subversions to give the slip to conceptual closure and thus authoritarianism. From this angle, the ethical virtue of postmodernism is that, although many believe it has cut the epistemological ground from under itself, its primary focus is the Other—that is, listening to, interpreting, and translating the differences and heterogeneity of social repression and cultural exclusions.

We are now in the realm of what I shall call "ethics as individualization." Ethics as individualization, as I seek to develop it, exemplifies concern, mutuality, and trust. But that is not all. Ethics as individualization promises a creativity to social relations that is considerably more radical than the preoccupation we find with communal solidarity and procedural fairness in other versions of political thought. The emphasis here is on curiosity, innovation, and imagination. In contrast to the controlled and competitive structures of ethics as sociality, with its hankering for tradition, rootedness, and community, the frames of mind that make up ethics as individualization work off person-to-person dialectics of morality and ethics, with considerable toleration for the ambivalent, the contingent, and the undecidable. In this postmodern rendering of social relations there lies the self-conscious attempt to situate a range of possible identities in relation to the cultivation of newly emerging moral sentiments and ethical issues. More concretely, there is a kind of *open psychological space,* I shall argue, in the most sophisticated portraits of the postmodern condition, portraits in which selves engage critically with the ethical dilemmas and moral difficulties which arise in relation to the culture of modernity.

The idea of ethical obligation or responsibility seeks to grasp something operating outside predefined social experience, something in the field of the Other. In so far as ethical responsibility for the Other is regarded as at the core of moral life, civic duty becomes organized around future consequences—a concern, for example, about the state of the world for future generations, the plight of our children and our children's children. But if the future is itself postulated (that is, imagined), what truly binds the subject to the Other?

The philosopher Emmanuel Levinas, in his magisterial *Otherwise Than Being,* presents an erotically charged solution to this dilemma, one that centers on the face. Face-to-face relations for Levinas are at the core of the ethical relation. "The Other," writes Levinas (1981: 83), "becomes my neighbour precisely through the way the face summons me, calls for me, begs for me, and in so doing recalls my responsibility, and calls me into question." Contrary to first impressions, in referring to the face Levinas does not mean physical appearance, the body, or looking at another; on the contrary, he maintains that hearing and smell are more important than sight in the realization of ethical responsibility. "The face," Levinas says (1986: 23–24), "is not in front of me, but above me." Paradoxically, the face is at once presence and absence, subject and object. The face for Levinas is Being, touch, caress, or eroticism; such intimate interaction restores the proximity of the self to another, and it is within this intersubjective relation that the Other's call presses in on the ethical self.

Face-to-face relations, the Other's call, the caress—Levinas's worldview centers on the vulnerability of the self in relation to others and to the world. It is this vulnerability of self, says Levinas, that leads men and women to feel responsibility for the Other. This is a primordial urge, an urge which for Levinas arises prior to ontology and before individuals are socialized into 'rules' and 'responsibilities'; such an urge is the nonfoundational core of moral anxiety. The sheer giveness of the vulnerability of self, coupled to the Other as a 'face' in close proximity, stirs up the most remarkable form of moral commitment: *being-for the Other*. Being-for, which Levinas sharply distinguishes from being-with others, implicates the self in forms of open-ended, imaginative, and radical social care. There is nothing contractual or reciprocal (as in ethics as sociality) in Levinas's being-for the Other. Ethical responsibility for Levinas is unlimited; the demands of the Other are unending and continue unto death; there is no rest or hiding place from the disturbance of ethics, no position from which the self might feel safe or secure in the knowledge that responsibility has been discharged. The ethical self is hostage to the Other; our natural inclination to care for others places the Other as asymmetrical and hierarchical in relation to the self.

"To be human," Levinas writes in *Ethics and Infinity* (1985: 100–1),

> means to live as if one were not a being among beings. . . . Responsibility is what is incumbent on me exclusively, and what, humanly, I cannot refuse. This charge is a supreme dignity of the unique. I am I in the sole measure that I am responsible, a non-interchangeable I, I can substitute myself for everyone, but no one can substitute himself for me.

In these reflections Levinas allows that ethics is ambivalent and can even be unbearable. It can be unbearable because Levinas sees no safe refuge for the individual within socially endorsed ethical norms—for norms or guidelines or foundations can only be a retreat from ethics. The ambivalence between self and other breeds insecurity and instability, yet it is in this messy, affective, and incongruent hiatus opened up from within the intersubjective relation, this impossibility of ever locating a comforting security of being, which provides the very source of the critical power of ethics.

If for Levinas an "ethical position" is a scandalous contradiction, so in a different sense is the subjective labour of founding the moral self. For Levinas, ethics is precisely ethics because of its indeterminancy, its stretching beyond self-identical identities and enlightened rationalities, and its impossibility of closure. It is not hard to see that Levinas's ethics is dramatically at odds with ethics as sociality. Where, in strong versions of ethics as sociality, responsibilities arise from contractual duties and secure legal foundations, the relation between self and other involves limited cooperation set within defined limits; in weaker versions of ethics as sociality, where responsibilities are seen as an outcrop of natural solidarities, the relation between self and other involves sympathy, trust, concern, and intimacy. By contrast, ethics for Levinas arises not from law and contract, nor from mutual understanding and sympathy but from the unsettled and unsettling mix of human autonomy, affect, vulnerability and frailty. As regards self and other, Levinas's being-for the Other binds people together, but leaves individuals free. This is ethics as paradox: the self is set half-in and half-out of the social relation.

In *Postmodern Ethics* (1993) and *Life in Fragments* (1995), the Polish sociologist Zygmunt Bauman builds upon the work of Levinas to assess the postmodern excavation of moral sentiments and ethical urges covered over by centuries of modernist denial and repression. Like Levinas, Bauman situates ethics before ontology. An ethical responsibility to the Other, says Bauman, is more unconscious than conscious; ethical sentiments are deeply innate, very much a largely unconscious affair, prior to ontological objectification. But while for Bauman ethics denotes the preontological, this does not necessarily guarantee the enactment of morality in advance, certainly not through any modernist book of rules nor any postmodern celebration of intuition. "There is nothing necessary," writes Bauman (1993: 76–77), "in being moral. Being moral is a chance which may be taken up; yet it may be also, and as easily, forfeited."

Bauman reserves some of his sharpest criticism for communitarianism and culturally relativist theories of moral responsibility, neither of which he thinks can adequately raise morality to the level of new, global challenges. These challenges presented by our globalizing world arise as a consequence of new information technologies upon self-experience and cultural pursuits and choices. It is here—in connecting moral dilemmas and ethical torments to the technological systemic forces of globalization—that Bauman advances beyond Levinas, raising vital political issues concerning the moral resources and ethical capacities of selves and organizations to exercise prudent and reflective judgment. In a world of TV satellites and cables that span the globe, says Bauman, we are made continually aware (and cannot help but be aware) of the suffering, pain and misery of distant other. As Bauman (2001: 1) notes:

> While our hands have not grown any longer, we have acquired "artificial eyes" which enable us to see what our own eyes never would. The challenges to our moral conscience exceed many times over that conscience's ability to cope and stand up to challenge. To restore the lost moral balance, we would need "artificial hands" stretching as far as our artificial eyes are able to. . . . Our sensitivity is assaulted by sights which are bound to trigger our moral impulse to help—yet it is far from obvious what we could do to bring relief and succour to the sufferers. Moral impulse won't be enough to assure that the commitment to help will follow the sight of suffering.

Moral responsibility, for Bauman as for Levinas, is a cleaving to the impulse to help others, without reward or recognition; such an ethical impulse is not on the whole something we can choose and thus is not something from which we can easily walk away. But in conditions of advanced modernity, it is far from clear how individuals and collectivities might connect up such moral impulses and the commitment and capacity to help others.

If "multiculturalism" and "cultural diversity" are part of what makes up the theories of today's moral theorists, the call to celebrate such diversity has gone astray, becoming disconnected from the issue of a universal human right to a dignified and secure life. While profoundly critical of the modernist political project to legislate universal standards of justice and responsibility, Bauman nonetheless argues that any serious defense of our moral responsibility to each other must start from ethical considerations of human frailty and individual self-esteem. To affirm the variety of cultural choice, without reckoning the elementary degree of human self-confidence and dignified life that makes such choices possible is the merest cliché in the mouths of academics, politicians, and policymakers whose key preoccupations are protecting the most affluent of society. The current "multiculturalist" rhetoric for Bauman is precisely such a discourse.

It is precisely from such a reconfiguration of difference, rights, and justice that the Italian cultural sociologist and clinical psychologist Alberto Melucci asserts that today we find ourselves in multiple bonds of belonging (communal links, associative networks, reference groups), in an infinity of worlds, travelers in the labyrinths of the metropolis—as "nomads of the present." In *The Playing Self* (1996), Melucci delves into questions about the self, subjectivity and intimacy, with particular attention devoted to the new challenges and opportunities for ethics and morality in the postmodern world. Melucci is essentially in agreement with the thesis of detraditionalization: the self/society links of family, state, and institutional politics are weakening, he contends, in terms of the power of custom and tradition, and accordingly the search for identity is now—and more than ever before—constructed in and through personal and institutional reflexivity. The shift from preestablished ways of doing things to open communication and dialogue accentuates the ambivalence of our decisions, choices, deliberations, and commitments; this shift produces a newly emergent fragility in which living increasingly becomes wrapped up in "living-with" others.

The thesis of "living-with" permits Melucci to challenge those, such as liberals and communitarians, tending to counter-pose individuality with community, identity with difference. As Melucci (1996: 116) develops this point:

> In order to meet otherness one needs to change form. We cannot communicate or relate to differences by simply remaining ourselves. In the issue of multi-culturalism, which implies some capacity and will to meet the "other," there is a profound moral implication: the necessity to keep and to lose, to cope with fears and resistances, but also with the ability of going beyond our given identities.

This is a very important conceptual move, I think, since Melucci specifically connects the issue of postmodern ethics to passion and emotion. The late modern or postmodern world for Melucci raises anew issues about ethics and morality because it reconstitutes our psychophysical relation with others. Drawing from psychodynamic research, he insists we are today facing a kind of "overmentalization" of relations of identity and difference—a process involving constant negotiation among different parts of the mind or versions of self, and dependent on the collecting, monitoring, processing, and translation of information pertaining to the self/other dialectic. The main implication of this psychic and emotional negotiation of identity and difference, according to Melucci, is that it raises the realm of the ethical to prominence. Without self-questioning, there is no problem of ethics.

At this point, let me comment on both the social utility and social limitation of ethics as individualization. We have seen that with Levinas and others, ethics becomes a kind of artfulness, a realm of pure autonomous interaction free of social conventions or cultural solidarity. Ethics is invention, creativity, playfulness, eroticism, open-endedness, utopianism. The principles of subjectivity and intersubjectivity are understood in this frame of reference in terms of the superiority of private virtues over social roles and of a moral responsibility over public opinion. Ethics as individualization does away with foundations; it is a realm without structure; it needs no rule book and presents social life as a world of vulnerabilities, torments, imaginings, differences, and unpredictabilities. For this reason alone, ethics as individualization is unlikely to win a sympathetic hearing in the world of institutionalized politics, with its relentless bureaucratic stress on ordered predictabilities. But there is also a radical political edge here, and this is surely that ethics as individualization is a *dissident cultural form,* one that contributes to imaginings that there are other forms of social life beyond the Left or Right, beyond competition or solidarity, as well as the critique of notions that individual subjectivity and social relations automatically correspond.

It can be argued, however, that while the elevation of private responsibilities over social roles in ethics as individualization is enlivening and radical, it also necessarily contains the seeds of its opposite—that is, the failure of intersubjectivity and social relations. Certainly the ethical relation in this mode of construction is complex, contradictory, intrinsically ambivalent, and exquisitely open-ended; but the moral impulse is acted on by individuals notwithstanding its inherent ambiguity, and it is surely for this reason that many believe it is possible to develop an ethically informed politics and even to insist on the articulation of ethical discourse within social institutions, private enterprises, and governmental agencies. Not so, according to postmodern ethics, which is relatively uninterested in social realism and is equally remote from politics—or so some argue. Perhaps this accounts for the esoteric feel of much postmodernist ethics; there is little concrete proposal or suggestion in the postmodern insistence on ethical indetermination, and for many critics such abstractness when joined with idealism only serves to produce a version of social theory that appears as little more than high-minded claptrap. From such an angle, the preoccupation with individuality, intuition, and autonomy that we find in much postmodern ethics, in fact, masks narcissism. To approach ethics as the protection of an essential preontological care for the Other is, in this critique, to maintain a pathologically fearful distance from a political culture that is viewed as debased and debasing. Thus, for all its talk of instant innovation and creative indeterminacy, such a standpoint simply fails to grasp the essential point that daily life for many people can be mind-numbingly monotonous, repetitious, routine, and dull.

CONCLUSION

In this chapter, the aim has been to connect ordinary moral dispositions and ethical orientations with the broader issues of political theory and philosophy, to link the ideas of theorists and philosophers with the substantially emotional and ethical meaning-creating activity of human subjects. By focusing on ethical diversity—the different moral views and different ways of life that individuals and collectivities hold to—I have tried to underscore something of the personal complexity and social complications of ethics and morality in contemporary political life.

References

Adam, B. 1998. *Timescapes of Modernity: The Environment and Invisible Hazards.* London: Routledge.

Alexander, J. 1996. Critical Reflections on "Reflexive Modernization." *Theory, Culture and Society* 13, no. 4: 133–38.

Althusser, L. 1984a. *Essays on Ideology.* London: Verso.

———. 1984b. Freud and Lacan. In his *Essays on Ideology.* London: Verso.

———. 1984c. Ideological and Ideological State Apparatuses. In his *Essays on Ideology.* London: Verso.

Amato, P., and A. Booth. 2000. *A Generation at Risk: Growing Up in an Era of Family Upheaval.* Cambridge, Mass.: Harvard University Press.

Anzieu, D. 1989. *The Skin Ego.* New Haven, Conn.: Yale University Press.

Archer, M. 1982. Morphogenesis vs. Structuration. *British Journal of Sociology* 33: 455–83.

Archer, M. 1990. Human Agency and Social Structure. In *Anthony Giddens: Consensus and Controversy,* ed. J. Clark, C. Modgil, and S. Modgil. New York: Falmer.

Arnason, J., and P. Beilharz. 1997. Introduction. *Thesis Eleven* 49: i–viii.

Bauman, Z. 1991. *Modernity and Ambivalence.* Cambridge: Polity.

———. 1992a. *Intimations of Postmodernity.* London: Routledge.

———. 1992b. *Mortality, Immortality and Other Life Strategies.* Cambridge: Polity.

———. 1993. *Postmodern Ethics.* Oxford: Blackwell.

———. 1995. *Life in Fragments.* Oxford: Blackwell.

———. 1996. On Communitarians and Human Freedom. *Theory, Culture and Society* 13, no. 2: 79–90.

———. 1997. *Postmodernity and Its Discontents.* Cambridge: Polity.

———. 1998. *Globalization: The Human Consequences.* Cambridge: Polity.

———. 2000. *Liquid Modernity.* Cambridge: Polity.

———. 2001. Quality and Inequality. *The Guardian,* December 29, p. 1.

Beck, U. 1986. *Risikogesellschaft: Auf dem Weges einem andere Moderne.* Frankfurt: Suhrkampf.

197

————. 1991. *Ecological Enlightenment: Essays on the Politics of the Risk Society.* Atlantic Highlands, N.J.: Humanities.

————. 1992. *Risk Society: Towards a New Modernity.* London: Sage.

————. 1994. *Ecological Politics in an Age of Risk.* Cambridge: Polity.

————. 1996a. Risk Society and the Provident State. In *Risk, Environment and Modernity: Towards a New Ecology,* ed. S. Lash, B. Szerszynski, and B. Wynne. London: Sage.

————. 1996b. World Risk Society as Cosmopolitan Society: Ecological Questions in a Framework of Manufactured Uncertainties. *Theory, Culture and Society* 13, no. 4: 1–32.

————. 1997. *The Reinvention of Politics.* Cambridge: Polity.

————. 1998. *Democracy and Its Enemies.* Cambridge: Polity.

————. 1999a. *What Is Globalization?* Cambridge: Polity.

————. 1999b. *World Risk Society.* Cambridge: Polity.

Beck, U., and E. Beck-Gernsheim. 1995. *The Normal Chaos of Love.* Cambridge: Polity.

————. 1996. Individualization and "Precarious Freedoms": Perspectives and Controversies of a Subject-Orientated Sociology. In *Detraditionalization: Critical Reflections on Authority and Identity,* ed. P. Heelas, S. Lash, and P. Morris. Oxford: Blackwell.

Beck, U., A. Giddens, and S. Lash. 1994. *Reflexive Modernization: Politics, Tradition and Aesthetics in the Modern Social Order.* Cambridge: Polity.

Benhabib, S. 1992. *Situating the Self.* Cambridge: Polity.

Benjamin, J. 1995. *Like Subjects, Love Objects.* New Haven, Conn.: Yale University Press.

————. 1998. *Shadow of the Other.* New York: Routledge.

Benvenuto, B., and R. Kennedy, eds. 1986. *The Works of Jacques Lacan.* London: Free Association Books.

Best, S., and D. Kellner. 1991. *Postmodern Theory: Critical Interrogations.* London: Macmillan.

Bollas, C. 1995. *Cracking Up.* London: Routledge.

Borch-Jacobsen, M. 1991. *Lacan: The Absolute Master.* Stanford, Calif.: Stanford University Press.

Bowie, M. 1991. *Lacan.* London: Fontana.

Boyne, R. 1991. Giddens's Misreading of Finsch Sociology. In *Giddens's Theory of Structuration,* ed. C. G. A. Bryant and D. Jary. London: Routledge.

Braaten, J. 1991. *Habermas's Critical Theory of Societies.* New York: State University of New York Press.

Bracher, M., M. Alcorn, R. Corthell, and F. Massardier-Kenney, eds. 1994. *Lacanian Theory of Discourse: Subject, Structure and Society.* New York: New York University Press.

Braun, D. 1991. *The Rich Get Richer* Chicago: Nelson-Hall.

Brown, N. O. 1990. *Love's Body.* Berkeley: University of California Press.

Bryant, C. G. A., and D. Jary. 1991. *Giddens' Theory of Structuration.* London: Routledge.

————. 1997. *Anthony Giddens: Critical Assessments,* 4 vols. London: Routledge.

Butler, J. 1990. *Gender Trouble: Feminism and the Subversion of Identity.* New York: Routledge.

————. 1993. *Bodies That Matter: On the Discursive Limits of "Sex."* New York: Routledge.

Cascardi, A. 1992. *The Subject of Modernity*. Cambridge: Cambridge University Press.

Castell, R. 1991. From Dangerousness to Risk. In *The Foucault Effect*, ed. G. Burchell, C. Gordon, and P. Miller. Hemel Hempstead: Harvester.

Castoriadis, C. 1982. The Crisis of Western Societies. In *The Castoriadis Reader*, ed. D. Curtis. Oxford: Blackwell, 1997, 253–66.

————. 1984a. *Crossroads in the Labyrinth*. Cambridge, Mass.: MIT Press.

————. 1984b. The Imaginary: Creation in the Social-Historical Domain. In *The Castoriadis Reader*, ed. D. Curtis. Oxford: Blackwell, 1997, 3–18.

————. 1987. *The Imaginary Institution of Society*. Cambridge: Polity.

————. 1989. Done and to Be Done. In *The Castoriadis Reader*, ed. D. Curtis. Oxford: Blackwell, 1997, 361–417.

————. 1991a. Dead End? In his *Philosophy, Politics, Autonomy: Essays in Political Philosophy*. Oxford: Oxford University Press, 243–75.

————. 1991b. *Philosophy, Politics, Autonomy: Essays in Political Philosophy*. Oxford: Oxford University Press.

————. 1994. Radical Imagination and the Social Instituting Imaginary. In *The Castoriadis Reader*, ed. D. Curtis. Oxford: Blackwell, 1997, 319–37.

————. 1995a. From the Monad to Autonomy. In *The Castoriadis Reader*, ed. D. Curtis. Oxford: Blackwell, 1997, 172–95.

————. 1995b. Logic, Imagination, Reflection. In *Psychoanalysis in Contexts: Paths between Theory and Modern Culture*, ed. A. E. and S. Frosh. London: Routledge, 16–35.

————. 1997. *World in Fragments: Writings on Politics, Society, Psychoanalysis and the Imagination*. Stanford, Calif.: Stanford University Press.

————. 1999a. *Figures du pensable: Les Carrefours du labyrinthe VI*. Paris: Seuil.

————. 1999b. *Sur le politique de Platon*. Paris: Seuil.

Chamberlain, D. 1987. The Cognitive Newborn: A Scientific Update. *British Journal of Psychotherapy* 4: 30–71.

Chodorow, N. 1978. *The Reproduction of Mothering*. Berkeley: University of California Press.

Cixous, H. 1980. The Laugh of the Medusa. In *New French Feminisms*, ed. E. Marks and I. de Courtivron. Brighton: Harvester.

Clark, J., C. Modgil, and S. Modgil. 1990. *Anthony Giddens: Consensus and Controversy*. New York: Falmer.

Cohen, I. 1991. *Structuration Theory: Anthony Giddens and the Constitution of Social Life*. London: Macmillan.

Cook, D. 2001. The Talking Cure in Habermas's Republic. *New Left Review* 12: 135–51.

Craib, I. 1992. *Anthony Giddens*. London: Routledge.

Crompton, R. 1996. The Fragmentation of Class Analysis. *British Journal of Sociology* 47, no. 1: 56–67.

Curtis, D., ed. 1997. *The Castoriadis Reader*. Oxford: Blackwell.

Dahl, R. 1957. The Concept of Power. *Behavioural Sciences* 2: 201–5.

Davies, A. 1972. *Essays in Political Sociology*. Melbourne: Cheshire.

de Lauretis, T., ed. 1991. Queer Theory. *Differences* 3, no. 2.

Deleuze, G. 1988. *Foucault*. Minneapolis: University of Minnesota Press.

————. 1990. *The Logic of Sense*. New York: Columbia University Press.

————. 1994. *Difference and Repetition*. New York: Columbia University Press.

Deleuze, G., and Guattari, S. 1987. *Anti-Oedipus: Capitalism and Schizophrenia*.

Derrida, J. 1998. *Resistances of Psychoanalysis*. Stanford, Calif.: Stanford University Press

Dews, P. 1987. *Logics of Disintegration*. London: Verso.

————, ed, 1999. *Habermas: A Critical Reader*. Oxford: Blackwell.

Douglas, M. 1986. *Risk Acceptability According to the Social Sciences*. London: Routledge.

————. 1992. *Risk and Blame: Essays in Cultural Theory* London: Routledge.

Douglas, M., and A. Wildavsky. 1982. *Risk and Culture*. Oxford: Blackwell.

Dryzek, J., and S. Leonard. 1998. History and Discipline in Political Science. *American Political Science Review* 82.

Dunn, J. 1985. *Rethinking Modern Political Theory*. Cambridge: Cambridge University Press.

Eagleton, T. 1991. *Ideology: An Introduction*. London: Verso.

Easton, D., J. Gunnell, and L. Graziano, eds. 1991. *The Development of Political Science: A Comparative Survey*. London: Routledge.

Elliott, A. 1992. Looking at Sex and Love in the Modern Age. *Times Higher Education Supplement*, September 11, pp. 18–19.

————. 1994. *Psychoanalytic Theory: An Introduction*. Oxford: Blackwell.

————. 1996. *Subject to Ourselves*. Cambridge: Polity.

————, ed. 1998. *Freud 2000*. Cambridge: Polity.

————. 1999. *Social Theory and Psychoanalysis in Transition: Self and Society from Freud to Kristeva*. London: Free Association Books.

————. 2001. *Concepts of the Self*. Cambridge: Polity.

————. 2002. *Psychoanalytic Theory: An Introduction*. 2d ed. Durham, N.C.: Duke University Press.

Elliott, A., and C. Spezzano, eds. 2000. *Psychoanalysis at Its Limits: Navigating the Postmodern Turn*. London: Free Association Books.

Elster, J. 1991. The Possibility of Rational Politics. In *Political Theory Today*, ed. D. Held. Cambridge: Polity.

Evans, D. 1996. *An Introductory Dictionary of Lacanian Psychoanalysis*. London: Routledge.

Ewald, F. 1986. *L'État Providence* Paris: Grasset.

————. 1993. *Der Vorsorgestaat*. Frankfurt am Main: N.p.

Felman, S. 1987. *Jacques Lacan and the Adventures of Insight: Psychoanalysis in Contemporary Culture*. Cambridge, Mass.: Harvard University Press.

Flax, J. 1995. Keynote address, Australasian Political Science Association Conference, University of Melbourne.

Forrester, J. 1990. *The Seductions of Psychoanalysis: On Freud, Lacan and Derrida*. Cambridge: Cambridge University Press.

Foucault, M. 1965. *Madness and Civilization: A History of Insanity in the Age of Reason*, trans R. Howard. New York, Panthian.

————. 1972. *The Archaeology of Knowledge*. Trans A. Sherridan Smith. New York: Panthian.

————. 1977a. *Discipline and Punish: The Birth of the Prison*. Trans. A. Sherridan. London: Alan Lane.

———. 1977b. Nietzsche, Genealogy, History. In *Language, Counter-Memory, Practice*, ed. D. Bouchard. Oxford: Blackwell.

———. 1980a. *The History of Sexuality: An Introduction*. London: Penguin.

———. 1980b. Two Lectures. Trans. C. Gordon et al. In *Power/Knowledge: Selected Interviews and Other Writings, 1972–1977*, ed. C. Gordon. New York: Pantheon.

———. 1985. Sexuality and Solitude. In *On Signs: A Semiotic Reader*, ed. M. Blonsky. Oxford: Blackwell.

Fraser, N. 1989. *Unruly Practices: Power, Discourse and Gender in Contemporary Social Theory*. Minneapolis: University of Minnesota Press.

Freud, S. 1921. *Beyond the Pleasure Principle*. London: Hogarth.

———. 1930. *Civilization and its Discontents*. London: Hogarth.

———. 1935–1974. *The Standard Edition of the Complete Psychological Works of Sigmund Freud*. London: Hogarth.

Frosh, S. 1987. *The Politics of Psychoanalysis*. London: Macmillan.

Fukuyama, F. 1992. *The End of History and the Last Man*. New York: Free Press.

Fuss, D. 1989. *Essentially Speaking*. New York: Routledge.

———. 1991. *Inside/Outside: Lesbian Theories, Gay Theories*. New York: Routledge.

Gallop, J. 1982. *Reading Lacan*. Ithaca, N.Y.: Cornell University Press.

Giddens, A. 1971. *Capitalism and Modern Social Theory*. Cambridge: Cambridge University Press.

———. 1972a. *Émile Durkheim: Selected Writings*. Cambridge: Cambridge University Press.

———. 1972b. *Politics and Sociology in the Thought of Max Weber*. London, Macmillan; New York: Pall Mall.

———. 1973a. *The Class Structure of the Advanced Societies*. London: Hutchinson University Library; New York: Harper & Row.

———. 1973b. *Positivism and Sociology*. London: Heinemann; New York: Basic Books.

———. 1976. *New Rules of Sociological Method*. London: Hutchinson; New York: Basic Books.

———. 1977. *Studies in Social and Political Theory*. London: Hutchinson; New York: Basic Books.

———. 1978. *Emile Durkheim*. London: Fontana; New York: Penguin.

———. 1979. *Central Problems in Social Theory*. London: Macmillan; Berkeley: University of California Press.

———. 1981a. *A Contemporary Critique of Historical Materialism*. London: Macmillan; Berkeley: University of California Press.

———. 1981b. *Profiles and Critiques in Social Theory*. London: Macmillan.

———. 1982. *Sociology: A Brief but Critical Introduction*. London: Macmillan; New York: Harcourt, Brace, Jovanovich.

———. 1983. *Profiles and Critiques in Social Theory*. London: Macmillan; Berkeley: University of California Press.

———. 1984. *The Constitution of Society: Outline of the Theory of Structuration*. Cambridge: Polity; Berkeley: University of California Press.

———. 1985. *The Nation-State and Violence*. Cambridge: Polity; Berkeley: University of California Press.

———. 1986. *Durkheim on Politics and the State*. Cambridge: Polity; Palo Alto, Calif.: Stanford University Press.

———. 1987. *Social Theory and Modern Sociology*. Cambridge: Polity; Palo Alto, Calif.: Stanford University Press.

———. 1988. *Sociology*. Cambridge: Polity; New York: Norton.

———. 1990. *The Consequences of Modernity*. Cambridge: Polity; Palo Alto, Calif.: Stanford University Press.

———. 1991. *Modernity and Self-Identity*. Cambridge: Polity; Palo Alto, Calif.: Stanford University Press.

———. 1992a. *Human Societies*. Cambridge: Polity.

———. 1992b. *The Transformation of Intimacy*. Cambridge: Polity; Palo Alto, Calif.: Stanford University Press.

———. 1994. *Beyond Left and Right*. Cambridge: Polity; Palo Alto, Calif.: Stanford University Press.

———. 1995. *Politics, Sociology and Social Theory*. Cambridge: Polity; Palo Alto, Calif.: Stanford University Press.

———. 1996. *In Defence of Sociology*. Cambridge: Polity; Palo Alto, Calif.: Stanford University Press.

———. 1998. *The Third Way*. Cambridge: Polity, 1998.

———. 1999. *Runaway World: How Globalization Is Reshaping Our Lives*. London: Profile Books.

Giddens, A., U. Beck, and S. Lash. 1994. *Reflexive Modernisation*. Cambridge: Polity; Palo Alto, Calif.: Stanford University Press.

Giddens, A., and D. Held. 1982. *Classes, Conflict and Power*. London: Macmillan; Berkeley: University of California Press.

Giddens, A., and G. Mackenzie. 1982 *Classes and the Division of Labour*. Cambridge: Cambridge University Press.

Giddens, A., and C. Pierson. 1998. *Conversations with Anthony Giddens*. Cambridge: Polity.

Giddens, A., and P. H. Stanworth. 1974. *Elites and Power in British Society*. Cambridge: Cambridge University Press.

Giddens, A., and J. Turner. 1988. *Social Theory Today*. Cambridge: Polity; Palo Alto, Calif.: Stanford University Press.

Grosz, E. 1990. *Jacques Lacan: A Feminist Introduction*. London: Routledge.

Gunnell, J. G. 1993. *The Descent of Political Theory: The Genealogy of an American Vocation*. Chicago: University of Chicago Press.

Habermas, J. 1971. *Knowledge and Human Interests*. Boston: Beacon.

———. 1987a. Excursus on Cornelius Castoriadis: The Imaginary Institution. In *The Philosophical Discourse of Modernity*. Cambridge: Polity, 327–35.

———. 1987b. *The Philosophical Discourse of Modernity*. Cambridge: Polity.

———. 1991a. *The Theory of Communicative Action: Volume 1. Reason and the Rationalization of Society*. Cambridge: Polity.

———. 1991b. *The Theory of Communicative Action: Volume 2. Lifeworld and Systems: A Critique of Functionalist Reason*. Cambridge: Polity.

———. 1992. *Postmetaphysical Thinking: Philosophical Essays*. Cambridge: Polity.

———. 1994. *The Past as Future*. Cambridge: Polity.

———. 1997a. *A Berlin Republic: Writings on Germany*. Cambridge: Polity.

———. 1997b. *Between Facts and Norms*. Cambridge: Polity.

————. 2001a. *The Liberating Power of Symbols: Philosophical Essays*. Cambridge: Polity.

————. 2001b. *On the Pragmatics of Social Interaction*. Cambridge: Polity.

————. 2001c. *The Postnational Constellation: Political Essays*. Cambridge: Polity.

————. 2002. *The Future of Human Nature*. Cambridge: Polity.

————. 2003. *Truth and Justification*. Cambridge: Polity.

Harvey, D. 1989. *The Condition of Postmodernity*. Oxford: Blackwell.

Held, D. 1995. *Democracy and the Global Order*. Cambridge: Polity.

————. 2001. Regulating Globalization? The Reinvention of Politics. In *The Global Third Way Debate*, ed. Anthony Giddens. Cambridge: Polity, 394–405.

————, ed. 1991. *Political Theory Today*. Cambridge: Polity.

Held, D., A. McGrew, D. Goldblatt, and J. Perraton. 1999. *Global Transformations: Politics, Economics and Culture*. Cambridge: Polity.

Held, D., and J. B. Thompson. 1989. *Social Theory of Modern Societies: Giddens and His Critics*. Cambridge: Cambridge University Press.

Hirst, P., and G. Thompson. 1996. *Globalization in Question* Cambridge: Polity.

Hollway, W., and T. Jefferson. 1997. The Risk Society in an Age of Anxiety: Situating Fear of Crime. *British Journal of Sociology* 48, no. 2: 254–66.

Honneth, A. 1991. *The Critique of Power: Reflective Stages in a Critical Social Theory*. Cambridge, Mass.: MIT Press.

Howard, D. 1977. *The Marxian Legacy*. London: Macmillan.

Irigaray, L. 1985. *This Sex Which Is Not One*. Ithaca, N.Y.: Cornell University Press.

————. 1993. *The Ethics of Sexual Difference*. New York: Routledge.

Jonas, H. 1984. *The Imperative of Responsibility*. Chicago: University of Chicago Press.

Keat, R. 1981. *The Politics of Social Theory*. Oxford: Blackwell.

Kovel, J. 1988. *The Radical Spirit: Essays on Psychoanalysis and Society*. London: Free Association Books.

Kristeva, J. 1984. *Revolution in Poetic Language*. New York: Columbia University Press.

————. 1989. *Black Sun: Depression and Melancholia*. New York: Columbia University Press.

————. 1993. *New Maladies of the Soul*. New York: Columbia University Press.

————. 1995. Psychoanalysis in Times of Distress. In *Speculations after Freud: Psychoanalysis, Philosophy and Culture*, ed. S. Shandasani and M. Munchow. London: Routledge.

————. 2000. *Crisis of the European Subject*. New York: Other Press.

Lacan, J. 1949. The Mirror Stage as Formative of the Function of the I. In *Écrits*. London: Routledge.

————. 1953. The Function and Field of Speech and Language in Psychoanalysis. In *Écrits*. London: Routledge.

————. 1966. Of Structure as an Inmixing of an Otherness Prerequisite to Any Subject Whatever. In *The Structuralist Controversy*, ed. R. Macksey and E. Donato. Baltimore, Md.: Johns Hopkins University Press, 1970, 186–200.

————. 1975a. *Encore: Le Seminaire XX*. Paris: Seuil, 1975.

————. 1975b. *Le Séminaire: Livre XX. Encore, 1962–63*. Ed. J.-A. Miller. Paris: Seuil.

————. 1977. *Écrits: A Selection*. Harmondsworth: Tavistock.

————. 1979. *The Four Fundamental Concepts of Psychoanalysis*. Harmondsworth: Penguin.

———. 1988a. *The Seminar of Jacques Lacan, Vol. 1: Freud's Papers on Technique 1953–54.* Cambridge: Cambridge University Press.

———. 1988b. *The Seminar of Jacques Lacan, Vol. 2: The Ego in Freud's Theory and in the Technique of Psychoanalysis 1954–55.* Cambridge: Cambridge University Press.

———. 1990. *Television: A Challenge to the Psychoanalytic Establishment.* Ed. J. Copjec. New York: Norton.

———. 1991. *Le Séminaire: Livre XVII. L'envers de la psychanalyse, 1969–70.* Ed. J.-A. Miller. Paris: Seuil.

———. 1992. *The Ethics of Psychoanalysis 1959–60: The Seminar of Jacques Lacan.* London: Routledge.

———. 1993. *The Psychoses, 1955–56: The Seminar of Jacques Lacan.* London: Routledge.

Lambropoulos, V. 1997. Justice and Good Governance. *Thesis Eleven* 49: 1–30.

Laplanche, J. 1987. *New Foundations for Psychoanalysis.* Oxford: Blackwell.

———. 1999. *Essays on Otherness.* London: Routledge.

Laplanche, J., and S. Lecaire. 1972. The Unconscious. *Yale French Studies* 48.

Lasch, C. 1980. *The Culture of Narcissism.* London: Abacus.

Lash, S., B. Szerszynski, and B. Wynne, eds. 1996. *Risk, Environment and Modernity: Towards a New Ecology.* London: Sage.

Lash, S., and J. Urry. 1987. *The End of Organised Capitalism.* Cambridge: Polity.

———. 1994. *Economies of Signs and Space.* London: Sage.

Laswell, H. 1936. *Politics: Who Gets What, When, How.* New York: McGraw-Hill.

Lemaire, A. 1970. *Jacques Lacan.* London: Routledge.

Lemert, C. 1995. *Sociology after the Crisis.* Boulder, Colo.: Westview Press.

———. 1997. *Social Things.* New York: Rowman & Littlefield.

———. 2002. *Dark Thoughts.* New York: Routledge.

Lévi-Strauss, C. 1970. *The Raw and the Cooked.* London: Cape.

Levinas, E. 1981. *Otherwise Than Being, or Beyond Essence.* The Hague: Martinus Nijhoff.

———. 1985. *Ethics and Infinity: Conversations with Philippe Nemo.* Pittsburgh: Duquesne University Press.

Luhmann, N. 1993. *Risk: A Sociological Approach.* New York: Walter de Gruyter.

Lukes, S. 1974. *Power: A Radical View.* London: Macmillan.

Lyotard, J.-F. 1988a. *Reécrire la Modernité.* Paris: Lille.

———. 1988b. *Peregrinations.* New York: Columbia University Press.

———. 1990. The Dream-work Does Not Think. In *The Lyotard Reader,* ed. A. Benjamin. Oxford: Blackwell.

MacCannell, J. F. 1986. *Figuring Lacan: Criticism and the Cultural Unconscious.* London: Croom Helm.

Macey, D. 1988. *Lacan in Contexts.* London: Verso.

———. 1995. On the Subject of Lacan. In *Psychoanalysis in Contexts,* ed. A. Elliott and S. Frosh. London: Routledge.

Maffesoli, M. 1988. Jeux de Masques: Postmodernism Tribalism. *Design Issues* 4, nos. 1/2.

Marcuse, H. 1956. *Eros and Civilization.* London: Ark.

Marshall, T. H. 1973. *Class, Citizenship and Social Development.* Westport, Conn.: Greenwood.

Marx, K. 1963. *The Eighteenth Brumaire of Louis Bonaparte.* New York: International.

McCarthy, T. 1991. *Ideals and Illusions: On Reconstruction and Deconstruction in Contemporary Critical Theory.* Cambridge, Mass.: MIT Press.

McNay, L. 1992. *Foucault and Feminism.* Cambridge: Polity.

Melucci, A. 1996. *The Playing Self, Person and Meaning in the Planetary Society.* Cambridge: Cambridge University Press.

Merriam, C. 1934. *Political Power: Its Composition and Incidents.* New York: McGraw-Hill.

Mestrovic, S. 1998. *Anthony Giddens: The Last Modernist.* London: Routledge.

Metz, C. 1982. *Psychoanalysis and Cinema.* London: Macmillan.

Miller, D. 1993. Deliberative Democracy and Public Choice. In *Prospects for Democracy,* ed. D. Held. Cambridge: Polity.

Mitchell, J. 1974. *Psychoanalysis and Feminism.* Harmondsworth: Penguin.

———. 1984. *Women: The Longest Revolution.* London: Virago.

Mitchell, J., and J. Rose, eds. 1982. *Feminine Sexuality: Jacques Lacan and the école freudienne.* London: Macmillan.

Morgenthau, H. J. 1978. *Politics among Nations: The Struggle for Power and Peace.* New York: Knopf.

Munch, R. 1987. Parsonian Theory Today. In *Social Theory Today,* ed. A. Giddens and J. Turner. Cambridge: Polity.

Oakeshott, M. 1991. *On Human Conduct.* Oxford: Clarendon.

O'Brien, M., and S. Penna. 1998. *Theorising Modernity: Reflexivity, Environment and Identity in Giddens's Social Theory.* London: Longman.

Ogden, T. 1989. *The Primitive Edge of Experience.* Northvale, N.J.: Aronson.

O'Neill, J. 1986. The Disciplinary Society: From Weber to Foucault. *British Journal of Sociology* 37: 42–60.

Orbach, S. 1994. *What's Really Going On Here? Making Sense of Our Emotional Lives.* London: Virago.

Paolini, A. 1993. Foucault, Realism and the Power of Discourse in International Relations. *Australian Journal of Political Science* 28, no. 1.

Pensky, M. 1999. Jürgen Habermas and the Antinomies of the Intellectual. In *Habermas: A Critical Reader,* ed. P. Dews. Oxford: Blackwell.

Petersen, A. 1996. Risk and the Regulated Self. *Australian and New Zealand Journal of Sociology* 32, no. 1: 44–57.

Poster, M. 1990. *The Mode of Information: Poststructuralism and Social Context.* Cambridge: Polity.

Ragland-Sullivan, E. 1986. *Jacques Lacan and the Philosophy of Psychoanalysis.* Chicago: University of Illinois Press.

Rawls, J. 1971. *A Theory of Justice.* Cambridge, Mass.: Harvard University Press.

Reich, W. 1968. *The Function of the Orgasm.* Panther Press.

Riceour, P. 1970. *Freud and Philosophy: An Essay on Interpretation.* New Haven, Conn.: Yale University Press.

Ritzer, G. 1993. *The McDonaldization of Society.* London: Sage.

Robertson, R. 1992. *Globalization: Social Theory and Global Culture.* London: Sage.

Robertson, R., and B. S. Turner. 1991. *Talcott Parsons: Theorists of Modernity.* London: Sage.

Rojek, C., and B. S. Turner. 2001. *Society and Culture (Theory, Culture and Society)*. London: Sage.

Rorty, R. 1991. *Philosophical Papers: Vol. 2. Essays on Heidegger and Others*. Cambridge: Cambridge University Press.

Rose, N. 1996. Re-figuring the Territory of Government. *Economy and Society* 25, no. 3: 327–56.

Roudinesco, E. 1997. *Jacques Lacan*. Oxford: Polity.

Schluchter, W. 1979. *Entwicklung des okzidentalen Rationalismus Eine Analyse don Max Weber Gesellschaftsgeschichte*. Tübingen: Mohr Siebeck.

Schneiderman, S. 1980. *Jacques Lacan: The Death of an Intellectual Hero*. Cambridge, Mass.: Harvard University Press.

Sedgwick, E. K. 1990. *The Epistemology of the Closet*. Berkeley: University of California Press.

Sennett, R. 1998. *The Corrosion of Character: The Personal Consequences of Work in the New Capitalism*. New York: Norton.

Singer, B. 1979. The Early Castoriadis: Socialism, Barbarism and the Bureaucratic Thread. *Canadian Journal of Social and Political Theory* 3, no. 3: 35–56.

Smart, B. 1992. *Modern Conditions, Postmodern Controversies*. London: Routledge.

———. 1993. *Postmodernity*. London: Routledge.

———. 1999. *Facing Modernity: Ambivalence, Reflexivity and Morality*. London: Sage.

———. 2000. Postmodern Social Theory. In *The Blackwell Companion to Social Theory*, ed. B. S. Turner. Oxford: Blackwell, 447–80.

Stern, D. 1985. *The Interpersonal World of the Infant*. New York: Basic Books.

Stevenson, N. 1995. *Understanding Media Cultures*. London: Sage.

Sullivan, E.-R. 1986. *Jacques Lacan and the Philosophy of Psychoanalysis*. Chicago: University of Illinois Press.

Thompson, J. B. 1984. *Studies in the Theory of Ideology*. Cambridge: Polity.

———. 1989. The Theory of Structuration. In *Social Theory of Modern Societies: Giddens and His Critics*, ed. D. Held and J. Thompson. Cambridge: Cambridge University Press.

———. 1995. *The Media and Modernity: A Social Theory of the Media*. Cambridge: Polity.

Tucker, K. 1998. *Anthony Giddens and Modern Social Theory*. London: Sage.

Turkle, S. 1978. *Psychoanalytic Politics: Freud's French Revolution*. New York: Basic Books.

Turner, B. S. 1992. *Regulating Bodies*. London: Routledge.

———. 1993a. Contemporary Problems in the Theory of Citizenship. In *Citizenship and Social Theory*, ed. B. S. Turner. London: Sage.

———. 1993b. *Max Weber: From History to Modernity*. London: Routledge.

———. 1994. *Orientalism, Postmodernism and Globalism*. London: Routledge.

Tustin, F. 1980. Autistic Objects. *International Review of Psycho-Analysis* 7: 27–40.

———. 1984. Autistic Shapes. *International Review of Psycho-Analysis* 11: 279–90.

Urry, J. 1995. *Consuming Places*. London: Routledge.

———. 2000. *Sociology Beyond Societies: Mobilities for the Twenty-first Century*. London: Routledge.

Waltz, K. N. 1979. *The Theory of International Politics*. Reading, Mass.: Addison-Wesley.

Weeks, J. 1977. *Coming Out*. London: Quartet.

———. 1985. *Sexuality and Its Discontents*. London: Routledge.

———. 1995. *Invented Moralities: Sexual Values in an Age of Uncertainty*. Cambridge: Polity.

Westergaard, J. 1995. *Who Gets What?* Cambridge: Polity.

Whitebook, J. 1985. Reason and Happiness: Some Psychoanalytic Themes in Critical Theory. In *Habermas and Modernity,* ed. R. J. Bernstein. Cambridge: Polity, 140–60.

———. 1995. *Perversion and Utopia: A Study in Psychoanalysis and Critical Theory*. Cambridge, Mass.: MIT Press.

Wilden, A., ed. 1968. *The Language of the Self: The Function of Language in Psychoanalysis*. Baltimore, Md.: Johns Hopkins University Press.

Winnicott, D. W. 1971. *Playing and Reality*. Harmondsworth: Penguin, [1974].

Wright Mills, C. 1956. *The Power Elite*. New York: Oxford University Press.

Zizek, S. 1989. *The Sublime Object of Ideology*. London: Verso.

———. 1991. *Looking Awry: An Introduction to Jacques Lacan through Popular Culture*. Cambridge, Mass.: MIT Press.

Index

abstract systems, 49–50

action: constraints on, 46, 55; rational choice theory, 172–73; structure and, 10–11, 45–46

Adorno, Theodor, 98, 112, 115, 124–26, 160

advanced modernity. *See* reflexive modernization

agency, 11, 56, 186; stratification model, 47–48, 57; structure and, 47, 55

"The Agency of the Letter in the Unconscious, or Reason since Freud" (Lacan), 68

Alexander, Jeffrey C., 13–14, 26

Althusser, Louis, 72, 93

Amato, Paul, 145

American ego psychology, 12, 64

anxiety, 37, 57, 59–60; postmodern, 35–37, 167

Anzieu, D., 96

archaic societies, 103

Archer, Margaret, 55

Arendt, Hannah, 116–17

Aristotle, 86, 88

automobilities, 3–4

autonomy, 51, 86, 125–26, 128, 157; Castoriadis's interpretation, 100–103, 104; individualization and, 39–40; meaning and, 40–41; as open-ended process, 101–2

Bauman, Zygmunt, 5, 37, 152, 156, 162–63, 168, 180, 184, 193–94

Beck, Ulrich, 7, 10, 14, 15, 19–20, 162, 177, 181; critique of, 24–42; individualization theory, 20, 23–24, 146, 157–59; outline of social theory, 20–24; power and domination in works of, 28–32; reflexive modernization, 22–23; risk, reflexivity, and reflection, 25–28; risk society thesis, 20–22; subpolitics, concept of, 30, 32–33, 37; works, 20

Beck-Gernsheim, E., 24

being-for, 192

Bell, Daniel, 53, 172

Benjamin, Jessica, 96, 155

Beyond Left and Right: The Future of Radical Politics (Giddens), 45, 52–54

Beyond the Pleasure Principle (Freud), 153

binary oppositions, 175

biopower, 176

Bodies That Matter (Butler), 144

body, 144–45, 160, 176

Bollas, Christopher, 155

Booth, Alan, 145

boundary problems, 15, 111

About the Author

Anthony Elliott is research professor of social and political theory at the University of the West of England, Bristol, where he is director of the Centre for Critical Theory. Born in Australia, he came to England on a Commonwealth Scholarship in 1987 to undertake doctoral research at Cambridge University. Since that time, he has held various academic positions, including an Australian Research Council Fellowship from 1992 to 2000. His research interests span social theory, psychoanalysis, politics, and cultural studies, and his articles and books have been translated into ten languages.